D0254888

Building
OHIO

Building

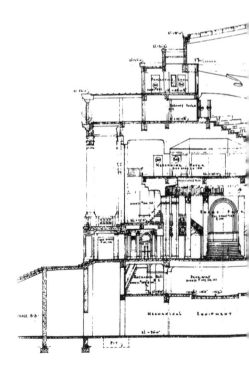

O H I O

A Traveler's Guide to Ohio's
Urban Architecture

by Jane Ware

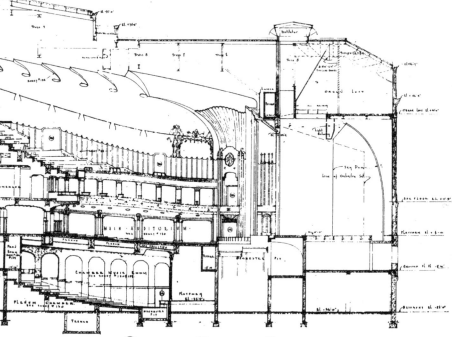

Orange Frazer Press
Wilmington, Ohio

HARRIS-ELMORE PUBLIC LIBRARY
328 TOLEDO STREET
BOX 45
ELMORE, OHIO 43416

ISBN 1-882203-74-7
Copyright 2001 by Jane Ware

No part of this publication may be reproduced in any material form (including photocopying or storing in any medium by electronic means and whether or not transiently or incidentally to some other use of this publication) without the written permission of the copyright holder except in accordance with the provisions of the Copyright, Designs and Patents Act 1988.

Additional copies of Building Ohio: A Travelers Guide To Ohio's Urban Architecture or other Orange Frazer Press books may be ordered directly from:

Orange Frazer Press, Inc.
Box 214
37 ½ West Main Street
Wilmington, Ohio 45177

Telephone 1.800.852.9332 for price and shipping information
Web Site: www.orangefrazer.com

Library of Congress Cataloging-in-Publication Data

Ware, Jane.
   Building Ohio : a traveler's guide to Ohio's urban architecture / by Jane Ware.
      p. cm.
   Includes index.
   ISBN 1-882203-74-7
   1. Architecture--Ohio--Guidebooks. 2. Ohio--Guidebooks. I. Title.

NA730.O3 W37 2001
720'.9771'091732--dc21

                                        2001036356

Acknowledgements

This is a book I could never have done without help; it's depended on the generosity of hundreds of people. My thanks to Frank Elmer, architect and friend, the first person I talked to and the one who, in the end, pulled extra talent out of his sleeve and did many drawings. My thanks to Douglas Graf, who gave me the courage to proceed, as well as help evident throughout these pages; and finally, he read the whole manuscript. My thanks to Walter Leedy and to Jeanne Reed, whose advice on formatting I followed. Some people suggested buildings, indulged me with tours and/or multiple interviews, and provided help for more than one locality for years; my special thanks to Craig Bobby, Jeff Brown, Robert C. Gaede, Glenn A. Harper, Ted J. Ligibel, Mary Ann Olding, James A. Pahlau, Mary Anne Reeves, Rebecca Rogers. My thanks to all those in these pages and to many others, who for this volume included:

Akron, Barbara Baskin, Cary Dell, Mark Heppner, John P. Mazzola, John Miller, James A. Pahlau, Harold Rasmussen, Margaret Tramontine;

Canton, M.J. Albacete, Joseph Andaloro, June S. Brogden, Jeff Brown, Heidi Ewald, Marguerite Fulk, Jon Jacob, Lisa K. Holl, Mary Margaret Myers, James A. Pahlau, Sarah Titus;

Cincinnati, Cecie Chewning, Amy Fisher, John Fleischman, Charles Fox, Price Gaines, Marie Gallagher, Bruce Goetzman, Burt Gross, Marge Hammelrath, Greg Hand, Cheryl Hatfield, Janet Hauck, Carolyn Kindle, Walter E. Langsam, Paul Loechle, Jack McAfee, Bob McKeever, Marie Matsunami, Dennis Matthews, Declan Mullin, Paul Nohr, Mary Ann Olding, Judith Osborne, Patty Pritz, Millard Rogers, Patrick Rose (the Swedenborgian), Patrick Rose (the Railroad Club), Fred Rutherford, Ruthann Sammarco, Liz Scheurer, Abby S. Schwartz, Tom Sessman, Janet E. Setchell, Beth Sullebarger, Ken Tieman; Ernie Toplis, Chad Yelton;

Cleveland, Marita Ahmad, Lawrence Albert, George Bradac, Shirley Branyi, Craig Bobby, Rabbi Armond E. Cohen, Bob Fahey, William John Fuller, Robert C. Gaede, Jane Gaydos, Gladys Haddad, Dennis Harrison, Carol Jacobs, Rev. Jason Kappanadze, Susan Koletsky, Robert D. Keiser, Sandra L. Koozer, Christine L. Krosel, Walter Leedy, Steven Litt, Kathy Miller, Harvey G. Oppmann, Jeremy Parkhurst, Michael Perry, Ellen Petler, Tina Russell, Roger Sherman Schnoke, Carolyn Sloan, Barbara Thomas, R. Van Petten, Richard Worswick;

Columbus, Abbott Lowell Cummings, Gary Cunningham, Priscilla Smith D'Angelo, Roger Farrell, Carol Gabriel, Sherri Geldin, Ruth Gless, Erin Hanover, Kaye Henderson, Craig Hodgetts, Bertha Ihnat, Lin Jackson, Edward J. Keirns, Robert D. Loversidge Jr., Julia Brooks Katz, Amy Kobe, Andrew Macioce, George Nickerson, Jay Panzer, Barbara Powers, Bruce Ratekin, Jeanne Reed, Michael Rosen, Franco Ruffino, Bryan Saums, Lavon Shook, Dave Stephenson, Lea Ann Sterling, Rosa F. Stolz, Mari Sunami, William W. Taschek, Michael Tsao, Cara Vanasdale, Donald C. Welsch;

Dayton, Kathleen M. Fox, Loren Gannon, John Gower, Bill Hager, Glenn A. Harper, Karen Johnson, Sharon Kierce, Marguerite Krein, Marianne Lorenz, Bill Mangen, Helen L. Pinkney, Marion Schaeffer, Wayne Shuller, Oma Sollenberger, Noël D. Vernon, Claudia Watson;

Toledo, Larry Adams, Randy Alexander, Patricia Appold, Sharon Armstrong, Tara Barney, Chris Barry, Reynold Boezi, Judge Andy Devine, William Frisk, Stefan Gerlica, Bill Hamilton, Randy Hinderer, William Hirt, John Kiely, Sandra Knudsen, Jim Larson, Ted J. Ligibel, Tom Lingeman, Irene Martin, Larry R. Michaels, Michael and Donna Mills, Don Monroe, Michael Murray, the late Robert Shiffler, Charles H. Stark III, Lawrence R. Stine, Judy Stone, Bill Thomas, Sally Vallongo, Barbara Van Vleet, John Widmer, Chuck Williams, Stanley Woody, Mark Yeary, Michael Young;

Youngstown, Dexter A. Hollen, Louis Kennedy, Pamela L. Pletcher, Carol Potter, Jim Ramhoff, Joan Reedy, Rebecca Rogers.

Thanks to Nathalie Wright and the Ohio Historical Society Preservation Office, which keeps the state's National Register files; to Akron-Summit County Library; Bexley Public Library; Public Library of Cincinnati and Hamilton County; Cleveland Public Library; Dayton and Montgomery County Public Library; Ohio State University's Science & Engineering Library, which includes architecture; Toledo-Lucas County Public Library Local History Room; Public Library of Youngstown and Mahoning County, Information Services Department; and especially to Sam Roshon, who has developed a superb Ohio local history collection at the Columbus Metropolitan Library.

Thanks for particular help with illustrations: Andrew Borowiec, David Day, Linda Essai, Robert C. Gaede, Scott Hisey, Sylvia Johnson, Joanne M. Lewis, Craig MacIntosh, James A. Pahlau, Cervin Robinson, Sam Roshon and the Columbus Metropolitan Library, Janet E. Setchell, Eleanor Shankland, Toledo Museum of Art, U.S. Coast Guard Historian's Office, Carl N. White and the Landmarks Preservation Council, Lucas County-Maumee Valley Historical Society.

Thanks to those who not only helped prepare this book, but then read parts of it: Robert D. Keiser, Cleveland; Walter E. Langsam, Cincinnati; Ted R. Ligibel, Toledo; James A. Pahlau, Akron and Canton; Rebecca Rogers, Youngstown; Jay Panzer and Rosa Stolz, parts of Columbus.

Special thanks to John Baskin of Orange Frazer Press. This book was his idea; from the writer, he asked for the commitment that's kept me at it for years. And in the end, by putting these pages together with elegant pictures, he was the one who, I think, made Ohio look good.

And finally, thanks to my husband, Brendan, who's learned way more about architecture than he ever expected. And liked it.

illustration: David Day, Frank Elmer, and Craig MacIntosh.

photography: Ian Adams, Andrew Borowiec, Robert Flischel, Bill and Tom Patterson, Cervin Robinson, Eric Weinberg.

cover: Cincinnati's Union Terminal by Gordon Baer.

The books, *County Courthouses of Ohio* and the photographs by Tom and Bill Patterson, published in 2000 by Indiana University Press, and *Cleveland, Ohio*, by Cervin Robinson, published in 1989 by the Cleveland Museum of Art, would make handsome additions to anyone's architectural library. They were of immeasureable help in the making of this book, as were Andrew Borowiec's photographs from *Historic Architecture in Canton, 1805-1940*, published in 1989 by the Canton Art Institute; the photographs and text of *Look Again: Landmark Architecture in Downtown Toledo and Old West End* by Eric Johannesen and Allen L. Dickes and published by Ober Park Associates, Inc., in Pittsburgh in 1973; and Craig MacIntosh's *Dayton Sketchbook*, by Landfall Press in Dayton, 1985.

Contents

CLEVELAND 110

COLUMBUS 178

DAYTON 228

Author's Note: On Choosing Buildings

Early in 1996, I sat down and picked most of the buildings listed in this guide.

By then I'd spent a year and a half asking architects, preservationists, and local historical societies for suggestions, vetting the literature, and driving around taking pictures—ultimately, I would have thousands of pictures from all of the 88 Ohio counties.

Douglas Graf, associate professor of architecture at Ohio State University, has seen almost all my pictures; he became, in effect, a co-selector of these buildings, especially for modern ones. That is not to say he would endorse every last one of these choices; I'm sure he would not; but he would agree with almost all. I am convinced that his input enhanced the overall level of selection.

What I was looking for, was varied examples of good and interesting architecture for a guide (this is *not* an architectural history). I started with architects and architectural features—styles and sites, for instance—but I've also included buildings designed by non-architects. A distinctive building had an edge.

I set up categories, mostly building types of the nineteenth or the twentieth century, and chose up to 15 good examples for each. Types included houses, hotels, churches and cemeteries, courthouses, small (Main Street) and large commercial buildings, schools and colleges, skyscrapers, recreation (park pavilions, restaurants, theaters), stores. Some categories were themes: rural Ohio or innovative reuses or small or unusual buildings, such as a tiny octagonal chapel in the woods of Portage County, a little restaurant in a Columbus alley, and lighthouses. Other categories were ways of enhancing the look of places and buildings: town planning, site, ensembles.

A problem with categories is that some types are underrepresented, especially courthouses. So are houses. This guide has more houses than any other building type. But then too, so does Ohio.

Another factor in selecting was the availability of information. Almost always, I used research by local individuals and historical societies.

Some choices—often those written about briefly—were included to augment tours, especially in cities. But by and large, selections were made in a statewide context, so that although this work can claim to be a guide to Ohio architecture, it can't pretend to be definitive for any one place, especially cities.

Introduction: Places That Matter

Six-foot-three, Douglas Graf folds himself into his road-wise Civic and sets out to find the good stuff, architecturally speaking. He expects to find it in places others overlook— places, even, like Ohio.

He knows that Ohio has architectural masterpieces, and he names some. Union Terminal in Cincinnati. The Netherland Plaza Hotel ("spectacular"), also in Cincinnati. The Toledo Art Museum. Terminal Tower in Cleveland.

And he knows Ohio has wonderful places, like University Circle in Cleveland or Mill Creek Park in Youngstown or Spring Grove Cemetery ("second only to Boston in quality") and Eden Park in Cincinnati. And it has buildings and ensembles that are unique, like the Barberton barns, the many college campuses, Cincinnati's Dixie Terminal, the Western Reserve's New England villages.

Graf knows all this partly because of his profession—he's an associate professor of architecture at Ohio State—and partly because he travels. At every pause in the academic calendar, his Civic is out there; it's taken him all over Ohio and across the country. Beyond the United States, he's seen architecture all over Europe. He knows what's been written. And he's observed that his students are among those who don't realize that Ohio has exceptional architecture, that Ohio was once on the cutting-edge. They discount this place, architecturally. They are not alone.

So it is time for a guide to Ohio architecture, in the hope that more Ohioans may realize that this is a place with architecture that matters. That is what this book is about.

It looks at the built Ohio at its best—the happy collusions of good design, taste, and, usually but not always, money.

To prepare this book, I needed many guides myself, and among them Doug Graf was principal. For over five years, I've been writing down what he said when I was around, which was all right if I didn't call it an interview. It turns out that, though he grew up mostly in Washington, D.C., and studied at Princeton (architecture) and Harvard (a master's degree), Graf is an Ohio native. His passion for places began in Seven Mile, Ohio, between Middletown and Hamilton. Seven Mile was the right size for someone who was six. "It was just big enough to have some public space, a monument, and a flag pole," Graf says. It also had two stores, a bank, a barber shop, a consolidated school, a cement block plant, and a train he could watch passing through every day. After first grade his family moved away. Thirty years after he'd left Ohio, in 1984, he came back to teach at Ohio State.

He has some singular aptitudes. One is, that even on cloudy days, he always knows where north is, which means, he always has a good sense of where he is. So, when he walks into a house for the first time, he can comment on a window's having north light. He is voracious for new places, but then his sense of direction takes the kick out of it. "The deliciousness of a new place is lost so quickly," he says. "You get the layout and have to move on to the next one." Another of his aptitudes is, that when he looks at a good building, he finds a narrative. "There's a dialogue between pieces," he says. "The design starts to discuss itself. It starts moving and changing. In good architecture, I should be able to make a long story happen."

One day, when we were having lunch at the Wexner Center's cafe and looking at pictures of Ohio buildings, I asked Doug Graf what, if anything, was unique about Ohio architecture, and he gave a spontaneous talk, a lecture, really—still another aptitude. Ohio, he announced, is not just like everywhere else architecturally, for three factors have given it a unique stock of good buildings.

First, the state was located so that it was settled at the

right time, when the nation was new, and moving west of the Alleghenies was not yet a commonplace. People came to Ohio with tremendous confidence in the future and in this new place. "Each town had the potential of being the new Athens," Graf said. Each town had to prepare for greatness with public space and public building (the green and the courthouse), with institutions (college, seminary, opera house), with quality structures. That sense of optimism diminished as settlement moved west; the farther west you go, the less interesting the towns are; and private colleges become rarer and rarer. "By the time you get to the West Coast," Graf said, "the optimism was completely dead. In San Francisco and Seattle there's almost no public space. They're just plats, with very little design."

Second, Ohio had industrialization that made it rich; at one time or an other, every county had money. Agriculture and industry were strong and widely dispersed, an unusual pattern; in other places, wealth was more concentrated. As late as 1950, Ohio was the only state with so many as six cities with populations of more than a quarter million. Moreover, these large cities and many smaller ones stayed prosperous with industrial niches in, say, glass, cash registers, tires. Communities competed with one another.

Colleges were—and are—everywhere. "When you get to a small city in Indiana, you don't expect to find a college," says Graf. "But in Ohio, every town has a college, many of them fairly good. So you have money in a cultured venue that values the town. Then buildings will matter, will be thoughtful, will be a natural embellishment of the place."

Finally, Ohio has many examples of innovative hybridization, which depended on a general interest in what was going on in the rest of the world. The hybridization was reinterpreting styles or, say, combining elements of both New England and Virginia town layouts. The latter had central greens containing an important building, while New England towns had a central green with public buildings facing into it and a commercial street off to the side. Worthington, for example, has a side commercial street combined with greens reminiscent of Virginia.

Gambier has a wonderful, completely original layout—a hybridized concoction. This village, which is mostly the Kenyon College campus, has a mile-long Middle Path that links two pavilions, Kenyon Hall at one end and Bexley Hall at the other. The town is midway between, where two parallel two-way streets flank a green.

Or, says Graf, take the towns of Lancaster, Granville, Newark, and Mount Vernon, four central Ohio towns that are within an hour of each other. Three resemble other places. Thus Graf sees Lancaster as a Virginia town and Granville as a New England village. Newark has the broad streets and emphatic grid more typical west of Ohio—Newark could be Iowa. As for Mount Vernon, Graf calls it "a perfect Ohio town, which means it's actually quite unusual." Its central green is a neutral hub between commercial and governmental buildings. "These towns," says Graf, "are all very close but completely different. That wouldn't happen other places without incredible time differences."

Ohio's hybridization can be seen in building design too, Graf says, and he cites the Columbus architects J.W. Yost and Frank L. Packard, who practiced together in the 1890s. Yost's Orton Hall on the Ohio State campus is a very good Richardsonian Romanesque building, but, says Graf, "you'd never confuse it with H.H. Richardson's work. Yost didn't have the fine New England stone Richardson had, so he couldn't reproduce the style exactly. But he turned that into an opportunity. He transformed it into something wonderful."

When you add together optimism, money in cultured venues, and hybridization, Graf says, "You see that for a long time a lot of good architecture was being produced in Ohio." From the 1820s through the 1920s, Ohio was almost always part of what was happening nationally in architecture. Ohio buildings appeared in professional journals; good architects came here from other places; talented natives stayed.

But with the Depression all that came to a halt. The three major tower complexes that were being finished about

1930—Carew in Cincinnati, Terminal in Cleveland, LeVeque in Columbus—represented Ohio's last "big display of embellishment of the city for 50 years," Graf says. "Now, good things aren't being built here. We're getting deteriorating downtowns, unpleasant suburbs, and a disappearing rural landscape. It's funny when you think of it. There's been this cataclysmic decline from cutting edge to dreg and it's provoked no public scrutiny in the state. It's as though every organization and everybody here has been lobotomized."

Doug Graf is not about to coddle us.

This volume looks at architecture in eight Ohio cities. Their buildings show just how great—how ambitious, how rich and how smart, how much fun—those cities once were. And this volume was written with the knowledge that they can be, and the hope that they will be, again.

Jane Ware
Columbus, Ohio
July, 2001

xx

Key

Building Ohio is an architectural guide to Ohio, in two volumes. Volume I includes the state's eight largest cities, and Volume II includes towns and rural areas. In this volume, cities are listed alphabetically.

All buildings are visible from street, though some are partly obscured by summer vegetation. Private houses, and their yards, are private and not accessible to the public. A few owners are willing to show their houses to visitors at least occasionally; in those cases, a phone number is included.

How Buildings are Listed:

1) Loew's Ohio, now Ohio Theatre, 1928

2) Thomas W. Lamb, New York

3) 39 East State Street, NHL, NRHP

4) Theater; regular venue for orchestra, ballet, Broadway series, classic films; for information about tours, some free, call CAPA, 469-1045

1) Building's historic name; present name; year construction was completed

2) Architect, builder, or other designer who planned building and where they worked, if known; "attributed to" means there's no proof

3) Street address (sometimes *not* where the door is) and National Register listing, if any (see below); for groups, Register listing is often mentioned in preceding text

4) Present use; if interior is accessible to the public, days (but not times) when open; phone number for museums and public buildings

"Access" is how to find a site or sites. "See also" is used for cross-references. Because this complete guide is in two volumes, a "see also" followed by a volume reference refers to the one not in hand.

National Register of Historic Places

Maintained by the U.S. Department of the Interior, the National Register of Historic Places recognizes the architectural worth of many historic buildings; Register status is included in this guide. Abbreviations are:

NHL = National Historic Landmark

NRHP = National Register of Historic Places

HD = Building is listed as part of a Historic District

CD = Building is listed as part of a Commercial District

PD = Building is listed as part of a Preservation District

MRA = Building is on Register through a Multiple Resource Area, a type of group listing no longer used

TR = Building is on Register through a Thematic Resource, a group listing no longer used

Building
OHIO

Akron

Just in time to make automobile tires, American rubber manufacturing concentrated in Akron; the city had found the product that made it rich, populous, and known. The rubber business also gave Akron two early twentieth-century structures that rank with Ohio's architectural wonders—Goodyear Airdock, a special kind of factory, and Stan Hywet Hall, a special kind of house. ¶ Akron's layout is of interest to Ohio State's Douglas Graf. He describes the plat as "quite sophisticated and extremely unusual in the Midwest." Alone among Ohio cities, Akron doesn't have a fully developed grid—even downtown the grid is distorted. It does have Market Street, which runs all the way across the city on an east-west diagonal. Market Street, says Graf, is "really Medieval. It widens and bends. It's a *very* interesting street plan." ¶ Also, to drive all through Akron on Market Street, is to see the city in cross section: the sublime, the gritty, the schlock—mostly the latter two. The route encompasses suburban malls, beautiful older residential areas, dreary neighborhoods, downtown, and industry, including rubber. This guide divides Akron into three sections: Downtown, East, and West.

Access: To reach downtown Akron from I-76 take Main-Broadway exit and drive about a mile north to central Akron. Coming from the north on I-77, take Market Street/State Route 18 east to downtown.

Downtown

Historian James A. Pahlau has often marveled at the surge of energy in Akron between 1928 and 1931, when the city had enough oomph and wherewithal to build eight major Art Deco buildings—all of them downtown. Three are listed here. Downtown today has too many gaps, of course, but the city has recently done a fine job with the new Canal Park, where the minor league Akron Aeros play baseball. The field fronts the sidewalk on South Main Street at University Avenue with a row of brick shops.

Access: Market Street/18 is useful for getting around; it goes everywhere or connects with streets that do. It connects with the major streets downtown, which are, from west to east, Main, High, and Broadway; the places below are on those streets south of Market, except for the YMCA, which is a right/west turn off Main onto Bowery Street. Sites here are in order for a loop tour on foot. To see Firestone Park drive south on Main, past I-76 to Firestone Boulevard; turn left to area around shield-shaped park.

CASTLE HALL, 1878

Jacob Snyder, Akron
57 East Market Street
Commercial and apartment building

Showy though it is, Castle Hall might not be noticeable today if the owner, John Mazzola, hadn't restored the facade. That was no simple matter. When Mazzola bought the building in the 1970s, it was white, covered with a stucco of perlite and portland cement, a mixture that Mazzola says is sometimes slathered onto deteriorating masonry. By the 1980s this stucco was peeling off in places, adhering resolutely in others. Getting all of it off, plus regrouting, painting, and restoring the tin cornice, went on longer than Mazzola likes to remember. Castle Hall is one of downtown Akron's two oldest commercial structures, according to Jim Pahlau. Designed by one of the best local architects (see also the Hower House), it is High Victorian Gothic in red brick with sandstone trim. Until they moved out in 1891, the Knights of Pythias used the castle-like high-ceilinged room on the top floor. Akronites associate the building with Hammel Business College, here from 1919-1981.

OLD POST OFFICE, NOW AKRON ART MUSEUM, 1899, 1981

James Knox Taylor, Supervising Architect, Treasury Department, Washington; 1981 renovation, Peter van Dijk of Dalton, van Dijk, Johnson & Partners, Cleveland
70 East Market Street at High, entry at rear, NRHP
Art Museum open daily except Monday; 330/376-9185

Under a low roof with a wide overhang, this one-time post office is in an elegant Italian Renaissance Revival style that makes it worthy of the Art Museum. In 2001, three European architectural firms were competing to design an addition facing High Street. Part of this project, due for completion in 2005, would be a renovation (not the first) of the old post office interior.

CENTRAL DEPOSITORS BANK & TRUST, NOW FIRST NATIONAL TOWER, 1931

Walker & Weeks, Cleveland
106 South Main Street
Office building; lobby accessible during business hours

At 330 feet, the 28-story Central Depositors Bank & Trust Tower was the tallest of the eight Art Deco buildings that sprouted downtown around 1930. Moreover, it was designed by Walker & Weeks, whom Jim Pahlau dubs "the most prestigious firm ever to practice out of Cleveland." The plans were intended originally for a Cleveland site, but when that project was abandoned the design was recycled for Akron. It had to be adapted for this irregular site: two corners are obtuse angles and two acute, a deviation that is not very noticeable. The building has typical Art Deco features, including setbacks and vertical lines of windows and spandrels, which are the spaces above and below windows. Limestone was used at street level and at the top setback; the rest is gray brick. Windows and interior have been redone, but by taking his tours down the stairs to the right of the front door, Pahlau shows them some of the original Art Deco grillwork, railings and doors.

FIRST CENTRAL TOWER, AKRON, OHIO   B-733

▶ FIRST NATIONAL TOWER

YOUNG MEN'S CHRISTIAN ASSOCIATION, 1931
(Albert H.) Good & (Edwin D.) Wagner, with designer John R. Luxmore, Akron
80 Center Street, off West Bowery, NRHP
YMCA and private apartments

On the outside this building is a striking 16-story tower, limestone at the
base and brown-orange brick for the ascent, with contrasting Aztec-and-
Mayan style terra-cotta trim. It's a favorite of Jim Pahlau's. The interior,
now part-YMCA, part private apartments, also had fine Art Deco detailing,
but only a little can be seen now in the lobby.

LOEW'S AKRON, NOW AKRON CIVIC THEATRE, 1929

John Eberson, Chicago and New York
182 South Main Street, NRHP
Theater, with programming through University of Akron E.J. Thomas Performing
Arts Hall; one-hour tours for a fee by prearrangement; if possible will show lobby
and auditorium to individuals during the day; 330/535-3179

Only a 21-foot storefront wide on Main Street, the Akron Civic Theatre at
first seems inconsequential. Then you enter, pass the box office, and walk the
length of a 105-foot corridor. Finally you pass through a door and behold
the Moorish splendor of the Grand Lobby. It's an enormous room, 42-by-72
feet, four stories high. In the dim light you'll make out the grand staircase at
the far end; you'll see ornamented pillars, curlicues and hexagons, statues in
niches, birds, a lush patterned carpet. This must be as close to the seraglio as
anyone can be on Main Street. The Grand Lobby's best illusion may be in
disguising the fact that it's really a bridge. It's so long because a series of
concrete pillars, unseen and underneath, are carrying it over a canal. (One
result, says board member Barbara Baskin, is that the lobby's hard to
heat.) The auditorium, beyond the lobby on the far side
of the canal, also goes Moorish on the walls.
The ceiling has the simulated sky of an
"atmospheric"

theater: tiny stars twinkle and clouds float lazily by. Right. The seraglio and heaven all at once. Architect John Eberson invented the atmospheric, which uses a projector to set clouds afloat. Born in 1875 in Austria, schooled in Dresden and Vienna, Eberson came to the United States in 1901 with $7 in his pocket. He settled in German-speaking St. Louis, where displays of inexpensive plaster opulence at the 1904 World's Fair made a lasting impression on him. Always a theater designer, Eberson became the stuff of legend in 1923 when he built the first atmospheric in Houston. He built his last in 1929, but the idea was widely imitated. Eberson moved his practice to Chicago and built atmospherics, each one unique, all over America. A staff of Hungarian draftsmen produced working drawings; Michelangelo Studios cast ornaments in plaster mixed with straw. In two- and three-foot lengths, the castings were shipped to the building site where Eberson's migratory 30-person crew assembled them under the direction of his son, Drew, who also mapped the stars. Eberson died in 1954, the year the first of his great theaters was torn down, the Paradise in Chicago. Theater historian John Naylor describes this Akron theater as one of John Eberson's three best, for its "balance and grace" and "fantastic intricacy."

THE A. POLSKY CO. STORE, AKRON, OHIO   63

▶ POLSKY BUILDING

A. POLSKY COMPANY STORE, NOW POLSKY BUILDING, 1930

Starrett & Van Vleck, New York
225 South Main Street
University of Akron classrooms, offices, archival services

The interior of this one-time department store has been altered extensively, but the Art Deco exterior, with its singular siding of terra-cotta scales, is wonderful.

SUMMIT COUNTY COURTHOUSE, 1908

J. Milton Dyer, Cleveland
209 South High
Street, NRHP
County courthouse;
330/643-2500

The Summit
County Courthouse
is set up on a hill,
proudly overlooking
High Street; a grand
staircase that once
ascended to it was
removed in the
1970s. The
sandstone
courthouse is
Second Renaissance
Revival in style;
interior features a
multi-story atrium

▶ SUMMIT COUNTY COURTHOUSE

surrounded by balconies at every floor and crowned with a stained-glass skylight. A fine, well treed urban park is adjacent to the courthouse, which, with a state office tower, encloses the park and makes it courtyard-like.

ST. BERNARD'S CATHOLIC CHURCH, 1905

William P. Ginther, Akron
44 University Avenue at South Broadway, NRHP
Church; open daytimes; 330/253-5161

St. Bernard's Catholic Church, perched between downtown and the University of Akron campus, becomes a distinctive landmark with its pair of eight-story towers. Late Romanesque Revival in style, St. Bernard's has a spectacular Baroque interior. Jim Pahlau says that altogether architect William P. Ginther designed some 300 Catholic churches, mostly built in Ohio but also in places like New York, Illinois, and California. For this German Catholic parish, Ginther drew inspiration from contemporary churches in Germany.

AKRON HILTON INN AT QUAKER SQUARE, NOW CROWNE PLAZA QUAKER SQUARE, 1930, 1980

1980 remodeling by Curtis and Rasmussen Inc., Cuyahoga Falls
135 South Broadway
Hotel; 330/253-5970

▶ AKRON HILTON

This silo-Hilton is a particularly imaginative building reuse. It turns a complex of old grain silos into a hotel with 196 rooms, all of them round. Thus the Hilton Inn at Quaker Square can describe itself as "A unique experience— like no other hotel in the world!" It wasn't just tires that Akron gave America; it also made oatmeal. Quaker Oats built this complex of 36 silos in 1930 and filled them with grain that the adjacent mill processed into cereal. In 1970 Quaker stopped production in Akron, and five years later Curtis and Rasmussen, Cuyahoga Falls architects, helped turn the National Register-listed mill into the shopping center known as Quaker Square. The idle silos next door presented the next challenge. The first idea for them, recalls Harold Rasmussen, was apartments; but then, to lure a restaurant into Quaker Square, the apartments evolved into a hotel. The 120-foot-high silos have eight floors of rooms (they're not filled all the way to the top) that are 24 feet in diameter, which makes them bigger than standard hotel rooms. Bathrooms fit in the interstices between silos. Halls, sliced out of a row of silos, are lined with arcs which, as Rasmussen says, help preserve the character of the place.

FIRESTONE PARK, BEGUN 1915

Vicinity of Firestone Boulevard east of South Main Street

As Akron's population tripled in the 1910s, demand for housing far exceeded the supply. So both Goodyear and Firestone developed housing estates for employees, and neither stinted when it came to design. Harvey S. Firestone, Sr., founder of the eponymous rubber company, called on talent he'd used for his own house (since razed), landscape architect Alling S. DeForest of Rochester. Firestone Park focuses on a park in the shape of a shield, the company symbol. Many of the houses, produced by Sears, were special designs used only in this development.

THE TREASURE: JAMES A. PAHLAU

—Among the architectural treasures of Akron, one is two-legged. He is James A. Pahlau, who knows more about Akron's buildings than anyone. For hundreds of the city's structures, he knows the date and architect, style and construction material; and he knows where they fit in city history. Of Akron he says, "We're *very* strong in twentieth-century architecture." He's been doing everything he can, to make that fact less of a surprise.

Now in his early 70s, Jim Pahlau is slight in build; he wears a short white beard and horn-rim glasses that ride down on his nose. He has overflowing enthusiasms. At Akron's Stan Hywet house museum, where he has studied not only the building and its history, but the master drawings on linen, Pahlau would take his local architecture classes on tours that included everything from the wine cellar to the hospital room on the tower's fourth floor. Scheduled from 9 to noon on a Saturday, these tours always took five hours, even when he hurried.

Pahlau is self-taught in architectural history. Part of his learning was driving around looking at buildings, especially houses, in an unhurried way, pausing and later returning, which in residential areas the police may notice. Akron cops came to know him, but once when he was in the Cleveland suburb of Bratenahl, where houses are hard to see from the road, he had a serious run-in with the police. After checking him out, they let him go with a warning not to drive so far into driveways just to turn around.

And part of his learning was books. Over the years Pahlau acquired an architectural library, the major investment of his lifetime. In 1995 he donated his accumulations, which his small apartment couldn't hold, even in boxes, to the University of Akron Archives. By then his collection included 4,849 books, just over half on architecture, the rest on decorative arts and musical theater; 800 historic architectural journals, blueprints, and photographs. The Akron *Beacon Journal* ran a front-page story on him ("the area's foremost architectural historian,") and his dedicated book collecting (he was quoted: "I don't drink. I don't smoke. I don't run around. This is what I do.") Altogether his library was valued at $85,000, but could well be worth twice that. After the article appeared a reader wrote in objecting that someone with $85,000 worth of books should have access to subsidized housing. Then another letter appeared in his defense, saying that many lunches were missed so Mr. Pahlau could buy those books. Which is true.

After the books went to the Archives, Pahlau himself shelved them so he could see them all again; he is still sorting papers and drawings. Now his collection is on the internet's OhioLINK, where sometimes his is the only copy of a book available in the state. For Pahlau this is gratifying but also ironic, for he bought many of the titles at sales of library discards.

When Pahlau was born in Massillon he made the papers: Stark County's first baby of the 1930s decade. By the 1940s, he'd found architecture. From junior high on he would do his homework after school at the Massillon library and then walk the mile and a quarter to his home. His route took him along Fourth Street, past five blocks of exceptionally good houses, including the Massillon Woman's Club by Cleveland architect Charles F. Schweinfurth. At dusk the lights would go on and he could look inside, and the more he saw, the more interested he became.

Except for two English courses at Kent State, Pahlau did not go to college. With straight A's all through school, he did have 17 scholarship offers, not from places like Yale, he says, but from the University of Pennsylvania, Kent, and other Ohio schools. He turned them all down and spent a year in New York studying interior design, which he worked at when he came back to Massillon. A stint as an inventory clerk at Republic Steel financed book buying, but ultimately he gravitated into part-time caretaking jobs. One, as resident caretaker at the Perkins House, the Summit County Historical Museum, brought him to Akron in 1979. When I met him, he was working at Stan Hywet, where, until he retired in 1997, he went around with a bundle of keys on his belt loop and a shirt that said "Stan Hywet" over the pocket. Never was Pahlau caretaker for just any place; the job had to link him with architecture or historic buildings. And it had to be part-time to leave time for architectural history.

In Akron his expertise became well known. He taught 27 non-credit courses at the University of Akron; he wrote building descriptions for Progress Through Preservation, a local group; he wrote house descriptions for tours; local architects paid to hear him lecture. When author Virginia McAlester came to Stan Hywet, preparing to include it in her book on architectural styles in American houses, the people she talked to were Curator Margaret Tramontine and Jim Pahlau.

Pahlau's partiality for early twentieth-century Georgian and Tudor Revival houses is so well known that sometimes, he says, "People are surprised when I rave about Art Deco." He researched architects until some friends dubbed him, "Champion of Unknown Architect, Deceased." One of his two favorite unknowns is Herman J. Albrecht (1885-1961) of Cleveland and Massillon, where he designed Tudor and Georgian Revival houses on Fourth Street and the library. The other is Akron's Roy G. Firestone (1897-1970), no relation to the tire company. Pahlau knows 21 documented Firestone houses on Akron's Merriman Road; he especially likes a 1929 Spanish Colonial Revival at 985 Merriman. "Firestone does a house the way I'd have done it, if I could have," Pahlau says. But with 17 scholarship offers, couldn't he have been an architect? No, he says. He graduated from high school in 1948, when "everything I liked was earlier, and I knew it was gone."

At Stan Hywet, Jim Pahlau and I walk around the grounds and look at the back of the house. He fusses over a few details that aren't historically authentic, like gravel instead of grass in a path. But overall he loves this house. Of course, it is Tudor Revival. He admires two lions on the entry posts, each distinctive. He relishes the materials—the wood, the stone, the original brick, which contains sizable gravel. He values the site and the way the west facade gets "rosier and rosier" at sunset. He appreciates the design, the clusters of octagonal brick chimney pots. Or on the south facade, a curved soffit over the windows and the "great composition" above: three gables and a gargoyle. He recognizes the house's allure, as in a view of it from the greenhouses. From there, just the chimneys and gables are visible, poking up over the trees. The glimpse is so enticing, he says, that it's "almost erotic. You can hardly wait to see it."

Market Street East
Architecturally, this is Goodyear Country.

Access: From downtown take Market Street east to Fir Hill; turn right; Hower House is at first intersection. Continue east on Market to Goodyear Boulevard to see National City Bank and Goodyear Hall. To see Goodyear Heights take Goodyear Boulevard to vicinity of Pilgrim and Newton streets.

JOHN H. HOWER HOUSE, 1871
Jacob Snyder, Akron
60 Fir Hill at Forge Street, NRHP
House museum owned by University of Akron; open all year except January on Wednesday-Sunday afternoons for tours; fee; 330/972-6909

This brick and sandstone house has several distinctive features. First, it is an excellent and well maintained example of the Second Empire style, which is characterized by mansard roofs and was at the height of fashion in 1871. Secondly, the house has black walnut woodwork that on the first floor is carved almost as though it is draped over and around a doorway, flowing down, rounding the corners and, at the bottom, curving out to join the baseboard. Finally, the first floor has an unusual central hall that's not an entry but a hub. It has doors cutting off its four corners, making it octagonal. Double doors centered in the four walls lead into octagonal rooms (except for the diningroom, whose far end has been squared so it is merely hexagonal.) The single doors at the corners lead to three square spaces (including the entry) and a porch. Born in Columbia County, Pennsylvania, architect Jacob

▶ HOWER HOUSE

Snyder (1820-1890) studied theoretical architecture at Dickinson College and practiced in his home state before moving to Akron in 1853. There he was to design Ohio State University's first building, University Hall, 1873 (razed 1971), in Columbus. But Snyder's greatest claim to fame is that in 1868, he and a local industrialist, Lewis Miller, developed the Akron Sunday School Plan. Miller's daughter later married Thomas Edison, which perhaps explains why he's sometimes given all the credit for the Akron Plan. Because of the diagonals, the octagons, and the way the hall opens to adjoining rooms, the Hower House's first floor is sometimes likened to the Akron Plan. This church design typically featured a sanctuary, often octagonal with altar and facing pews on a diagonal axis. One wall could be opened so as to include Sunday school classes in the service. Snyder and Miller first used the Akron Plan in an annex of the First Methodist Episcopal Church, which burned in 1911. But the idea became popular with Protestant churches, which were installing Akron Plans into the 1920s; many are in this guide. Jim Pahlau reports that nationwide, 2,500 churches ultimately used the Akron Sunday School Plan, which could well be Ohio's single most influential contribution to American architecture. Built for industrialist John Henry Hower, the house was occupied by his descendants until 1973, when it was willed to the University of Akron. The most exceptional Hower of all was Blanche Bruot Hower, left a widow and named president of her husband's auto parts company in 1916. She stayed in that post until she died, aged 93, in 1953. She promoted vocational education, served on the Akron School Board, and, at the age of 74 in 1934, was elected to the Ohio General Assembly.

GOODYEAR HALL, 1919

Walker & Weeks, Cleveland
1201-27 East Market Street
Company office and recreation building, with Goodyear World of Rubber museum open during business hours; 330/796-7117

▶ GOODYEAR HALL

Built across the street from the factory, Goodyear Hall was a perk for employees: a combination school, clubhouse, theater, gym, and bowling alleys. Such a facility was no accident—Firestone had a similar one—because attracting and keeping employees was critical as Akron's rubber industry grew in the 1910s. Goodyear's sales, $9.5 million in 1909-10, increased to $168.9 million in 1918-19, a seventeenfold increase in ten years. To produce such volume, the number of wage earners in Akron's rubber industry jumped from 20,000 in 1914 to 75,000 in 1920. Goodyear Hall housed dances, Christmas parties, and meetings. Clubs brought together not just stamp collectors, bridge players, and bowlers, but also foremen (there was also an auxiliary for their wives), veterans, and the deaf and dumb. The Industrial University occupied four floors of classrooms and labs where as many as 2,000 people a year learned how to be foremen, caught up on basic academics they'd missed, and studied bookkeeping, typing, or engineering fundamentals. The design of the six-story building is eclectic, with decorative brick work and, overall, a fanciful quality. The first floor and windows have been altered. The building is still company-owned, used for recreation and meetings, offices, and a museum open to the public.

▶ OHIO STATE BANK

OHIO STATE BANK & TRUST, NOW NATIONAL CITY BANK, 1918

Walker & Weeks, Cleveland
1177 East Market Street at Goodyear Boulevard
Bank; lobby open during business hours

Though this is now National City Bank, people in Akron still call it by its old name, Goodyear State Bank. Next to Goodyear Hall, at the corner of Goodyear Boulevard, and just down the street from the Goodyear Clock Tower, which was once surrounded by company factories, it's in the very heart of Goodyear Country. Both this bank and the hall next door were Walker & Weeks designs. This Beaux Arts bank has a wedge-shaped footprint, with high arched windows along both sides and an entry—also under a high arch—at the narrow end. The door is flanked by fluted and banded columns and pilasters that Jim Pahlau labels "Mannerist." Detailing on the bands is vermiculated, which laymen will be interested to know means a pattern of wavy lines, like a mess of worms. The lobby inside has been changed, though the unusual shape, the windows, and interior columns remain. Whoever did the decorating saw fit to apply green paint over 14-carat gold trim up on the crown molding. Pahlau compares the bank to Cleveland's Carnegie West Branch Library, 1910 (see also), which similarly has banded columns.

GOODYEAR HEIGHTS, BEGUN 1913
Vicinity of Goodyear Boulevard and Pilgrim and Newton streets

Can we imagine an employer today calling in nationally recognized design talent to plan housing for employees? That's what Goodyear founder Frank Seiberling did. Having acquired a hilly tract of land near Goodyear offices and factories, he asked landscape architect Warren H. Manning of Boston to lay out Goodyear Heights—Manning had also done the grounds of Seiberling's own house, Stan Hywet. In 1912 Seiberling announced his intentions to plant foremen; he promised employees "an opportunity to become home owners at as low a cost and by as easy means as possible." For no money down, buyers had a choice of 20 different architect-designed plans, and monthly payments were only a little above the lowest rents. Then from Goodyear Heights they had only a ten-minute walk to work. The neighborhood is still attractive; see, for example, the shady curves of Hillside Terrace.

Access: To see Goodyear Airdock continue east on Market to Seiberling Street; drive south to Triplett Boulevard; turn left to see old airport terminal. The best way to approach the Airdock is by turning south/right from East Market onto Seiberling Street, which is some two miles from downtown. Then, after just driving along, you round a bend and suddenly, at the end of a streetful of bungalows, a mountain looms: the Airdock, still almost a mile away and an astonishing sight. Visible also from U.S. 224, it's always a good excuse for taking that road. Or, to reach an overlook, at the foot of Seiberling turn right onto Triplett, left on Kelly Avenue and then left into the parking lot of Carousel Dinner Theatre. Says a theater spokesman, "People drive in here all the time. Sometimes they even park and eat their lunch." Triplett, Kelly, and the theater lot all offer Airdock views, but the closest viewpoint is to the east, along Massillon Road. From Seiberling turn left onto Triplett which becomes State Route 241; stay on 241 and turn right at Springfield Lake, then right onto Massillon. You'll come to an open area where you can peer through a chain-link fence to your heart's content. You'll be looking at one of Ohio's marvels: the world's largest building with no internal supports.

GOODYEAR AIRDOCK, NOW OWNED BY LOCKHEED MARTIN TACTICAL DEFENSE SYSTEMS, 1929

Designed by Dr. Karl Arnstein, director
of engineering for Goodyear-Zeppelin Corporation; structural design by Wilbur
Watson & Associates, architects and engineers, Cleveland
1210 Massillon Road, NRHP
Private industrial facility; no provision for visitors

The Airdock has the shape of the top half of a long watermelon, but an immensity all its own. It's 20 stories high and, at 1,175 feet, long enough to hold two Carew Towers, end to end. It was designed as a place to build two U.S. Navy dirigibles, the *Akron* and the *Macon*. As they were 785 feet long, the Airdock needed more uninterrupted floorspace than was under roof anywhere. A building that broke records was expected to be just the beginning, for even as work began here in 1928, the German dirigible *Graf Zeppelin* made a spectacular 6,630-mile transatlantic crossing. For airships, the future seemed to hold unlimited promise. Akron's rigid-frame dirigibles were to be the creation of German know-how and American money. In the early 1920s, Goodyear took the initiative in forming an alliance with Zeppelin, a German manufacturer with a long record of successes. Goodyear also hired Zeppelin's engineering brain, Dr. Karl Arnstein, a Czech by birth. Arnstein's interests included not only dirigibles but also the hangar to build them in—a hangar whose round, aerodynamic shape would minimize the effects of air currents. To accommodate airship takeoffs and landings into the wind, the Airdock is set on a southwest-northeast axis, in line with the usual wind direction; for craft entering and going out, it has doors at both ends. And these doors don't flap open, which could generate enough turbulence to make it impossible to get a 785-foot ship out of the hangar. Instead, they are rounded, shaped like segments of orange peel, a pair at each end. To open they pivot on pins; each 600-ton door travels on 40 wheels to slide back against the wall. Ground preparation—the site had to be absolutely level—was the first step, in fall, 1928; actual construction began the following

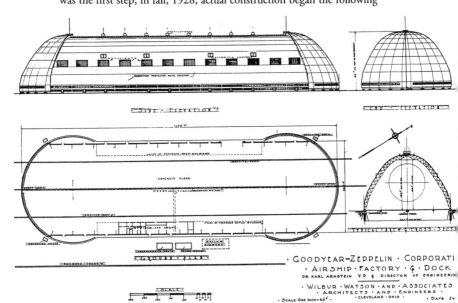

▶ THE AIRDOCK UNDER CONSTRUCTION

spring. Eleven parabolic arches of steel trusswork support the Airdock. Of those only the three central arches are anchored in a fixed position; the others flow on rollers, expanding and contracting. When construction of the *Akron* began in 1929, the building, still open at the north end, was two months from completion. Even when the north end was closed in, the building, reasonably enough, was not heated, though it holds one-story sheds and offices that are. Contrary to myth, clouds do not form in the Airdock, but condensation happens in the upper rafters; when this water falls, it may feel like rain. Owner Lockheed Martin acquired the Airdock and other facilities here in 1996 from Loral Corporation, which bought them from Goodyear nine years earlier. Lockheed staffer Cary Dell says the Airdock is leased to a company that makes aircraft brake systems. He also reports that, on first sight of the Airdock's interior, the response is standard: "Gee, that's big." The building is not open to the public, but the public has always been interested. When Mrs. Herbert Hoover, the president's wife, christened the *Akron* in August 1931, the city's largest crowd ever, 150,000 people, came to watch as she released 48 pigeons, one for each state. Then, as Margaret Bourke-White took pictures, the new ship emerged from the Airdock. A year and a half later, it crashed in an Atlantic Ocean thunderstorm; 73 of the 76-man crew were lost. Later the *Macon* flew two years before it went down in a Pacific Ocean squall in 1935. The U.S. never again tried the large, rigid-frame ships. Today they are remembered here because the big hangar was, in the end, the greater success, aerodynamically.

MUNICIPAL AIRPORT TERMINAL, NOW CAFE PISCITELLI, 1931
Michel M. Konarski, Akron
1800 Triplett Boulevard
Restaurant open daily except Sunday; 330/798-1986

This Art Deco airport terminal, which Jim Pahlau calls "a little masterpiece", was slated for demolition about 1990; the restaurant represents a happy rescue. Michel M. Konarski (1890-1970) was Akron's school architect from 1919 to 1938.

Market Street West

West of downtown, Akron's past is variously honored in the cemetery and the founder's house. Stan Hywet Hall is the kingpin of a still fine early twentieth-century residential neighborhood.

Access: From downtown take Market Street west to Rand Street, just after crossing over State Route 59; turn left; then take first right, Glendale Avenue, to cemetery; turn at Locust for cemetery entrance. Alternatively, west of Rand take Maple Street south to Glendale Avenue; turn left.

GLENDALE CEMETERY MEMORIAL CHAPEL, 1876
Frank O. Weary, Akron
150 Glendale Avenue at Locust, NRHP
Cemetery; open daily; 330/253-2317

Glendale Cemetery has one of the state's best clusters of cemetery buildings, and two of the four structures represent the best remaining work of the prolific Akron architect Frank O. Weary. The four are a chapel, a bell tower, a superintendent's lodge, and an office, all close to the entrance gates. The pride of the four is Weary's Memorial Chapel, built to honor Akron's Civil War dead. High Victorian Gothic in style, true to its era, it embodies a romantic expression of loss. So long as people lived who survived the Civil War, it was one of Akron's showplaces. The war was not so long past when the Buckley Post of Union Veterans decided to build the chapel. All the money—$25,000—was raised quickly, between February and July, 1874. Several architects submitted plans, and the design committee chose this one by Frank Orlando Weary (1849-1921), who had gone to war himself as a 14-year-old drummer boy. Born in Sheboygan, Wisconsin of parents who later returned to Akron, Weary had studied architecture with Heard & Blyth in Cleveland for two years, and then for a year in Boston; finally he spent three years working in Chicago after the 1871 fire. This chapel was his first major commission in Akron. Of rough stone blocks with smooth stone trim on the corners, the chapel has a cruciform plan, a front porch with polished rose-colored granite columns, and a very steep slate roof. In the early 1990s the roof got a $125,000 repair—part was replaced and the cupola was redone. But that was not before leaks had

▶ GLENDALE CHAPEL

undermined ceiling beams, and in 1994 the cemetery had to close the building. By early 1997 a foundation started raising the $700,000 needed for repairs, due for completion in 2000. The ceiling (of butternut), the stained-glass windows (of glass from Scotland), and the names of soldiers engraved on the walls are the chapel interior's principal features. As naturalists looking for old plant species have discovered, a cemetery can be a good place for keeping things. Except for the crypt underneath, this chapel has been little altered since 1876. Founded in 1839 as Akron Rural Cemetery, Glendale also has a striking collection of mausoleums along both sides of the road just beyond the chapel. People whose names come up in connection with buildings—for instance, the Seiberlings and Ohio Columbus Barber, founder of Barberton—are buried here.

GLENDALE CEMETERY SUPERINTENDENT'S LODGE, 1869, NRHP
Private

The cemetery's oldest building, the Superintendent's Lodge is to the right of the entrance. A story and a half high, built of stone, it has Gothic features and a towerlet with a mansard roof. "They knew how to mix styles and have it come out right," is Jim Pahlau's assessment. The lodge would never have been built had it not been for the Akron Ladies' Cemetery Association. Founded in 1866 by Mrs. Mary Ingersoll Tod Evans, whose brother David Tod was a governor, the group raised money by a series of concerts. The lodge initially cost $12,000, and the benefactresses later added a kitchen for

AKRON, O.

▶ GLENDALE CEMETERY ENTRANCE

$1,400 and heating for $300. The Cemetery Association also contributed $50 for a headstone for their founder. Mrs. Evans died early in 1869, before the lodge was finished.

GLENDALE CEMETERY BELL TOWER, 1883

Frank O. Weary, Akron
Not accessible to the public

Partly hidden by trees, the bell tower is on a hillside just southeast of the chapel. It is round, built of rustic stone, and at the top has an observation deck under a flared hip roof that narrows to a point. Pahlau mulls the style and comes up with "kind of Adirondack lodge." He says the bell was still ringing into the 1940s. Glendale Foreman Jim Finnerty reports that the Bell Tower contains three platforms, the lower ones revealed by window slits. Though the tower has not been open to the public in recent years, trespassers became so persistent that the door was welded shut. Nor is the exterior available for the public—like the YMCA class Finnerty found one day, practicing their rappelling. Cemetery insurance does not cover rappelling on the Bell Tower.

GLENDALE CEMETERY OFFICE, 1903, NRHP

The office is in a fine, house-like stone building with a wraparound porch. It's always been an office and still is, though the inside has been remodeled and is not so interesting as the outside. Stylewise, Pahlau calls it "noncommittal. Early progressive maybe. Sometimes it's hard to come up with one easy style."

Access: From cemetery take Glendale Avenue left/west to Maple Street; turn left/west. Road name changes to Copley; Perkins House is at Portage Path. To reach Stan Hywet take Portage Path north from Perkins House (or from Market Street).

PERKINS MANSION, 1837

Isaac Ladd, Warren
550 Copley Road, NRHP
Owned by the Summit County Historical Society, which offers afternoon tours
daily except Monday; fee; 330/535-1120

This stone Greek Revival house was built for Colonel Simon Perkins, son of Akron's founder. He came to Summit County to manage lands owned by his father, Warren's General Simon Perkins, who used his considerable influence to make sure the canal came to Akron, so that the value of his holdings might be enhanced. The Perkins family sold the house to the historical society in 1945. Note the unpolished marble fireplaces.

PERKINS WASHHOUSE, 1895

550 Copley Road, NRHP
Former laundry accessible to visitors touring house

This is a mere outbuilding, a laundry, done with flair. On top of the tower there's a windmill that was used to pump water. Jim Pahlau says the first floor was the washroom, so it had a waterproof brick floor and an enormous fireplace—"a walk-in fireplace," Pahlau jokes—for heating water. A large room upstairs was used for hanging laundry. The architect is unknown but Pahlau speculates that it could have been William Redding of Akron, or Frank Weary, also of Akron.

STAN HYWET HALL, 1915

Charles S. Schneider, architect, Cleveland; Warren H. Manning, landscape,
Boston
714 North Portage Path, NHL, NRHP
Tours daily; fee; 330/836-5533

Ohio has three truly superb planned landscapes. They are three places of great beauty, all well maintained and open to the public. One is the lakes area at Spring Grove Cemetery in Cincinnati; another is the Cleveland Museum of Art and the Wade Park lagoon area in front of it; and the third is the grounds of Stan Hywet Hall in Akron. Because of these grounds, Stan Hywet is Ohio's best house-and-garden ensemble, at least of those the public can see. Boston landscape architect Warren H. Manning chose the house site, and the one he selected is without peer in the state. The landscaping he planned offers vistas, allées, gardens, and ponds. Grounds and house are intertwined, showing each other off and making Stan Hywet one house that definitely has to be seen from all sides. From every angle the architecture is distinctive, and so is the landscape composition it relates to. Landscape highlights include the west terrace, in the back, leading down to an overlook that sees to the blue horizon. So does the overlook north of the house, at the end of the birch allée, where lagoons appear in the foreground below. The walled English garden (which not long ago had a $300,000 restoration) and the rose garden are worth seeking out. To walk all the gardens without much lingering takes about an hour and a half; house tours take an hour.

THE WELL-PLANNED COTTAGE

THE WELL-PLANNED COTTAGE—With over 65,000 square feet, Stan Hywet is hardly a modest house. Thus it's a little surprising that among the high styles for early twentieth-century houses, Stan Hywet's Tudor Revival was considered the homiest, the most comfortable domestic architecture. The style meant cottage rather than palace, though originally in Tudor England, it was often a cottage that expanded, accumulating wings, dormers, bay windows, porches, chimneys, and balconies, in an assortment of materials, and with varying roof heights. Stan Hywet has all these features, by design. It's considered the best work of Cleveland architect Charles S. Schneider. It also represented a happy collaboration between the architect and his clients, Goodyear founder Frank Seiberling and his wife Gertrude.

Stan Hywet's success was no accident; the Seiberlings prepared for it for years. In 1907 they bought the land, a rural area where Frank had hunted as a youth. That same year, Gertrude enrolled in Buchtel College (later University of Akron) to study architecture, interior design, horticulture, and gardening. Then in 1911 the Seiberlings hired Boston landscape architect Warren H. Manning, a former associate of park designer Frederick Law Olmsted, to plan the site for them. The following year they selected the old English design proposed by George B. Post & Sons, a New York architectural firm. Charles Schneider, head of Post's Cleveland office, took charge.

Almost immediately, Schneider, the Seiberlings, and their daughter Irene, then 22, went to England and France to look at mansions and castles. Some of Stan Hywet's features derive from that trip, such as the windows in the tower, which are copies of those at England's fifteenth-century Ockwells Manor in Berkshire.

Frank Seiberling launched Goodyear in 1898 by borrowing some money—$3,500 for a cash down payment on an idle factory in east Akron. Thirty-nine years old, he'd previously been in business with his father, but they'd lost everything two years earlier. Now he determined to use the vacant factory for a rubber company named for Charles Goodyear, who figured out how to vulcanize rubber and died penniless in 1860. Goodyear Tire and Rubber started out with carriage and bicycle tires, but in 1901 it produced its first automobile tire. Fifteen years later, the company became the world's largest car tire producer, a title it held until 1990, when Michelin became number one by acquiring Goodrich. Seiberling himself was forced out of Goodyear in 1921, after heavy losses. He rebounded immediately with Seiberling Rubber, which by the end of the decade was tenth in production.

In late 1915 the Seiberlings moved into Stan Hywet with their six children. After Frank Seiberling died in 1955 (his wife died in 1946), those children agreed to give the house to a foundation, for use as a museum and cultural center. If at the end of ten years the effort was succeeding, the family promised to donate the house's contents also. Though not without setbacks, the project

Music

did succeed; and in 1967 the foundation became complete owners. The family remains interested in the house—two grandchildren are docents, or volunteer tour guides. And until just recently, Irene Seiberling Harrison, who scouted European architecture with her parents more than 80 years earlier, was still resident in the gate lodge. She died early in 1999, just before her 109th birthday.

Today Stan Hywet Hall and Gardens is a $2.1 million operation; only the guides and people who run special events are volunteers. Until 1979 the house had no professional curator; today it has Margaret Tramontine and her assistant, Mark Heppner, who promote Stan Hywet as an early twentieth-century American country house. An old rumor keeps getting in the way—the fiction that the house was an antiquity imported from England brick by brick. In its early years as a museum, even docents unknowingly misrepresented some artifacts as Medieval, while in fact virtually all the furnishings are modern reproductions. The house is a modern one, with electricity, a vacuum system, 36 telephones, and central heating. Admittedly, radiators are hidden behind paneling or window seats—so are a telephone and even an elevator. The house does have some antiques—for example, two sixteenth-century Flemish tapestries and a pair of eighteenth-century Chinese Chippendale cabinets.

Doug Graf sees Stan Hywet's interior as contrasting with the exterior. He admires the inside for, he says, its "wacky 1920s style, with a Norman Rockwell quality to it, while the outside is relatively subdued." In their book *Great American Houses*, Virginia and Lee McAlester report that Stan Hywet's music room "is considered by one critic to be among America's most beautifully decorated rooms." For sure, no one calls the interior dull.

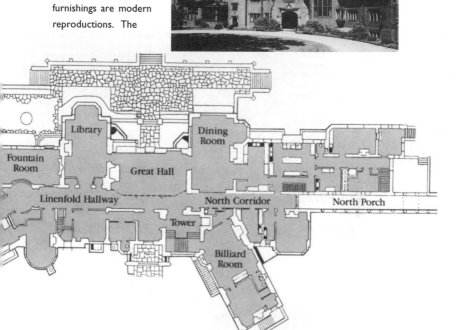

Canton

William McKinley may have been born in
Niles, but in 1867 he went to Canton to live
and practice law. He must have felt welcome,
for two years later he was elected county pros-
ecutor. Of course, that was just the beginning.
In 1875 Canton sent McKinley to Congress; in
the early 1890s Ohioans twice elected him
governor. As Ohio went, so went the nation,
for in 1896, after running a front-porch cam-
paign from his Canton home, McKinley was
elected president. Described by one historian
as a man who was "handsome, portly, and
sleek," he is well remembered in Canton, where
he is identified with buildings. He argued cases
in Courtroom No. 1 at the courthouse; he went
to the Church of the Savior United Methodist
downtown on West Tuscarawas at Cleveland
Avenue; and after his assassination in 1901, he
was buried in a tomb on the west side. (See
below.) As for the McKinley house with the

porch, that was razed in the 1930s. Thus, says local preservationist Jeff Brown, Canton became the only city to level a presidential residence. ¶ "Forty years ago," says Brown, now a staffer with the Stark County Planning Commission, "Canton must have been one of the most beautiful cities in Ohio." But later it became too eager to tear itself down, especially downtown, so that now much if not most of Canton's best architecture is in early twentieth-century residential areas like Ridgewood on the near north side and Hills and Dales to the west (see below). The houses are good because good architects, like Herman J. Albrecht of Massillon and Cleveland and Charles E. Firestone of Canton, were producing the designs. ¶ This tour divides Canton into Downtown, West Side and Western Suburbs.

Access: From I-77 exit at Tuscarawas Street/State Route 172 and drive east to downtown Canton. From U.S. 30 take I-77 north to Tuscarawas or turn north on State Route 43.

Downtown

Much celebrated when it was new in 1963, the Central Plaza along Market at Tuscarawas Street has been brightened anew by a revitalization in 2000. As for the rest of downtown Canton, it does have some good architecture, some striking examples of how not to alter buildings, and Bender's, my favorite barroom in Ohio.

▶ First National Bank Building; COURTHOUSE TOWER IN BACKGROUND

Access: These buildings are listed in order for a downtown loop tour on foot. Start at Tuscarawas and Market Avenue, the site of both Central Plaza and the Stark County Courthouse, 1893, designed by George F. Hammond of Cleveland. (It was built over and around an earlier courthouse.) At this intersection numbered cross streets begin counting in two directions, with an N or S visible on the street signs. Court, Cleveland, and McKinley avenues, in that order, parallel Market to the west; after walking north to Palace Theatre turn left.

FIRST NATIONAL BANK BUILDING, NOW BANK ONE, 1924

Frank L. Packard, Columbus
101 Central Plaza South
Bank offices; Canton Club closed in October 2000

This building has two special virtues. One is the painted beams of the Renaissance ceiling in the two-story marble banking room. The other is the quarters of the Canton Club on top of the building. They are accessible to visitors interested in architecture—a treat indeed, for this club space is little altered. In the corridor behind the banking room, take the elevator to the 12th floor, where the paneled lobby leads to club rooms. The club's diningroom is on the 14th floor, which is in a rooftop pavilion that's set back and faced mostly in stone. Inside, besides pilasters and cornice, the diningroom has high, arched windows that, unlike their counterparts on the ground floor, retain their original panes and dividers. On the outside, this Neoclassical Revival building has recessed colonnades at the 12th and 13th floors. Sheathing is granite and limestone at the base, then buff brick with stone quoins, or corner trim, for the tower.

GEORGE D. HARTER BANK & TRUST, NOW KEY BANK, 922

Walker & Weeks, Cleveland
126 Central Plaza North, at 2nd Street N.E.
Bank

Designed by Cleveland's Walker & Weeks, this bank has a distinctive facade dominated by a single three-story arch for door below and windows above. A relatively modern addition to the north, with a steep metal mansard roof, seems (to put it politely) awkward. As for the interior, Akron architectural historian James A. Pahlau found photographs of the original banking room. (He knows his way around the literature; they appeared in the single issue of *Architectural Revue of the Mississippi Basin*, published in 1930.) These pictures showed the still evident high blind arches (that is, arches filled in by wall) along the sides of the room and an amazing ceiling, with beams supporting a glazed gable roof. The ceiling and beams also are still there, though they've been painted white. Perhaps, under the paint, that skylight is still there too.

▶ RENKERT BUILDING

RENKERT BUILDING, 1912

Walker & Weeks, Cleveland
300 Market Avenue North at 3rd Street N.E.
Office building

Canton's first skyscraper, the Renkert Building has distinctive and quite wonderful brick work. The brick was all made by the first occupant, the Metropolitan Paving Company, which in 1917 became the world's largest paving-block producer. This 11-story Chicago Style building took the name of company president Harry Renkert. The exterior has lots of fabulous brick, laid decoratively.

▶ PALACE THEATRE

PALACE THEATRE, 1926

John Eberson, Chicago
605 Market Avenue North and 6th Street N.W., NRHP
Theater for movies, ballet and symphony; if convenient, will show to impromptu
visitors on weekdays; or prearrange; 330/454-8172

The Palace Theatre is one of those John Eberson designed to transport
audiences to the exotic locales of his dreams. You won't miss it, with its
immense sign, marquee, and tan terra cotta—in a sinewy scalloped cornice
and decorated piers—against brown brick walls. The festive ornament
continues inside, in multi-colored tile floors, decorative painting, ogee
arches. The 1,500-seat auditorium is an "atmospheric", a system Eberson
invented in 1923 to simulate star-like lights twinkling amid floating clouds
on the ceiling. Jim Pahlau, a Stark County native, dubs the style Hispano-

Moresque or Churrigueresque,
the same as Loew's Akron, also
by Eberson (see also). Canton
is lucky to have the Palace
Theatre, which, until local
people rallied to the rescue, was
slated for demolition in 1979; a
sister showplace, Loew's Plaza,
was torn down. Originally the
Palace was the gift of Harry H.
Ink, who made his money with
Tonseline, a medicine for sore
throats, and wanted to give

Canton a "state of the art" theater. Amid the decorative panels inside is a
picture of a giraffe with a bandaged throat: the Tonseline trademark.

ST. JOHN THE BAPTIST CHURCH, 1872, SPIRE ADDED IN 1890

Renwick and Kiely Associates, Brooklyn, New York
627 McKinley Avenue N.W. at 6th Street, NRHP
Church; to see interior on weekdays ask at rectory; 330/454-8044

This High Victorian Gothic Catholic church provides a chance to drop the name of James Renwick (1818-95), a leading American architect in his day. A Gothic Revival pioneer, Renwick designed St. Patrick's Cathedral in New York. Canton's St. John the Baptist is especially fine inside.

STERN AND MANN, 1925

Abram Garfield, Cleveland
Tuscarawas Street West at Cleveland Avenue N.W.
Office building

Once upon a time, says Jeff Brown, this clothing store was one of the best buildings in Canton. Now, the ground floor having been altered in the 1980s, you'll have to keep your eyes up, directed toward the second and third floors, still in marble and terra cotta, still like a Venetian palazzo. Architect Abram Garfield was the son of President James Abram Garfield.

TIMKEN VOCATIONAL HIGH SCHOOL, NOW TIMKEN SENIOR HIGH SCHOOL, 1939

Charles E. Firestone and Laurence J. Motter, Canton
521 Tuscarawas Street West at McKinley Avenue N.W.
High school

The Art Deco Timken Senior High School has its original windows, a marble hallway, multi-story glass-brick windows lighting stairways, and murals—large ones in the auditorium, smaller ones in the library. Until he found that he was afraid of electricity, Charles E. Firestone (1890-1970)

▶ TIMKEN SENIOR HIGH

wanted to be an electrical engineer. He settled for his second-choice profession, architecture, which he studied at the University of Michigan. According to M.J. Albacete, who prepared two editions of his book on historic Canton buildings, Firestone was the only Stark County architect to become a fellow of the American Institute of Architects.

FRANK T. BOW FEDERAL BUILDING, 1933

Charles E. Firestone, Canton
201 Cleveland Avenue S.W. at 2nd Street S.W.
Federal office building

Here's another example of architect Charles Firestone's work—like most good designers, he was master of more than one style. This Neoclassical Revival building faces its intersection with a recessed porch that has a curved colonnade in front.

THE BELMONT, NOW BENDER'S TAVERN, 1899

Guy Tilden, Canton
137 Court Avenue at
2nd Street S.W.,
NRHP
Bar and restaurant;
330/453-8424

▶ BENDER'S, 1902, MUCH AS IT IS TODAY

One night in Bender's barroom, I watched four well-dressed men at a corner table. While one officiated, the other three tried to identify wines poured from unlabeled bottles. At least, in Bender's they had a worthy setting for their sophisticated game. This vintage barroom has a grand bar, tile floor, coffered ceiling, colored and leaded glass, while diningrooms have sprawled north into two other buildings on Court Avenue's one-time "Whiskey Alley." In an essay on architect Guy Tilden (1857-1929), Cleveland architectural historian Eric Johannesen talked about Bender's barroom. "For some," he wrote, "this bit of Americana alone would justify the architect's reputation." It's just as well. Although Tilden was Canton's leading architect from the 1880s to the 1920s, much of his work has been lost. The last big demolition took the Frank Case Mansion, built in 1902 for a lawyer who made a successful career shift into manufacturing dental chairs.

▶ CANTON REPOSITORY

CANTON DAILY NEWS, NOW CANTON REPOSITORY, 1927

Schultze & Weaver, New York
500 Market Street South at
5th Street S.E.
Newspaper offices

The newspaper has a handsome Italian Renaissance Revival building with a 1957 addition at the back.

West Side

Access: **From downtown drive west on 6th Street N.W.; at Fulton the road jogs north onto 7th Street, which continues west to the McKinley tomb. On leaving the tomb take 7th half a block east to Monument; drive north to 12th Street; turn west; street becomes 13th on the other side of I-77 and almost immediately comes to The Stables.**

▶ MᴄKɪɴʟᴇʏ Mᴇᴍᴏʀɪᴀʟ

WILLIAM MCKINLEY TOMB, NOW MCKINLEY NATIONAL MEMORIAL, 1907

Harold Van Buren Magonigle, New York
800 McKinley Monument Drive N.W., NHL, NRHP
Tomb, open daily, free

Ten years after this Neoclassical Revival tomb was built, McKim, Mead & White did a McKinley Birthplace Memorial in Niles. That is a splendid building, while this one is less so. It's a pink granite Neoclassical Revival structure, round-domed, cylindrical, and, at 96 feet high and 79 feet in diameter, squat—a feature best appreciated from the back.

HENRY H. TIMKEN ESTATE BARN, NOW THE STABLES, 1919

Frank Gilchrist, Pittsburgh
2317 13th Street N.W., NRHP
Sports bar and restaurant; 330/452-1230

A St. Louis man named Henry Timken perfected the modern roller bearing and, at the turn of the century, moved his manufacturing to Canton to be closer to suppliers. Within a decade Timken was the town's leading industry. After World War I, the founder's son, Henry H. Timken, built himself an estate; almost all that remains today is this doughnut-shaped barn with four towers, in a Rural French Neoclassical style. Timken died in 1940, and for decades his old stable stood, but stood unused. Then in 1993 the barn became a sports bar intended to lure patrons also visiting the Pro Football Hall of Fame just to the north—"a football field away," as the promotional literature puts it. The Stables roofed the open space in the doughnut's middle and installed a curved row of booths and bigger-than-life football action statues. One tower contains the foyer; another, a meeting room. The

▶ TIMKIN STABLES

exterior is brown brick with contrasting masonry ornament on the towers. Roofs, both those on the barn and the conical ones on the towers, are slightly concave. Even while it was empty, people have always liked this building. In the parking lot, my camera was only one of several focused on Timken's fanciful barn.

Western Suburbs

Access: From The Stables, take I-77 north from Twelfth Street to the next exit, Fulton Drive/State Route 687, and drive west. After roughly two-and-a-half miles on Fulton, turn left/south on Everhard Road. You'll pass a corner of Tam O'Shanter Golf Course and some apartments on the left. Then, just before a Carriage Hill Club sign, make a sharp turn left between stone gates and drive uphill to the house.

CLARENCE HERBRUCK HOUSE, NOW CARRIAGE HILL CLUB, C. 1923

Frank B. Meade and James M. Hamilton, Cleveland
5228 Everhard Road N.W.
Clubhouse for adjacent apartment development; first and second floors open to
visitors; 330/492-2377

When Jim Pahlau was a boy in Massillon, he would bicycle around this area gazing at the stone gates here and at Hills and Dales nearby—he'd have given a lot to see the houses within. By now, he's well familiar with them. He showed me this house: Tudor Revival with a predominantly Georgian interior. It has been converted into an apartment development's clubhouse, so a swimming pool and gym area occupy an addition at the left. At least in summer, greenery makes the pool wing relatively discreet. The house, stone and half-timbered under a steep roof of heavy, roughly finished slates, has what might be described as a bow-shaped footprint, narrow in the middle. It has many highlights. I especially liked the elongated octagonal hall in the middle, where windows overlooking the landscaped grounds at the back are opposite the door. At the ends of the hall, doors lead off to partly glimpsed enticing places: a paneled study, a bending corridor, a diningroom, a curved stairway, a sunken livingroom. The house is also striking from the rear, with the half-timbered round stair tower on the left (ribbons of timbering curl down around the tower) and a part-octagon on the right. The grounds, hilly and well-treed, with a sunken garden near the house, are interesting too. Pahlau says the house has been called a small Stan Hywet.

▶ CARRIAGE HILL CLUB

Access: From Carriage Hill turn left/southwest on Everhard; at Wackerley turn left/southeast to Hills and Dales Road. Turn left/ east; Hills and Dales gates are on right opposite Tam O'Shanter entrance. Hills and Dales is a small village of winding roads; you should intersect Foxhill either by going straight, turning left, or persisting.

▶ T.K. Harris's 1926 house

T.K. HARRIS HOUSE, 1930

Albrecht and Wilhelm, Massillon
2601 Foxhill Drive N.W., Hills and Dales
Private house

Early in the 1920s, Canton's T.K. Harris visited Dayton and saw Hills and
Dales, a park with adjacent residential areas that the Olmsted Brothers
designed for John Patterson and his company, National Cash Register. (See
also Oakwood, a Dayton suburb.) So in 1922 Harris bought a 202-acre
farm just west of Canton, named it for the Dayton place that had inspired
him, and hired Cleveland landscape architects Pittkin and Mott to lay out a
residential community. He specified roads following the terrain's contours
and large lots—127 were set out in the end; of those several became
parkland. M.J. Albacete writes that lot sales began in 1925 and houses
followed shortly. The first house Harris built for himself was at 2615
Brentwood Road N.W.; finished in 1926, it's a brick and half-timbered Tudor

Revival by Albrecht,
Wilhelm and Kelly of
Massillon. This house on
Foxhill Drive was the third
that Harris built for
himself in Hills and Dales;
he lived in it for 40 years.
It's a great favorite of Jim
Pahlau, for whom it's "the
one greatest house in all of
Stark County." Pahlau is
especially partial to the
work of architect Herman
J. Albrecht, who practiced
in Massillon and Cleveland
and whose houses are
found in all Canton's early

▶ Harris's 1930 house

twentieth-century residential neighborhoods; in Hills and Dales alone he did
two dozen. Built of sandstone and limestone, this one is Georgian Revival—
"a perfect house of its style," Pahlau says.

Cincinnati

Cincinnati is Ohio's best place for buildings. That's not because it has the most opulent architecture (it doesn't); nor can architects take all the credit, for what's most remarkable about Cincinnati is the high quality of background buildings in older neighborhoods. ¶ For example, I saw a modest two-story house that I especially liked. It was brick, with two windows on the first floor and a mansard roof and dormer upstairs, while the tiny facade had carved detailing, brackets, decorative brick work; it was at once small and elegant. (The address is 2051 Harrison Avenue, on the west side of town.) Ultimately, I saw a version of this house in nineteenth-century neighborhoods to the north, east and west. Often it was frame, sometimes it was dilapidated; but for me, it had extraordinary charm. ¶ Cincinnatians Walter E. Langsam, an architectural historian, and preservationist Mary Ann Olding, both attribute the city's exceptional vernacular architecture—that's the stuff nonprofessionals build—

to the German influence. German preferences also account for the widespread use of brick, which endures and which, Olding says, is "hard to do foolish things with." ¶ The generally high level of vernacular architecture sets Cincinnati apart. But that is not all. Until the Depression, buildings here that every community has, such as firehouses, schools, park buildings, and water-pumping stations, were designed by the city's best architects and were very well done, not just in the best neighborhoods but everywhere, again and again and again. So for example, in spring 1998, the Cincinnati Preservation Association surveyed all 81 public schools and found 34 eligible for the National Register because of their architecture. That's amazing. ¶ Rookwood Pottery helped. Cincinnati-based, the country's leading art pottery almost routinely lavished fine glazed terra cotta tile inside and outside the city's buildings. It has helped that, though Cincinnati has razed a lot, it razes less than other Ohio cities. Perhaps that's because it's harder to tear down buildings on hilly terrain. ¶ Finally, there's an elemental fact of history; among Ohio cities, Cincinnati had a head start. In the 1840s and 1850s, it was already civilized; it reigned as the Queen City of the West. Sixth in the nation in population, a port where 8,000 river steamers docked in a year, it was a likely destination for the parents of an English child and future architect named Samuel Hannaford, or a German landscape architect who would invent "American" landscape design, or a Bohemian rabbi who would invent American Judaism.

To see more in Cincinnati—The best architectural guide any Ohio city has had is the two-volume *Bicentennial Guide to Greater Cincinnati: A Portrait of Two Hundred Years,* published by the Cincinnati Historical Society in 1988. It is in many libraries and may still be purchased from the shop at the Museum Center; 800/733-2077. The Cincinnati Preservation Association distributes a good booklet on downtown, *Historic Walking Tours of Downtown Cincinnati* and another on parks, *A Guide to Art and Architecture in Cincinnati*, both free. The CPA is at 342 West Fourth Street, 513/721-4506. *Cincinnati Observed* is John Clubbe's passionate collection of architectural walking tours. And finally, Walter E. Langsam, whom everybody regards as the city's ultimate living architectural history resource, has published *Great Houses of the Queen City*, which describes 70 of them, illustrated with photographs by Alice Weston.

Start your Cincinnati architectural tour with the old Union Terminal, a glorious building that rises improbably on a flood plain. It's a little out of the way—you won't see it from downtown streets—but from its front steps you'll see Cincinnati laid before you: the towers of downtown, the red-brick backside of Music Hall straight ahead and Mount Adams looming above it on the horizon, and the hills all around.

Access: To reach Union Terminal—and the Cincinnati Museum Center—from the north, drive south on I-75 until you see downtown, exit onto Ezzard Charles Drive (Exit 1H); you'll see the building on your right. Coming from the south or from I-71, follow Dayton signs (the interstates merge underneath the city), look for Ezzard Charles Drive exit, turn left on Drive. Terminal is immediately ahead.

CINCINNATI UNION TERMINAL, NOW CINCINNATI MUSEUM CENTER, 1933

Alfred Fellheimer and Steward Wagner, with Roland Wank, New York, and with Paul Philippe Cret, Philadelphia
1301 Western Avenue at Ezzard Charles Drive, NHL, NRHP
Museum complex with Cincinnati Museum of Natural History, Cincinnati Historical Society Museum and Library, Omnimax Theater; Children's Museum due to open fall, 1998; rotunda always open to the public with tours weekend afternoons; 513/287-7000, 800/733-2077

▶ Union Terminal

In 1971 New England photographer Gregory Thorp decided to hitchhike from Vermont to California. He never reached California, because a driver suggested that if trains were what Thorp liked, he should go to Cincinnati. So, wrote Thorp two decades later, "Thirty hours on the road brought me to the boulevard leading to Cincinnati Union Terminal. I stood astonished. I had never even seen a picture of Union Terminal. How could such a marvel exist without being famous?" Set apart from downtown, this marvel is still not famous, though it does make many of the books on Art Deco architecture. It's a building often described as Cincinnati's best: the Art Deco train station that gave seven railroads one local terminal. Set on a flood plain, it was an engineering feat first, its site raised as much as 58 feet with

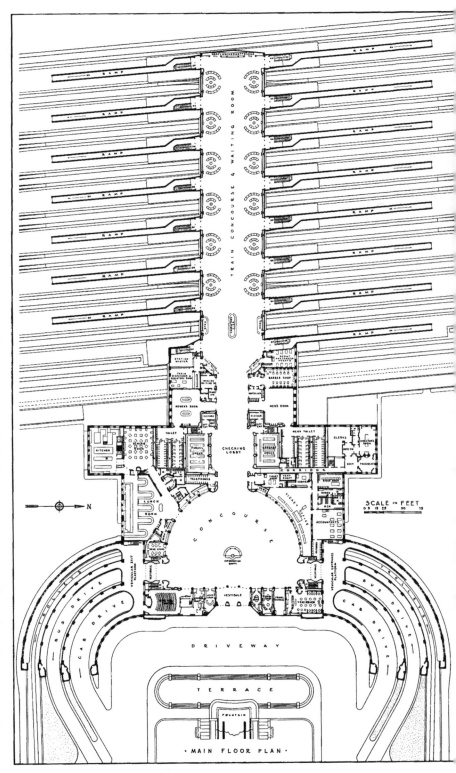

· MAIN FLOOR PLAN ·

▶ UNION TERMINAL SHOWING TERMINAL

THE BIGGEST EXHIBIT: UNION TERMINAL—Declan

Mullin has a corp-speak title—Director of Facilities and Operations—but as he sees his job, it fits right in at the Cincinnati Musem Center. For what he's in charge of is the biggest exhibit: the building itself, the old Union Terminal.

Mullin has always worked for big public places—soccer stadiums, convention centers—but this one is his favorite. He's soaked up its history, especially its finest hour as a passenger station during World War II. Then 200 trains a day came or went, as did up to 30,000 people, many of them troops. The station became the scene of sad separations, some of them final, and joyous reunions. Then after the war, passenger service declined sharply and in 1972 stopped altogether. The crown of Cincinnati railroading was only 39 years old.

But more than history got under Mullin's skin here. It was also design details, such as how contrasting paths in the terrazzo floors show people where a gate was, or a ticket line. Or it was the steelworkers' names carved on girders between the rotunda ceiling and the roof. Or it was the significance of, say, baggage carrousels first used here and now commonplace at airports. Standing in the rotunda, he can claim that this is the world's largest half dome. On the outside it's 138 feet high, covered in a skin of aluminum—a 1944 afterthought because the concrete leaked.

Mullin admires the original clock in the middle of the rotunda: a four-sided digital clock, set in a circle of gleaming stainless. It was one of the world's first LED clocks, run by a remote roomful of cans, each fitted with small gear teeth, each turning and clicking to control one lamp in the clock, and it still works.

What didn't work, Mullin fixed. Neon signs saying "To Trains" went dark around 1942, but in 1997 his crew got them working again. A sign never dreamed of when the station opened in 1933—for the 1998 Children's Museum—can look like 1933 because he found the original letter faces among the architects' drawings. He restores light bulbs—post World War II flourescent out, original incandescent back in. He is impatient with the common assumption that anything 65 years old is bound to be inferior.

Declan Mullin has been with Union Terminal since August, 1996. He's responsible for engineering, security, housekeeping, exhibit maintenace, catering, tenant relations, parking, and, lately at the rate of 580 a year, event sales—renting space, even the main concourse or a museum, is a major revenue source for the city-owned building. In the late 1980s and early 1990s Mullin ran Cincinnati's Riverfront Stadium and Convention Center. Then he spent two years in Memphis and two more in Atlantic City at the Convention Center, also a grand old building.

Mullin scoots up a hall off the

CINCINNATI UNION TERMINAL

rotunda. He's off to check on his pet project of the moment, in mid-1998: a restoration. He has rediscovered a suite of rooms that include the original board room and terminal president's office. Taking his cue from the rotunda dome, the president gave himself a round office fully paneled in walnut, maple and ash veneers—above the door, the building facade is depicted in different veneers. Here the desk is round; the couches curve to fit against the wall. A crew is at work, and Mullin confers with the chief restorer. He hopes to open this suite for tours and possibly for rentals to sedate groups. He wants it to *stay* restored.

With his father Mullin had a train set when he was a boy, but because he grew up in Derry, Northern Ireland, he also had real trains, which were usually the fastest way to go somewhere. Before he first came to Cincinnati in 1988, he worked at sports facilities in Britain; but his accent now is American—the Irish slips out only when he's excited about an especially amazing fact. At work, he wears a white shirt and tie. He takes some satisfaction in Union Terminal's having real, though limited passenger

train service today. Since 1991, a few days every week, a Washington-Chicago train makes a Cincinnati stop—westbound at 1:25 a.m., eastbound at 5:25 a.m.

He shows off the one-time lounge facilities originally between the rotunda and the train platforms. Amid zebrawood paneling, men could use a barbershop or a shoeshine stand. The women had flooring in rose, white and gray terrazzo. Their lounge had a bank of telephone booths that had been walled in, so Mullin first saw them in an old photograph. Now that wall is down. He's looking for 1940 telephones for these booths, and then he'll install mannekins that will seem to be using them.

In the 1980s a shopping mall opened in Union Terminal, just in time for the depression that would help close it several years later. When the shopping center developer was filling dumpsters with artifacts, the Cincinnati Railroad Club, which had been meeting in the terminal since 1938, mobilized as dumpster divers. They accumulated gates and gate signs, the original architects' drawings, furniture, light fixtures. They had so much stuff that they began renting storage space to hold it all.

And people gave memorabilia to club members. "We usually acquired it after someone said, 'Hey, you guys like trains,'" recalls Patrick Rose, a former president. Club accumulations expanded to books and photographs. In the 1960s a member made prints of all the Union Terminal construction photo negatives. Now the negatives have disappeared and his photos are the only set. Today some of the Railroad Club's collections are coming out of storage, piece by piece, and returning to Union Terminal.

In 1986 Cincinnati voters passed a bond issue that saved Union Terminal and converted it into a museum center. In 1990 the Cincinnati Historical Society Museum and the Cincinnati Museum of Natural History opened in three-story facilities that were mostly underground, under the curved wings at the sides and under the fountain in front, in one-time parking and auto service areas. After the 1998 opening of the Children's Museum, the three museums occupied over 10 acres of floorspace culled from old garages.

Though Union Terminal's main rotunda concourse is still standing, not all the station was saved. At the back, giving it a T-shaped footprint overall, the terminal had a 450-foot hall that led to 15 gates and 30 tracks. This hall, Mullin avers, was the model for today's airport concourses. This was where the prototypical luggage carousel was. But today, beyond the stairs that lead down the the Historical Society library, beyond the Omnimax theater, Union Terminal ends with a block wall.

Though passenger service is minimal, the freight yards remain in use. Freight trains use high piggyback container cars that require even higher cranes, and none of this fit under the platform concourse. So, after its

mosaic murals were removed and reinstalled at the Cincinnati airport in Kentucky, the innovative concourse, with circles of seats at each gate, was torn down.

To reach the old control room, Declan Mullin catches an elevator to the third floor and then trots up two flights of stairs, into Tower A. Since 1991 this place has been the Cincinnati Railroad Club's meeting room, open to the public every Saturday. Mullin calls it his favorite place. He pulls up the blinds at the windows overlooking the acres of tracks and freight trains below. He's talking now about a railroad museum, about setting aside 1,500 feet of track for a real steam engine and perhaps a couple of diningcars. He points west toward Bald Knob Hill, whose top was lopped off to raise the ground level here to 16 feet above the flood plain. In the 1937 flood that was high enough for the building but not for the tracks, trains came to a temporary halt.

On the wall is a display board: the yard's tracks as they used to be. The Railroad Club restored it as a static display with colored lights. Red, says Pat Rose, means a moving train, amber shows the direction of traffic, pairs of green lights mean the way is clear. Today's railroad yard still uses signals, but, says Mullin, they're controlled by satellite from Florida.

A large windowless closet that Mullin calls "my room" is off the control room. It's the Railroad Club library, with its collection of books and clippings, of everything published on the terminal. This was where he found Union Terminal's history and, specifically, his restoration projects. It helps him see behind walls.

It's where he transformed himself into the curator that he is.

5.5 million cubic yards of fill. Then it was an artistic triumph. It is, as Thorp found, astonishing: a 13-story half-dome rising at the end of a boulevard like the sun of a new day—or, as we are looking west, a setting sun, luring us to faraway destinations. Architects Alfred Fellheimer and Steward Wagner specialized in train stations, and their original drawings for Cincinnati showed a Neoclassical structure, like the station they'd just done in Buffalo. After construction started, the design changed. Philadelphia architect Paul Cret, an adviser to the architects, advocated the modern and less expensive Art Deco style; and in the Depression era, budget considerations were important. But at $41 million, this project was never a cheap one. Union Terminal's limestone facade curves down to step-like notches and concludes with one-story wings that arc forward, originally for buses, trolleys and automobiles dropping off passengers. Inside, the main concourse rotunda is a glorious space, with painted rings of gold and orange overhead, above Winold Reiss's glass mosaic murals. Historic in themes, the murals lead back to the great square arch that once directed passengers to the train platforms off a long concourse at the back. By the early 1970s passenger trains stopped. In the late 1980s, the then idle building was converted into a museum and library center, with an Omnimax theater and rental facilities. As the Cincinnati Museum Center, it draws 1.2 million visitors a year.

Access: To reach downtown and Fourth Street from Union Terminal, drive east, away from the Terminal, on Ezzard Charles until it deadends into Central Parkway at the rear of the imposing Music Hall. Turn right on Central and follow it as it turns and crosses the downtown blocks, then turn right on Sycamore. (Remember that in Cincinnati the east-west streets are numbered; the north-south streets fall according to the acronym, "Big Strong Men Will Very Rarely Eat Pork" —Broadway, Sycamore, Main, Walnut, Vine, Race, Elm, Plum.) From Sycamore, turn left on Fifth Street, then right on Pike, which will put you in front of the Taft Museum.

Downtown

This tour can be done on foot, though probably not all at once.

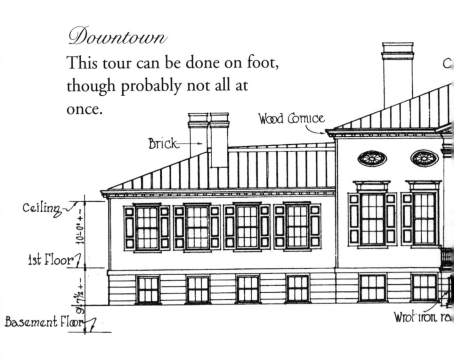

BAUM-TAFT HOUSE, NOW THE TAFT MUSEUM, 1820

316 Pike Street, NHL, NRHP
Art museum, fee, open daily
except some holidays,
513/241-0343

The Baum-Taft House is one of Ohio's finest. It easily gets As for site (a landscaped oasis at the edge of downtown) and age (for Ohio, 1820 is old.) It's in excellent condition, historically significant and, for over 60 years now, has served well as an art museum. Besides, it's a lovely house. Martin Baum came to frontier Cincinnati in the mid-1790s and prospered as an industrialist and land speculator. But then he built himself this country house east of town coincidentally with a financial panic; if he did live here, it was only briefly. Later in the century, in 1873 Charles Taft married Anna Sinton, whose father then owned the house, and the young couple settled in. Taft's name stuck to the house. Partly that was because his half-brother, William Howard Taft, became president in 1909. But it was also because after 1900 Anna and Charles Taft assembled a superb art collection which is now the crux of the museum. The Taft is one of America's great house museums. In the late nineteenth century, when good architecture was assumed to emanate only from name architects, this Federal style house was variously credited to James Hoban, who designed the White House, or to Benjamin Latrobe, who worked on the U.S. Capitol and who actually visited Cincinnati in 1820. Both those attributions have been quashed, and an architectural historian named Richard C. Cote has come up with a modern, though less specific attribution. In 1820, he says, almost all houses, including Martin Baum's, were designed by builders. This particular builder's name is unknown; presumably he was one of the 100 then in the Cincinnati directory. He worked in a Virginia mode, for the higher middle section and long hall for ventilation are both Virginia-like. And he used builders' handbooks, from which he copied the oval windows on the second floor and plaster ceiling decorations on the first. Cote believes that those oval windows and ceiling plaster are probably the house's only remaining original features. In redoing the house as a

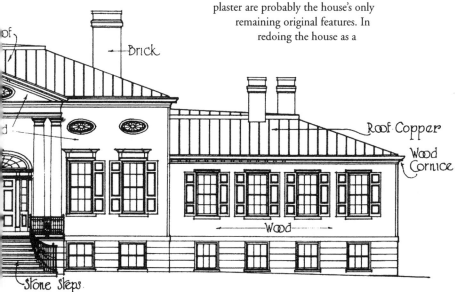

museum in the 1930s, Garber & Woodward supposed they were restoring it to its 1820 original, even though there really are virtually no records on the 1820 house. Restoration has fashions of its own. In the 1930s, Italianate mantels were out, and using mantels from other old Federal-style houses was in, an approach used at Williamsburg but frowned on today, as are the added display cabinets with some Art Deco styling. A room we would love to see today, but one out of style in the 1930s, was lost: the Tafts' Victorian library, which had very dark carved woodwork and tooled leather on the walls. Miraculously, restorers have saved the mid-nineteenth-century hall murals by Cincinnati artist Robert Duncanson, whose work had been hidden under layers of wallpaper.

Access: Cross Pike Street and start walking west on Fourth Street. The 1820 Federal style red brick house on your right, at 500 East Fourth Street, is the historic Literary Club; flanked by tall buildings it appears even more anomalous than the Baum-Taft House, which is set back on its lawn.

Fourth Street

Fourth Street was Cincinnati's signature street. Almost two hundred years old and one mile long, it was where smart shops wanted to be, where businesses wanted their headquarters, where people wanted to be seen. This is less true now, especially on West Fourth, where the current theme is For Rent signs, though the urban ambiance and the architecture remain. Wrote John Fleischman, "In matters of real estate both then and now, morality usually takes a back seat to value, but Fourth Street's ability to retain pieces of its former lives is unique."

GUILFORD SCHOOL, NOW GUILFORD BUILDING, 1914

Garber & Woodward, Cincinnati
421 East Fourth Street, NRHP
Private offices, health club

This Italian Romanesque-inspired building in brick and terra cotta introduces Cincinnati's extraordinary array of schools. It was built for city children who weren't well off, except in their elegant school. The formerly open, roofed terraces atop the wings were playgrounds.

▶ Cincinnati Gas & Electric

CINCINNATI GAS AND ELECTRIC, NOW CINERGY, 1930
Garber & Woodward, Cincinnati, with John Russell Pope, New York, consultant
139 East Fourth Street at Main
Utility company headquarters

A row of severe Doric columns fronts the recessed entry, which has a series of fine bronze doors. The tower has setbacks and a temple-like, pyramid-shaped section at the top.

DIXIE TERMINAL, 1921
Garber & Woodward, Cincinnati
49 East Fourth Street at Walnut
Terminal for buses to Kentucky, offices, shops

Dixie Terminal, built for buses to Kentucky, has a Neoclassical interior that's one of Fourth Street's highlights: under an ornamented barrel vault ceiling, a hall leads straight to the back of the building. There a plate glass window looks out over the Ohio River, the Roebling Suspension Bridge, and Kentucky, which was the travelers' destination. The hall also has arcades alongside and a second-floor balustrade. Upstairs the vaulting is visible close

▶ DIXIE TERMINAL BUILDING

at hand, and the stairways are marble. The building exterior is less striking. It's brick, with some limestone facing and Rookwood tiles in the entry arch. With its massive stone piers, the Roebling Suspension Bridge was builder John A. Roebling's practice run for New York City's Brooklyn Bridge, which he designed shortly before his death in 1869. Built under the direction of his son, Washington A. Roebling, the Brooklyn Bridge was not completed until 1883—almost 20 years after the Cincinnati prototype went into service. In the 1910s and 1920s, Frederick W. Garber (1877-1950) and Clifford B. Woodward (1878-1954) became Cincinnati's most important architectural team. Having both trained at MIT and started as draftsmen for Elzner & Anderson, Cincinnati, they become brothers-in-law who practiced together from 1904 to 1932.

FOURTH NATIONAL BANK BUILDING, 1905

D. H. Burnham & Co., Chicago
18 East Fourth Street
Office building

From the sidewalk what you'll see is the white-shingled roof of Gold Star Chili; look up and you'll find that the shingles emerge, absurdly, from polished granite columns. This slender, 12-story building was the last of four Chicago Style buildings that Daniel H. Burnham's firm designed in Cincinnati. It has brick in the middle, ornamented terra cotta on the top three stories. Burnham's other 1901-05 Cincinnati high-rises are Union Savings Bank, now Fourth and Walnut Building, 36 East Fourth Street; First National Bank, now Clopay Building, 101 East Fourth Street; and Traction Building, now Tri-State Building, 105 East Fifth Street at Walnut.

INGALLS BUILDING, NOW A.C.I. BUILDING, 1903

Elzner & Anderson, Cincinnati
6 East Fourth Street at Vine, NRHP,
National Historic Civil Engineering
Landmark
Offices

The Chicago-style Ingalls Building was the world's first high (16 stories) structure of concrete strengthened with steel. Many people believed it would

▶ INGALLS BUILDING

collapse of its own weight, so the city stalled for two years on a building permit. When the Ingalls Building opened, an eager newspaperman watched it all night, hoping to have a scoop when it collapsed. Far from disgracing its architects and builder, it made them famous. Ten years earlier Toledo's Gardner Building (see also) similarly pioneered reinforced concrete, but the Gardner Building is only six stories high.

UNION CENTRAL LIFE INSURANCE BUILDING, NOW FOURTH AND VINE TOWER, 1913 —

Cass Gilbert, New York, and Garber & Woodward, Cincinnati
1 West Fourth Street
Offices

Long known as the Central Trust Tower, the 38-story Fourth and Vine Tower is one of Cincinnati's landmarks. It's distinctive at the street level, where the white marble blocks are so deeply grooved, and so curved at the edges, that they look like oversized marshmallows. The tower's summit, until 1930 the city's highest, has a white pyramidal roof easily picked out in the Cincinnati skyline. Below the pyramid is a tower with three-story colonnades on all four sides; above it is a relatively small, coppery-green structure that also has columns. John Clubbe describes it as both a fanciful reproduction of a fourth century B.C. mausoleum and a smokestack cover. Zanesville-born architect Cass Gilbert was working on his famed New York City Woolworth

▶ GIDDING-JENNY BUILDING, FOURTH STREET

Building when he designed this Cincinnati skyscraper. The Woolworth Building tops the Fourth and Vine Tower by 22 stories—the equivalent of a full-fledged skyscraper.

GERMAN NATIONAL BANK, 1903

Rapp, Zettel & Rapp, Cincinnati
401 Vine Street at West Fourth
Coffee shop on ground floor

What a lovely row this is—three old buildings with elegant stone facades at the northwest corner of Fourth and Vine; they give a New York feel to this Cincinnati sidewalk. (The exalted urban atmosphere extends also around the corner and into the fabulous lobby of the Omni Netherland Plaza hotel.) Nearest the corner is the Beaux Arts Classical German National Bank, which gets all the impact possible out of three stories—the high round-arched windows help. The German Bank renamed itself during World War I, when it reemerged as Lincoln National Bank.

SUIRE BUILDING, LATER HERSCHEDE BUILDING, 1857
James Keys Wilson and William Walter, Cincinnati
4 West Fourth Street
First floor shops; offices

Next from the corner is an early five-story Italianate by two of Cincinnati's nineteenth-century architectural heavyweights, James Keys Wilson and William Walter. Look closely at the keystones over the windows; they're carved heads.

GIDDING-JENNY, 1880s, 1907
Frank M. Andrews, New York
18 West Fourth Street
clothing store

Third from the corner is the old Gidding-Jenny, a smart women's clothing store that in 1907 hired New York architect Frank Andrews (who earlier had a Dayton office and designed the Dayton Arcade, see also) to update their building's commercial Queen Anne facade. The redesign framed second-and-third-floor display windows with fruits and vegetables in luscious color tiles by Rookwood Pottery artist John D. Wareham.

East Fifth and Sixth Streets

CAREW TOWER AND NETHERLAND PLAZA HOTEL, NOW OMNI NETHERLAND PLAZA, 1930
Walter W. Ahlschlager, Chicago, with Delano & Aldrich, New York
441 Vine Street at West Fifth for tower; and for hotel, 35 West Fifth Street;
entrance around the corner on Race, NHL, NRHP
Office, hotel, and commercial complex; Carew Tower observation deck open daily
with evening hours Fri-Sat; fee; 513/579-9735

Start at the top here, for at its summit the Carew Tower offers Ohio's only full-time observation deck. This 49-story tower is Cincinnati's tallest, high enough for a glorious view that takes in city, river, Kentucky towns and hills. Cincinnati hills too—note Immaculata Church atop Mount Adams to the east. Nearby just to the west on Fifth Street, the Hyatt Regency in cross section looks like Pak-Man. In this major multi-use complex, the really great stuff is in the hotel, the Omni Netherland Plaza, which has some of Ohio's best public interiors. John Clubbe called it "America's finest Art Deco hotel," though he hedged with "probably." He praised the decoration for its richness, sophistication, and unity—the interrelation of lighting, lettering, railings, carpets, wall and ceiling ornament. The lobby, upstairs from the sidewalk, is low-ceilinged; just off it is the two-story Palm Court, a room so good that it will take your breath away. Even on a weekday afternoon

▶ CAREW TOWER AND OMNI NETHERLAND PLAZA

sightseers, one after another, come in gawking. Interior materials, lots of marble and rosewood paneling, are superb. It's hard to believe that this hotel needed updating in the early 1980s—to remove the likes of 1950s vinyl wallpaper over terra cotta. The Carew Tower also has a good Art Deco lobby and the two-story Carew arcade, which has bright Rookwood tiles framing the arches at both ends. Recently Tower Place, an enclosed modern mall, has been installed, incorporating the Carew arcade and enabling the multi-use complex to function today much as it did originally. The exteriors are of course Art Deco, too, with the setbacks almost universally used because New York City zoning mandated them to let in light and air. The lower floors are faced in black and gray granites; the towers are glazed gold bricks.

FOUNTAIN SQUARE
East Fifth Street between Vine and Walnut, NRHP

Fountain Square, which takes its name from the fine bronze Tyler Davidson Fountain, 1871, designed and cast in Munich, originally was an elongated rectangular plaza laid out by architect William Tinsley. In the late 1960s it was moved one block west and remodeled with a result that now seems ill defined and inhospitable. Cincinnatians pay it lip service but aren't apt to linger.

PROCTER & GAMBLE, 1956, 1971, 1985
Kohn Pedersen Fox, New York
1 and 2 Procter & Gamble Plaza, northeast of East Fifth and Broadway
Corporate headquarters

The best view of Procter & Gamble's twin-tower headquarters is from just to the north on I-71, southbound, preferably as sunset is approaching. Obviously, there's no lingering, not even for a picture, on I-71. But there is time enough to grasp the relative importance of Procter & Gamble in this city. Remember, though, that one reason Procter & Gamble was founded in 1837, is that soap is a by-product of hog processing, and in the beginning it was hogs that put Cincinnati on the map. The Postmodern twin-tower complex was built to expand a 1956 office building on Sixth Street east of Sycamore; the new, L-shaped complex east of Broadway is more interesting than its predecessor. The two octagonal 17-story towers are set at right angles to each other; each has a six-story wing. In a nod to some of the skyline heavyweights, Cincinnati Gas & Electric, Central Trust, and Times-Star, the towers have pyramidal roofs. Up to the tenth floor, the two towers are connected by glassed-in corridors (they look like webbing); and in front at the ground floor level, they share a five-story entrance pavilion whose interior, surprisingly using Art Deco style-inspired decoration with steel banding, travertine flooring, white and pink marble, is better than the exterior. Altogether, Procter & Gamble occupies over two blocks northeast of Fifth and Sycamore. The buildings face a formal garden, with vine-covered pergolas; seldom used and closed on weekends.

▶ PROCTER & GAMBLE

GWYNNE BUILDING, 1913
Ernest Flagg, New York
601 Main Street at East Sixth, NRHP
Office building

Before Procter & Gamble moved to the
1956 building at Sycamore and Sixth,
this was their headquarters. The
Gwynne is an elegant Beaux Arts
building with a small temple on one
corner of the roof.

STANLEY J. ARONOFF
CENTER FOR THE ARTS, 1995
Cesar Pelli & Associates, New Haven,
Connecticut, and GBBN, Cincinnati
650 Walnut Street between East Sixth and
East Seventh
Theater complex

▶ GWYNNE BUILDING

In the Aronoff Center's lobby I met Marie Matsunami, a volunteer guide
wearing a red jacket. She showed me the theaters (one, the Procter &
Gamble Hall, seats 2,700), told me the complex's $82 million came from the
state ($40), the city ($20) and private donors ($22), and explained that
putting the Aronoff at this site has revitalized a declining city neighborhood.
Architecturally, Ohio State's Douglas Graf finds that the Walnut Street
facade's irregular pavilions seem unrelated. The complex, he says, "doesn't
live up to its promise." Nor does its sidewalk, recessed at the corner;
Americans are apt to take empty corners for gas stations. The Contemporary
Arts Center's new quarters across the street from the Aronoff Center, due to
open in 2003, is likely to attract a lot of attention. It will be the first U.S.
work by the Iraqui-born London-based architect Zaha Hadid. She is
probably, Graf said, the world's most provocative architect.

Downtown North and East

PUBLIC LIBRARY OF CINCINNATI AND HAMILTON
COUNTY, 1954
Woodie Garber & Associates, Cincinnati; associated with Samuel Hannaford &
Sons, Cincinnati
800 Vine Street at West Eighth Street
Library main branch; 513/369-6900

Architects who were young professionals in 1950s Cincinnati talk of two
contemporary buildings that impressed them. One was the Terrace Hilton,
which has been radically altered. The other was the Public Library of
Cincinnati and Hamilton County, which has been altered and expanded, but
retains some of its original character. Designed by Woodie Garber, the son of

Frederick W. Garber of Garber & Woodward, the International Style library received national attention. Bruce Goetzman, one of those who remembers, says it was the first with a street-level entrance rather than a grand stairway, and books were visible through the glass windows.

▶ THE CITADEL

SALVATION ARMY CITADEL, 1905
Samuel Hannaford & Sons, Cincinnati
114 East Eighth Street, between Walnut and Main
Private offices

For the Salvation Army, what but a citadel? Though the Salvation Army moved to Central Parkway over 30 years ago, this picturesque crenellated structure in buff brick and stone keeps the original name, Citadel, carved in bas relief between the two central turrets. In the 1980s it was combined with the former firehouse next door at 110, and remodeled as an office building.

TIMES-STAR BUILDING, NOW HAMILTON COUNTY COURT OF DOMESTIC RELATIONS, 1933
Samuel Hannaford & Sons, Cincinnati
800 Broadway at East Eighth Street, NRHP
County courts and offices; lobby accessible during business hours

Built for the *Times-Star* newspaper, this 16-story Art Deco tower fronts what was a printing plant at the back. Faced in limestone, the tower has setbacks and dark, vertical bands of alternating windows and aluminum spandrels. The pyramidal roof has sculpted turrets at each corner. Pass through the high round-arched entry and behold the wonderful Art Deco lobby inside.

HAMILTON COUNTY COURTHOUSE, 1919
Rankin, Kellogg and Crane, Philadelphia
1000 Main Street at the foot of Court
Courthouse; 513/632-8825

Would that justice could be meted out per column, for this massive Neoclassical building has 16 columns and four pilasters in its facade—justice galore. The columns are above the rusticated, or deeply grooved stonework on the first floor, which also has seven round-arched doors. The hall inside, clad mostly in pink marble, has a striking series of elliptical arches. For a dollop of high-ceilinged courtrooms with marble wainscoting, see rooms 340, 360, 370, and 380.

Downtown North and West

PHOENIX CLUB, 1893
Samuel Hannaford & Sons, Cincinnati
812 Race Street at West Ninth, NRHP
Restaurant and party rooms, 513/721-8901

The Phoenix Club, a group of Jewish men, built themselves a Second Renaissance Revival building with stained-glass windows and a marble stairway inside. According to Walter Langsam, the Hannafords took their inspiration from a fashionable Chicago club, the Calumet. Closed from 1983-86, the building was renovated and reopened in 1988.

COURT STREET FIREHOUSE, NOW CINCINNATI FIRE MUSEUM, 1907, 1980
Harry Hake, Cincinnati; renovation by Bruce Goetzman, Cincinnati
315 West Court Street, west of Plum, NRHP
Fire museum; open daily except Mon; fee; 513/621-5553

As the Court Street Firehouse shows, Cincinnati took pride in its firehouses. Harry Hake (1871-1955), who trained locally at Ohio Mechanics' Institute, did 17 of them, including this brick and sandstone gem in Second Renaissance Revival. This firehouse has distinctive front and back facades, both with doors for fire trucks. The Court Street side, with arcaded windows on the second floor, is the more elegant. Once Cincinnati's busiest firehouse, the Court Street station all but lost its service area in the 1950s when the crowded West End was diminished by removal in the name of renewal. Closed in 1962, it was rescued in the 1970s to become the Fire Museum.

EIGHTH AND PLUM INTERSECTION
One of the high points of Ohio architecture is the celebrated intersection at West Eighth and Plum Streets. Approach by backtracking to Elm so you can walk west toward Plum on West Eighth. Then you may look up and see three distinctive towers: brick minarets, a soaring classical spire, and the rough brown stones of a Richardsonian Romanesque clock tower. That's what Eighth and Plum is all about, at least on three corners. Through the first part of the twentieth century, until 1945, when the bedomed brick 1870 Congregational Church on the northeast corner was torn down, the intersection had four distinctive nineteenth-century structures built during a 50-year period. The fourth corner has a post World War II contribution: an auto repair shop.

CINCINNATI CITY HALL, 1893
Samuel Hannaford & Sons, Cincinnati
801 Plum Street at Eighth, NRHP
City hall; 513/352-5200

Cincinnati's City Hall is the very model of a Richardsonian Romanesque building: imposing and immense, it looks and feels like a courthouse. It has the swagger of power. This was a city to be reckoned with. City Hall takes up a whole block, and was designed with entrances on four sides. Built of

City Hall, Cincinnati, Ohio

▶ CITY HALL

rough-cut buff sandstone with brown stone for contrast and a granite base, it has a high corner tower, pyramidal roofs, rows of arched windows, carved detailing, turrets, and squat columns. The footprint is like a squared figure eight, giving the building two courtyards. Enter from Plum Street and see the painting on the foyer ceiling, the clusters of fat Romanesque columns, the arch over the marble stairs, revealing an enticing portion of the stained glass window over the landing. The model for City Hall was Boston architect Henry Hobson Richardson's Allegheny County Courthouse, completed five years earlier in Pittsburgh. As for the Hannaford architects, their name is so entwined with Cincinnati that in 1980, 55 of their buildings were linked as a thematic group that landed on the National Register in one fell swoop. Cincinnati's first Hannaford architect was Samuel (1835-1911), who, in the 1870s, his breakthrough decade, won the contract for Music Hall over the reigning dean of Cincinnati architects, James W. McLaughlin. From then on, Hannaford was the city's most popular architect, able to work in any style. He became one of the prominent burghers in Winton Place, a railroad suburb where he designed the bigger houses, became mayor, and fathered 11 children. In 1888 he went into partnership with his two oldest sons, and although he retired in 1896, Samuel Hannaford & Sons survived until 1964. Samuel himself, in his enormously productive life, designed 1,000 buildings still standing today, from Terre Haute to Charleston, West Virginia. He was the quintessential Cincinnati architect, one who executed beautifully, with great detail, the kind of fanciful buildings and apartments that made Cincinnati distinctive. He was also blessed with a combination of good craftsmen, good materials, and the regional prosperity to afford such craft.

ST. PETER IN CHAINS CATHEDRAL, 1845, 1957

Henry Walter, completed by William Walter, Cincinnati; addition and alterations by Edward J. Schulte, Cincinnati
325 West Eighth Street at Plum, NRHP
Catholic cathedral; descriptive flyers available in church; tours; 513/421-5354

Once a nationally acclaimed Greek Revival church (Talbot Hamlin called it "one of the handsomest and most monumental"), St. Peter in Chains

Cathedral had the misfortune to be enlarged in the 1950s, when 600 tons of black marble were installed on the interior. That project was done for the best of reasons: to enlarge the downtown church so that it might again be the archbishop's cathedral and, incidentally, rescue its worsening neighborhood. The rear wall was moved back 60 feet and transepts were added to expand seating capacity. But in style, materials and detailing, like adding tracery to the windows, the resulting changes mar the building. All this does not mean that St. Peter in Chains is without virtues, for it has a fabulous spire over a fine portico. Architect Henry Walter, who won the competition for the Statehouse in Columbus, specialized in Greek Revival. The multi-stage octagonal tower, 221-feet high, has cross-shaped windows at one level and colonnades at two others. On three sides the portico has twelve fluted Corinthian columns, in sandstone; they have the faint corduroy lines of the tooling when they were cut. The building's exterior stone is limestone; the addition's stone is compatible because the original quarry was reopened.

PLUM STREET TEMPLE OR ISAAC M. WISE TEMPLE, 1866

James Keys Wilson, Cincinnati
720 Plum Street at Eighth, NHL, NRHP
Synagogue; group tours, which individuals may join, may be arranged on weekdays; call main office at 513/793-2556

Astonishing both inside and out, the imaginative work of a significant architect, historically important, this synagogue is surely one of Ohio's best buildings. Besides, in "Plum Street Temple" it has an unforgettable name, universally recognized even though congregation B'nai Yeshurun officially named the building for their rabbi, Isaac Mayer Wise, who deserved the honor. Here from 1854-1900, Wise was the founder of Reform Judaism in America and of Cincinnati's Hebrew Union College, the nation's first rabbinical seminary. Wise was really inventing American Judaism—a Judaism that would never be relegated to ghettos. A Bohemian immigrant, he came to Cincinnati after a short, contentious stay in Albany. Then even as he introduced the astonishing changes of Reform Judaism—for the first time men and women sat together; a synagogue had instrumental music; the American flag was displayed—his Cincinnati congregation was supportive. They were still supportive when he proposed a new synagogue: a temple that seats 1,200 though the congregation numbered 220. It was absurdly optimistic. The temple is Gothic Revival in an Islamic cloak, deliberately exotic to give Judaism a distinctive architecture. It also recalls how Jews flourished in Moorish Spain—this was Wise's Alhambra. Red brick and sandstone, the exterior has Gothic arches, mosque-like minarets, and fabulous carving in the stone. The interior has a high nave, clerestory windows, and 13 hemispheric domes: large ones over the nave, smaller ones over side aisles. Domes and walls have stencilled decoration, mostly in Moorish motifs, with six-pointed stars of David and several five-pointed, American stars. For John Clubbe, the inside is "the city's single most arresting interior space." Burt Gross, a third-generation member who oversaw the two-million-dollar mid-1990s restoration, says the interior paint is a water-based tempera. To restore it, New York's EverGreene Studios sent Kristina Lemmon, who also did Memorial Hall. Here, for five months in 1995, she supervised 14 artists who used 65 colors of hand-mixed paint and 135 different stencils. Although the interior has been fastidiously restored, the exterior brick was sandblasted in the late 1960s, before people realized that

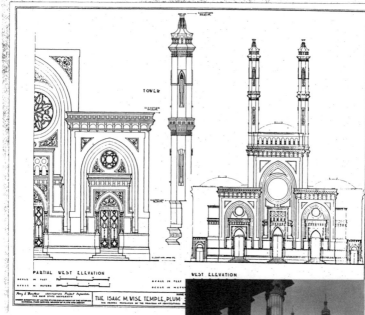

PARTIAL WEST ELEVATION   WEST ELEVATION

THE ISAAC M. WISE TEMPLE, PLUM

▶ Plum Street Temple

sandblasting takes off the brick's protective crust, permitting the erosion evident here. Migrating out of the central city, the congregation built another synagogue in Avondale in 1927; in 1976 they moved again, to Amberley Village. Plum Street Temple is used for special services and for occasions like weddings, which, Gross says, give people a chance to show it off to out-of-town visitors. Architect James Keys Wilson (1828-1894) was clearly an exceptional designer. Cincinnati-born, he studied in New York with Martin Thompson and James Renwick, a leading proponent of Gothic Revival. After spending 1847 in Europe, Wilson returned to Cincinnati, and much of his still standing work is in this guide. Curiously, Wilson stopped working after 1870, when he co-founded the Cincinnati chapter of the American Institute of Architects. He was only 42.

CINCINNATI BELL TELEPHONE, 1931

Harry Hake of Hake & Kuck, Cincinnati
209 West Seventh Street at Elm, NRHP
Cincinnati Bell Telephone Building

Harry Hake's firm designed more than firehouses; one of his other projects was this Art Deco building for Cincinnati Bell. Above the base, a decorative band of bas relief telephones encircles the building. The Art Deco lobby, accessible during business hours, is worth seeing.

Over-the-Rhine

"Over-the-Rhine is Cincinnati's great failure at urban redevelopment." So declared John Fleischman, a Cincinnatian, in *Ohio Magazine* in 1992. "Out-of-town preservationists drive around Over-the-Rhine with their mouths open, gazing at the nearly intact nineteenth-century streetscape," he said. ¶ What amazes them is the country's largest array of Italianate buildings, complete with commercial, residential, religious, and civic structures. Mostly, the buildings are two-to-five-story red brick with fancy cornices, brackets and window moldings. ¶ In 1870 the city was virtually bilingual. German immigrants concentrated in the neighborhood north of the canal where Central Parkway is now, and "Over-the-Rhine" was a natural nickname. It stuck even after World War II, when the last of the Ger- mans vanished into the sub- urbs, and

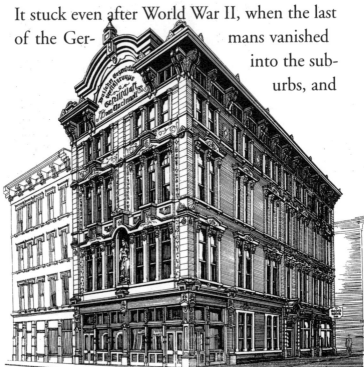

▶ GERMANIA

the neighborhood deteriorated into slumhood. Population dwindled from 90,000 to today's 9,000, 80 percent low income. As too many of its buildings fall into disrepair, the wonderfully intact neighborhood has remained in jeopardy, although new entrepreneurs along Main Street in the late 1990s spurred a turnaround. Art galleries, restaurants, clubs, and offices were joined by renovators; and more than 500 housing units at all income levels have been added since 1990. ¶ The spring 2001 riot in the neighborhood badly dented the neighborhood public relations, indicating the deeper problems the city seems unable to properly address. Visitors should by no means avoid Over-the-Rhine, but sample the atmosphere carefully and step gingerly.

ALMS & DOEPKE BUILDING, NOW HAMILTON COUNTY DEPARTMENT OF HUMAN SERVICES, 1878, 1912

Samuel Hannaford, Cincinnati; 1912, D.H. Burnham & Co., Chicago
222 Central Parkway between Sycamore and Main, NRHP/Hannaford & Sons TR
County offices

At the turn of the century Alms & Doepke was a major department store; by the mid-1950s it had closed and became government offices; in 1991 it had a complete renovation, including a gutting of the interior. The structure is actually five different buildings; the easternmost was designed by D.H. Burnham in 1912, all the others by the Hannafords. Second Empire in style, the Hannaford buildings are red brick with stone trim.

GERMANIA, 1877

Johann Bast, Cincinnati
1129 Walnut Street at Twelfth, NRHP/Over-the-Rhine HD
Private office building

This Italianate building distinguishes itself with a limestone facade and the statue in a second-floor niche: a proud and sturdy woman, fully draped and called Germania. At the time of World War I, when German-Americans wanted to affirm their loyalty to their new country, she was renamed Columbia. A German-language insurance company put up the building for $100,000; architect Johann Bast was a German immigrant.

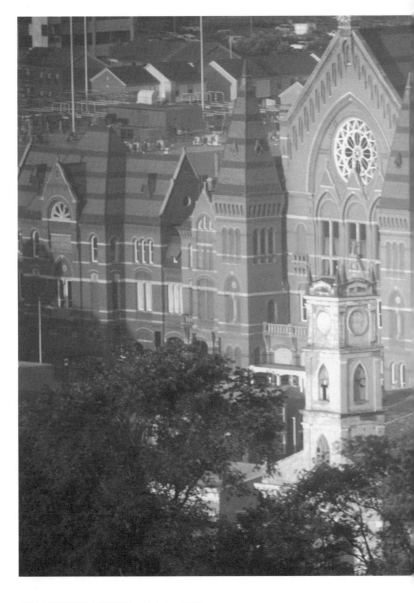

CINCINNATI MUSIC HALL, 1878

Hannaford & Procter, Cincinnati
1243 Elm Street, NHL, NRHP/Hannaford TR
Regular auditorium for Cincinnati Symphony and Opera; group tours by
prearrangement, 513/621-1919

In how many American cities today, can we come across a red-brick High
Victorian Gothic building, 372 feet long, 140 feet high, still being used for
its original purpose? It's such an uncommon experience that the first amazing
fact about Cincinnati Music Hall is that it still exists. John Clubbe minces no
words and calls Music Hall "Samuel Hannaford's masterpiece, the chief jewel
in Cincinnati's Victorian crown." He also avers that, with its 3,632 seats, the
auditorium is the country's largest regularly used for classical music. Through
all its length, the building facade is a succession of projecting and receding

▶ Music Hall

bays, round and pointed arches, small and medium gables, with the largest
and highest gable, complete with rose window, in the middle. The two
towers alongside, which have high pointed roofs, are helping to hold it all up.
Arched corbeling (rows of arches in brick canted outward to provide support)
outlines the central gable and cornices. Black brick mixed in with red forms
checkerboarding in the points of arches or decorative edging around arches
readily visible from the sidewalk. The back of the building, on the west side,
is a plain red brick, which the architect expected to take on a coral-like glow
in the afternoon light. But not everything seen—or expected—from the
sidewalk is wonderful. Too many windows have been bricked up. At the
north end in front there's an incongruous pink granite wheelchair ramp of
massive dimensions. In the beginning, this was the Cincinnati Music Hall
and Exposition Center—what people now call a multi-purpose complex.
Music was in the central part, behind the big gable. Along both sides 18-foot

alleys, under roof but otherwise open, separated music from museums. Horticulture Hall, initially for flowers and fruit and later an art gallery, was at the south end; mechanical exhibits were at the Fourteenth Street end. There Power Hall celebrated machinery, which was not merely on display but running, powered by a central steam boiler. (Machinery exhibits were at the north end so the coal ash would blow away.) Today the open alleys have long since been enclosed; the south wing is offices; and the making and storing of opera sets has taken over the north wing. Intermission promenaders may opt for the first-floor foyer inside, or the balcony overlooking it, or unimpressive halls alongside. The auditorium has been redone a couple times, first under Samuel Hannaford in the 1890s, when a proper stage was installed (originally the hall was elevated at one end but had no proscenium,) and electric lights replaced gas; the ceiling mural was painted in 1905. The second major restoration, in the late 1960s and early 1970s, enlarged the stage to accommodate the opera, which had been performing at the zoo. It also modernized with air conditioning, a hydraulic orchestra pit and a steel grid over the stage to hold scenery.

Memorial Hall; in drawing, Beemelin house is at far left

HAMILTON COUNTY MEMORIAL HALL, 1908
Samuel Hannaford & Sons, Cincinnati
1225 Elm Street, NRHP
Auditorium, meeting rooms for veterans and others; memorial exhibits; to see
interior (if building is not in use) ask at Music Hall offices or prearrange
by calling 513/621-1919

Just across the alley south of Music Hall, the Hannafords designed this Beaux
Arts Memorial Hall, with its two-story round-arched windows between
columns and pilasters. Inside it's had a restoration that's surely among the
most exquisite I've seen anywhere. The first floor has a fine hall and two
large rooms, all with memorial exhibits (one item: a wreath that was on
Lincoln's casket). Upstairs is the 600-seat auditorium, with gilded rosettes in
the proscenium and gilded swags on the balcony; writer John Fleischman
called it a "jewel box." Though still used by veterans' groups and a theater
company, by the late 1980s the building was in poor condition. Then in
1988, the Miami Purchase Association, now Cincinnati Preservation

Association, moved in. Mary Ann Olding, then association director, and Judy Ruthven, the chairperson, began raising money. Ultimately, they raised $700,000 in private donations, persuaded the county commissioners to contribute another $1.3 million, and oversaw seven years' work. Today the CPA is on Fourth Street, but chamber music and vocal groups use Memorial Hall's auditorium, and the Cincinnati Symphony's marketing department occupies the basement offices. The interior, says Olding, "was an amazing array of colors and designs." It could be so handsomely restored because, although it was sorely neglected, it remained the least altered of Ohio's 12 remaining Memorial Halls (there were 14 in all), and some of the original wall decoration and its geometric designs remained so that it could be recreated. The memorial halls were a tribute to the political clout of the Civil War veterans during the half-century that followed the great conflict; in 1884 they persuaded legislators to permit second-tier cities to issue bonds for construction of their halls, which meant that today they are still found largely in smaller cities such as Bellefontaine and Mansfield. The county-owned Memorial Hall is managed by the Cincinnati Arts Association, in the person of a governmentally dextrous man named Ernie Toplis, who also oversees the state-owned Aronoff Center and the city-owned Music Hall.

DR. RUDOLPH H. REEMELIN HOUSE, 1894
Samuel Hannaford & Sons
1209 Elm Street

Between Twelfth Street and Memorial Hall is a row of houses typical of those that make Cincinnati so interesting architecturally. See especially 1209, two-

and-a-half stories behind an elegant stone facade. The second floor has a projecting bay; the third, a mansard roof where a central dormer, in stone, has a fancy French surround. Walter Langsam calls it a "chateau in miniature."

To see more in Over-the-Rhine:
Two Over-the-Rhine churches, both Catholic, of special interest are Old St. Mary's, 1842, 123 East 13th

▶ OVER THE RHINE; OLD ST. MARY'S IN FOREGROUND

Street, originally a German church that still offers Latin and German, as well as English, masses, call 513/721-2988 to see interior; and St. Francis Seraph, 1859, Liberty at Vine, by Cincinnati architect James W. McLaughlin, renovated after the turn of the century by the Hannafords, who applied the orange brick. See also the Ohio Mechanics' Institute, 1909, the Tudor Revival building by Hannaford & Sons, 100 East Central Parkway at Walnut Street; it contains the symphony's former venue, Emery Auditorium. John Clubbe says the Emery is one of only four comparable theater-concert halls in the country; the others, which unlike this one are still in use, include New York's Carnegie Hall and Chicago's Orchestra Hall. In 2001, the building's upper floors had been renovated into apartments.

Access: To reach Dayton Street, take Central Parkway north (away from the downtown) from behind Music Hall. Just past Liberty Street, turn left/south at the second light, which is Linn Street; Dayton Street intersects on the right/west in a few blocks. To visit Hauck House museum, park on Linn or go around the block to park on south side of Dayton (no parking on north side).

HATCH HOUSE, 1851

Isaiah Rogers, Cincinnati
830 Dayton Street, NRHP/Dayton Street HD
Private apartments
Dayton Street was a Millionaire's Row in the late nineteenth century, even if pigs were driven down the street every day on their way to nearby packing houses. Both pigs and millionaires are long gone but happily the houses, often divided into apartments, are mostly intact. The Hatch House is the largest

▶ HATCH HOUSE

on the block and, with its pair of bow windows on the front, very unusual in Ohio. However, architect Isaiah Rogers (1800-1869) had begun practicing in Boston, where such round bays were and are relatively common. Massachusetts born, Rogers himself was unusual in his day, for he was truly a national architect, the designer of hotels in Boston, New York, Nashville, Toledo (where the Oliver House is the only surviving Rogers' hotel), and, in Cincinnati, the Burnet House. Rogers moved to Cincinnati while working on the Burnet House; he became the architect who completed the Ohio Statehouse in Columbus. Between the two bow windows, the Hatch House has an octagonal porch with fluted Corinthian columns, echoed above on a part-octagon bay. John Clubbe calls it "one of the most sophisticated Greek Revival designs in the country." The original owner, a soap-and-candle maker named George Hatch, became mayor in the 1860s but then moved to Canada, allegedly because of Confederate sympathies.

JOHN HAUCK HOUSE, 1870

812 Dayton Street, NRHP/Dayton Street HD
House museum operated by Historic Southwest Ohio; Dayton Street Walking Tour
available at house; admission fee; 513/563-9484

No wonder Germans came in such numbers; they had the likes of John
Hauck to inspire them. Aged 23 in 1852, he came to Cincinnati to work for
his uncle in a brewery. By 1858 he was brewmaster of his father-in-law's
brewery; after another five years he founded his own. So when he bought
this house in 1880, he had more than enough money to make the place more
elegant by installing stone over the original brick. Today the interior is being
restored gradually, recently under Janet Hauck, a great-granddaughter-in-law
of John Hauck. The first floor has 14-foot painted ceilings, parquet and tile
floors, pocket doors, and an original chandelier.

**Access: This is a city of hills; Ravine Street will introduce you to them.
From Dayton Street, turn left (north) on Central Parkway, look immediately for Ravine, heading up the hill to the right. This route leads to
the Cincinnati University area. Turn right on Warner Street, which is
two-thirds up the hill. The Fairview School looms over the hillside
from its prominent occupation of Stratford Avenue.**

Fairview

Look close or you'll miss one of Cincinnati's most
intact inner-city neighborhoods. Fairview *proper*
is considered by residents as that cluster of modest Queen Anne, mostly two-and-a-half story
homes on the west side of Ravine Street. It's
Warner, Ada, Fairview, and three or four little
cul-de-sacs that wrap around the hilltop. In the
late 1800s, it was a hillside farm envisioned by
beer baron Christian Moerlein as a new residential community above the city. To that end, his
connections saw that public services were provided long before the lots were occupied. In
effect, Fairview was a planned community without ever being known as such. Moerlein's development, however, never became the upper-class
enclave he had originally envisioned; instead it
was occupied by largely German stock: lower-to-

middle income brewery workers, shop foremen, and city functionaries who filled—and maintained—many of the two-family homes which never *looked* like doubles. Thanks to their descendants—spiritually if not otherwise—Fairview's stoutly built brick homes, enveloped on three sides by parkland, hold their own against urban assaults that have toppled mightier fortresses. To see, drive west on Warner, across Ravine, deadend in Fairview. To your left is the scenic overlook; turn around and drive slowly around the Fairview curve to the light on McMillan. Try to catch the light on red; pause to admire the corner police station whose upstairs was once a hayloft.

▶ FAIRVIEW SCHOOL

FAIRVIEW SCHOOL, 1888
H. E. Siter,
Cincinnati
2232 Stratford
Avenue at Warner
Public elementary school with bilingual program in German; 513/357-4380

Here's the distinctive Fairview School, an 1888 building that to Doug Graf looked modern, advanced for its day. The only buildings you'll see like it anywhere are other Cincinnati schools by Boston-trained architect H.E. Siter, who developed his own personal version of Richardsonian Romanesque. Red brick with stone basement and trim, the building has polygonal corner bays, round-arched entries, a steep roof with dormers. Inside the classrooms in the corner bays are spacious and high-ceilinged—just as wonderful as you'd expect.

2241 STRATFORD STREET
Private house

Just across the street from Fairview School is one of the vernacular two-story houses I liked so much, with a Second Empire mansard roof. This one has two windows downstairs and a round-roofed dormer upstairs in the mansard. That dormer is good enough to make up for the siding.

Access: For the best approach to Hughes High School from the Fairview/McMillan intersection, turn right on McMillan and drive just under a mile to Vine Street; turn left/north one block to Calhoun, which is one-way westbound. Alternatively, from I-71, exit at Taft Road and drive west; Taft becomes Calhoun.

HUGHES HIGH SCHOOL, NOW HUGHES CENTER, 1910

J. Walter Stevens, St. Paul, Minnesota, with Harry Hake, Cincinnati
2515 Clifton Avenue at Calhoun
Public high school with specialized magnet programs; 513/559-3097

Driving west on Calhoun, you may suppose that you're going to the University of Cincinnati. But the university is off to your right side, scarcely noticeable because the terrain dips. This street's true destination looms ahead, its high brick tower dripping in cream-colored terra cotta. If Hughes High School is not your destination, it deserves to be. In 1906 the school board held a design competition for Hughes High School, and everyone was surprised when an out-of-towner from St. Paul won it. Though J. Walter Stevens's building still has its grandeur, maintenance has been so neglected that when I was there in 1998 daylight glimmered like stars in the auditorium ceiling and librarian Carolyn Kindle had just thrown out books irretrievably damaged by water. Hughes High School has so much terra cotta that it looks as though it were luciously frosted—doors, windows, cornices all are in cream-colored terra cotta, as are gargoyles, griffins, hatchets and lo, books. The style is Collegiate Tudor, popular for schools in the early twentieth century. The interior, especially the library, is interesting. The Rookwood drinking fountains are fabulous, especially the boy riding a dolphin, in the first-floor hall. But I grieve for Hughes and the other glorious Cincinnati schools whose maintenance has been so neglected. Of course they're expensive to fix, but perhaps repairs would help with more than just the structure.

Access: The University of Cincinnati is accessible from Clifton
Avenue north of Calhoun. To see the Frank Gehry building turn east at
Dr. Martin Luther King, Jr. Drive and continue past Vine Street to Eden
Avenue; building is on northwest corner.

ARONOFF CENTER FOR DESIGN AND ART, UNIVERSITY OF CINCINNATI, 1996

Peter Eisenman, New York, with Lorenz & Williams,
Cincinnati
Clifton Avenue at King Drive,
southeast corner of intersection;
northwest corner of campus
University of Cincinnati art and
architecture school

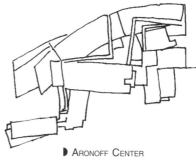

That a high school attracts all your
attention when approaching from
the east, reveals something
about the University of
Cincinnati

▶ ARONOFF CENTER

campus; it's not necessarily much to look at. And
walking on it can be oppressive, for it's
predominantly pavement and big, clunky
buildings. In recent years the university decided
to spark things up by inviting leading American
architects to provide designs that local architects

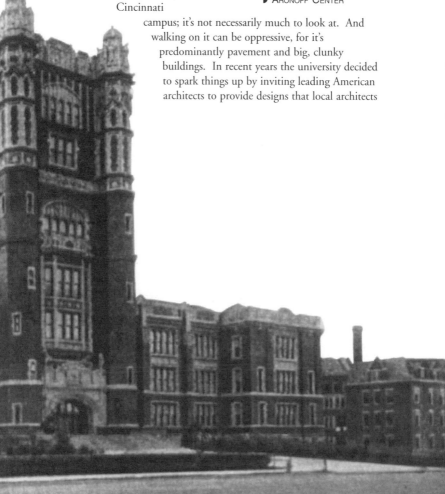

would do the drawings for. (This was partly to sidestep objections from local practitioners, who complain when a public facility hires out-of-state talent.) As of mid-1998 the Peter Eisenman building for art and architecture students is the most interesting result. It's best seen from Clifton to the north: a long segmented structure in pastels—pink, tan, green, blue—working its way along the hill above Martin Luther King Drive. When approached from the campus side, the building, actually behind and connected to a couple of older structures, is not so easy to spot; look for a blue pastel entryway. Inside the main feature is underground: a continuously changing 800-foot-long hall with lots of parallel fluorescent tubes overhead. Especially when you've seen Eisenman's other two Ohio buildings, the Wexner Center and the Convention Center in Columbus, you'll realize that halls are really what this architect does best.

VONTZ CENTER FOR MOLECULAR STUDIES, UNIVERSITY OF CINCINNATI, 1999

Frank O. Gehry & Associates, Santa Monica, and Baxter Hodell Donnelly Preston, Cincinnati
Eden Avenue at King Drive, northwest corner
University research building

Although Frank Gehry complained about his budget restrictions here, the Vontz Center for Molecular Studies is a characteristically Gehry-esque accumulation of boxes and other shapes, some bulging. Cladding over the reinforced concrete curves is brick that was pre-laid in frames---"brick wallpaper," Gehry called it. Computer-aided design made the complexity possible.

Clifton

If downtown Cincinnati was the basin, where coal smoke obscured even the river from sight, then the place to escape to was the surrounding heights, into clean air and the beauty of lawns and gardens. That's how John R. Stilgoe wrote of Clifton in *Borderland*. The idea was that, once removed from factories and saloons, people could create an ideal environment permitting virtuous lives. ¶ The people on the hills of Clifton were like those who escaped to other Cincinnati hills, except that they were richer. For a while, thanks to the landscaping of Adolph Strauch, they had a veritable paradise. What survives are the houses, by the city's best architects.

Access: From the campus, drive north on Clifton Avenue, past Burnet Woods; turn right/east at Jefferson to see Parkside Flats. Then return west to Clifton and continue north past Woolper Avenue; you'll come to Calvary Church just north of Greendale. Again go north on Clifton to Lafayette Avenue, where the road bends east.

PARKSIDE FLATS, 1895

3315-3317 Jefferson Avenue
Apartments

This sprawling Shingle-style apartment complex looks like nothing so much as an old resort hotel at the shore, though here the amenity is not the ocean but the park behind the building. Apartments like these were for people who couldn't afford houses but wanted the advantages of living outside the city; the shingles make Parkside seem more like houses.

CALVARY EPISCOPAL CHURCH, 1867

William Tinsley, Cincinnati
3766 Clifton Avenue, NRHP/Clifton
Avenue HD
Church; 513/861-4437

Calvary Episcopal Church's spire roof is, uncommonly, stone; Henry Probasco, whose house, also by William Tinsley, is a little further up the hill, donated the tower and bell. The style is Gothic Revival.

▶ CALVARY EPISCOPAL

RAWSON HOUSE, LATE 1860S

3767 Clifton Avenue, NRHP
Private house

It's hard to miss this Italian Villa, which meatpacker Joseph Rawson bought in 1876. Its significance is to remind us of Clifton's ascendant period when its grand country houses might occupy as much as thirty landscaped acres. The Rawson House is one of the few places left in Clifton that has kept its site largely intact.

SOL P. KINEON-JOHN URI LLOYD HOUSE, 1888

James W. McLaughlin, Cincinnati
3901 Clifton Avenue at Lafayette, NRHP
Private house

From a distance this hilltop house seems to be Clifton Avenue's destination, but then the road swerves to the side. Richardsonian Romanesque, the house is hard to see in summer because of foliage, but it's striking in winter. It has a central bay that's really a little off center; the bay's top floor is round and shingled under a conical roof. John Uri Lloyd was a pharmacist-author who bought the property in 1908.

▶ PROBASCO HOUSE

HENRY PROBASCO HOUSE, OAKWOOD, 1865

William Tinsley, Cincinnati
430 West Cliff Lane, NRHP
Private house

Henry Probasco's name lives on because he spent his money so well. As a young man he came to Cincinnati and went into partnership with a hardware merchant named Tyler Davidson. After Davidson died in 1865, Probasco sold the business and retired at 46. In Davidson's memory he had Fountain Square's fountain made, and then he  settled down to collecting art and the rare books that later effectively launched Chicago's esteemed Newberry Library. He built this house, Oakwood, for an awesome $500,000; to design the gardens on the 30-acre site, he called in Adolph Strauch, who became Spring Grove Cemetery's landscape artist. Thus Oakwood's grounds had rare imported tree species, thousands of roses, a fern garden. Today the gardens are long gone, the estate subdivided, the art sold, the library in Chicago. But here on West Cliff Lane is Probasco's house, readily visible from the street. Probasco chose architect William Tinsley, who had worked for titled aristocracy in his native Ireland and for Kenyon College in Gambier. For Probasco, Tinsley designed a Norman Romanesque Revival house in light brown sandstone with gray limestone trim. The house is L-shaped, with one wing for servants. In the bend of the L the house has a round stair tower, octagonal on the top level, with a flared and pointed eight-sided roof. The exterior trim has extensive carving, but the truly renowned carving here is on the woodwork inside, where every spindle in the stair railing is different. Father-and-son carvers Henry and William Fry are said to have spent three years on the stairway alone. At the top of the stairs, the second floor has a surprising two-story octagonal hall with a skylight and minstrels' gallery. In the late 1880s Probasco lost his wife, remarried, started a family, and lost his fortune. He sold off his possessions, even, in 1899, his home. He moved to a smaller house in Clifton and died three years later. Since then Oakwood has remained a private, single-family home except in the 1920s, when it became a school for women church workers. The other houses on West Cliff Lane, built on what was once Oakwood's lawn, date from the mid-twentieth century. Doug Graf, for one, laments the loss of the gardens, which now no one can remember.

GEORGE K. SHOENBERGER HOUSE, SCARLET OAKS, NOW SCARLET OAKS RETIREMENT COMMUNITY, 1870

James Keys Wilson, Cincinnati
440 Lafayette Avenue, NRHP
Retirement community; phone ahead to see interior, 513/861-0400

George K. Shoenberger came to Cincinnati to represent his father's Pittsburgh iron business, made a pile during the Civil War, and then spent an incredible $750,000 of it on Scarlet Oaks. The facade and entry porch look like nothing so much as a Gothic Revival church—it must be the stone tracery in the windows and the high, upward-reaching lines of the building. The house is on a bluff overlooking the Mill Creek valley and Spring Grove Cemetery, from which it is possible to look up and spot Scarlet Oaks's tower. When the Shoenberger family sold the house in 1908, the buyer donated it to Bethesda Hospital, to serve as a home for the elderly. None are living in the house now, but the retirement complex has sprawled out; in 1960, a long four-story orange-brick addition emerged from the side of the house. That is definitely a downside. A definite upside is that, since it is an institution, visitors may see the house close up and may even call ahead to see the inside; a printed guide is available. Though the interior has several sumptuous rooms, the high point is the three-story hall with a fabulous carved fireplace, stairway, and balcony above. In 1962 the retirement home learned in a newspaper article that four original paintings by Hudson River School landscape painter Thomas Cole were hanging in their chapel, which had been the Shoenbergers' art gallery. Rather than hire a guard and provide humidity controls, the home sold the paintings to a dealer for $400,000, and he in turn made a substantial profit in selling them to Washington's National Gallery. The home hung copies in their stead.

Access: Finally, continue on Lafayette and turn into Mount Storm Park to see the Temple of Love.

TEMPLE OF LOVE, MOUNT STORM PARK, 1845

700 Lafayette Avenue

In London in 1851, Cincinnatian Robert B. Bowler met landscape architect Adolph Strauch, who was working at the Royal Botanical Gardens in Regent's Park. As Strauch showed Bowler around, the two hit it off and Bowler invited Strauch to come to Cincinnati, if ever he visited the United States. The next year, by accident, Strauch found himself in Cincinnati and tracked down Bowler at his office. Bowler took Strauch home to his Mount Storm estate and persuaded him to stay as head gardener. As writer John Fleischman described it, Bowler already had the finest garden in the West: exotic plants, including 10 greenhouses with 90 varieties of camellias and eight producing banana trees. He also had a folly, the Little Temple of Love, set over a cistern that stored water for the plants. A small round pavilion with Corinthian columns in iron, it has a stone base below and a round-domed roof above. Strauch redesigned Bowler's garden, introducing the Lawn Plan, which looked natural by careful design. Impressed with the results, Bowler's neighbors—including Henry Probasco at Oakwood—wanted Strauch's help too, and gradually the adjoining estates of the Clifton barons became one large Lawn Plan garden, without fences, with groves of trees framing distant mansions. In 1854 Strauch moved on to design and run Spring Grove Cemetery, and ten years later Bowler was killed by an omnibus. His family sold the estate to the city to turn into a park in 1911, though by then the gardens and greenhouses were gone. After the house was torn down in 1917, the Temple of Love was the only remaining relic of Robert Bowler's glorious Mount Storm estate. Not far from the Temple of Love, the park has

▶ TEMPLE OF LOVE

a pavilion that serves as a shelter and a viewpoint; designed in 1935 by Samuel Hannaford & Sons, its style has been described as Depression Modern.

Access: From Mount Storm Park turn right continue in same direction on Lafayette to Ludlow; turn left/east to Clifton Avenue; then turn north to Woolper Avenue. To reach the Cincinnati Zoo, take Woolper Avenue east; cross Vine Street and road becomes Forest Avenue; at Drury turn right to zoo entrance. Alternatively, from I-75 take exit 6, Mitchell Avenue; take Mitchell east to first major intersection, Vine Street; turn right/south, then left/east onto Forest; at Drury turn south to zoo entrance. Maps of zoo available at entrance.

THE ZOO

3400 Vine Street; it's open daily year round 9-5, later in summer; fee; 513/281-4700 or 800/94-HIPPO

Second oldest in the county, a National Historic Landmark, the Cincinnati Zoo and Botanical Garden is hilly, with winding paths---Adolph Strauch was consulted on the landscaping---but it's also compact and easy to explore. It's an important zoo; before the Bronx Zoo opened in 1899, Cincinnati had the country's largest collection of animals. Hired as architect for the fledgling zoo, James W. McLaughlin of Cincinnati produced some picturesque animal houses in 1875. For birds he designed a row of small Chinese pagodas. One

Bird Cages, Zoo, Cincinnati, Ohio.

▶ THE ZOO

survives as the Passenger Pigeon Memorial, because Martha, the last passenger pigeon, died in one of these aviaries in 1914. Originally so numerous that they could darken skies with flocks of a billion, passenger pigeons were slaughtered to extinction by market hunters who prevented them from breeding. For monkeys McLaughlin concocted a Turkish-style Monkey House now used for reptiles. Best feature is the round roof: a dome with a cupola on top. The Pigeon Memorial, Monkey House, and Elephant House are all on the National Register.

HERBIVORA BUILDING, NOW THE ELEPHANT HOUSE, 1906

Elzner & Anderson, Cincinnati

The Elephant House has a series of round domes with a high, pointed dome in the middle. It might look like Moslem architecture, but it might also look like a row of enormous elephants, seen from the rear. A few years earlier Elzner & Anderson had designed the Ingalls Building downtown, the first reinforced concrete skyscraper. Thus the Elephant House, built of the same material, was the skyscraper's beneficiary. Architects Alfred O. Elzner (1962-1933) and George M. Anderson (1869-1916) certainly had great credentials for their day—or, judging by their work, for ours. Elzner attended MIT and trained with H.H. Richardson in Boston; he first came to Cincinnati in 1886 to supervise construction of Richardson's Chamber of Commerce building. In 1896 Elzner formed a practice with Anderson, who had studied at Columbia and the École des Beaux-Arts in Paris.

**SPRING GROVE: WORLD
CLASS**—Almost as an aside, Doug
Graf mentioned that Spring Grove is
one of the world's best landscaped
cemeteries. Though I didn't believe
him—I thought he must be exaggerating—I wrote down his remark. Surely if
Spring Grove were one of the world's
best, everyone would know it. But,
probably like most people, I know little
about landscape design or, for that
matter, cemeteries. In our era,
cemeteries have become places to
avoid. As for great landscapes, they've
become very hard to see, because they
are not being designed today and so few
remain. But Spring Grove, I was to
discover, is one of those few.

Just beyond the arch leading into
the burial grounds, this cemetery has a
beautiful area of small lakes, lawns and
trees, with occasional large monuments
and mausoleums. The white temple
that's the Fleischmann mausoleum is
glimpsed through trees on the far side
of a lake. Across another lake, the
curved white gable of the Burnet
mausoleum faces the water. As for the
trees, they're a mix of evergreen and
deciduous; little groves, not gravestones,
are set at corners formed by curving
roads. A lake can never be seen all at
once, for part of it meanders out of
sight, making it hard to grasp how tiny
the lake really is. But the lakes are ever
present, visible both from roads and
from high points; if they slip out of sight,
they soon reappear. And nothing that's
seen is accidental, not even these lakes
that look so natural. In this landscape
every sight, every effect, is by design.

It was all the creation of Adolph
Strauch, an authoritarian Prussian who
had rules for developing a beautiful
cemetery. One was not to have the
place chock full of gravestones. Strauch
wanted a family burial plot to have one
prominent, beautiful monument,
anchored six feet down so it would

never tilt. It was surrounded by as
many as eight graves which could be
identified on the single marker but
more often had flat stones in the
ground. He waged war on what he
saw as clutter: iron fences, hedges,
vines, even flowers, though Spring
Grove has some today. He set aside a
forest preserve, a dense beech and
oak grove in the middle of the
cemetery, forever off-limits to
internments and to monuments.

Strauch wanted dignity and fine
arts in Spring Grove. His standards
were challenged in 1859 when A.B.
Latta wanted his own memorial to
honor his main achievement in life: the
steam fire engine. Latta proposed
columns supporting an iron canopy,
under which would hang a replica of
his invention. According to Strauch
biographer, H.A. Rattermann, Strauch
opposed this with the passion
Laocoön mustered against the
enormous horse offered to Troy. But
the outcomes were different. The
Trojans ignored Laocoön and their city
was destroyed, while Strauch prevailed
and the steam fire engine was barred.

Following the intentions of the
cemetery founders, Strauch expanded
Spring Grove's arboretum. Between
1855 and 1865 he planted 200
different kinds of trees, from all over
North America, Europe and Asia; they
were grouped by families and placed
for effect. With alternating patches of
both sun and shade, the foliage was to
be backdrop and frame for beautiful
scenes and for fine sculptured
memorials. To Strauch, an international arboretum seemed especially
appropriate here. Planting the trees of
the world was comparable, he
thought, to people from many nations
settling in Cincinnati.

Strauch was himself an
immigrant. He was born in Silesia the
same year Frederick Law Olmsted was

born in Connecticut, 1822; he started working for Spring Grove as a landscaper in 1855, about the same time Olmsted started on Central Park. Strauch studied horticulture in school in Germany and then spent six years at the Imperial Gardens of Schoenbrunn in Vienna, where he met a leading European park reformer, Prince Hermann von Puckler Muskau. Later he went on to study gardens in German and Dutch cities, in Ghent, Paris and London. In 1851 he left for America, and the following year, just after he turned 30, he reached Cincinnati.

Intending to leave right away on a train to Niagara Falls, he arrived on a steamer from New Orleans. But he missed the train, looked up an acquaintance who offered him a job (as described above under Temple of Love, Mount Storm Park), and ended up staying for the rest of his life. At first he dazzled Robert Bowler, Henry Probasco and the other Clifton barons by turning their adjoining estates into a beautiful park. But when the Spring Grove job came along, he wanted it, and the barons could arrange it for him. Four years after starting, in 1859, he was named Spring Grove's superintendent, a post he held until his death in 1882.

Spring Grove was founded in 1845 as a rural cemetery, set outside of the urban grid. When it opened, the front third of its land was a swamp, with high ground and hills at the back. Cincinnati landscape architect Howard Daniels, who designed the old Montgomery County Courthouse (see also) in Dayton about the same time, laid out winding roads on the hills; the first graves were there. When Strauch was hired, he left Daniels's plan in place, though he tried to take out fences and clutter and reset many upright gravestones, so that they lay flat in the ground, facilitating mowing.

Where others saw swamp, Strauch saw the potential for a beautiful place. He planned the chain of small lakes, whose excavated soil was piled up to form solid ground where soft had been. Some of the lakes were dug as deep as 20 or 30 feet, to give them a more natural appearance. When completed with their plantings, they became such a success that they helped pull the cemetery out of debt—people wanted lake lots even if prices were higher. Ultimately the lakes generated the profits that paid for James Keys Wilson's buildings at the entrance gate. A grateful board of trustees gave Strauch the island in Geyser Lake, for his own family plot. An arched stone footbridge near the Fleischmann Mausoleum leads to Strauch Island.

Spring Grove was popular not only as a burial ground, but also as a destination for outings and prom- enades. Strauch reported that in 1867 the cemetery had 149,019 visitors, not counting funerals. Shelters were installed on the grounds; the gatehouse was converted to a restroom for women. But as Spring Grove and other cemeteries became pleasure grounds, mourners began objecting, and cities started planning parks. From 1871 to 1875 Strauch himself became Cincinnati's park superintendent. He designed Eden Park, Cincinnati's first, as well as Burnet Woods and Lincoln Park, the latter lost when Union Terminal was built in the 1930s. As planned, by the 1890s the number of people making pleasure jaunts to Spring Grove began to fall off.

Spring Grove's success gave Strauch a national reputation. Through a period of almost 20 years, Blanche M.G. Linden, a cultural historian now in Fort Lauderdale, researched Spring Grove; and in 1995 she published a history of it. She wrote that, as others tried to hire Strauch away, the cemetery raised his salary again and again. In 1863 they paid for him to go to Europe, and he was allowed to take other assignments. And of course in Strauch Island, the directors gave him the best burial site of all. For over half a century, Strauch's concept of a beautiful place influenced cemetery design. And, Linden wrote, his uncluttered Lawn Plan was acclaimed as the "American system."

Today the landscape he designed is intact and well maintained, though in a cemetery that's grown to 733 acres, the lakes area is a small proportion of the whole. Of course the cemetery is a resource for local historians. It's valuable also to horticulturists, for it has 25 national and state champion trees—more than any other single place in Ohio. Noticing all the horticultural tours, two art historians, Liz Scheurer and Cecie Chewning, inventoried a thousand pieces of sculpture in the mid 1990s, and they hope to develop a tour of art works. Spring Grove has room for many more than the 170,000 burials it's already accommodated. Because it's still selling plots, Scheurer says, it hasn't had to focus on itself as a cultural resource, as Boston's Mount Auburn Cemetery has.

Through the nineteenth century, Spring Grove was the cemetery others, even Frederick Law Olmsted, wanted to imitate. When consulted on Oakland's Mountain View Cemetery in California in 1864, Olmsted was interested because he'd been wanting

to work on a rural cemetery like Spring Grove. In 1875 he called Spring Grove the nation's best, "from a landscape gardening point of view." Olmsted was not the only one to notice. After a national tour in the 1870s, a reporter from Philadelphia wrote that Strauch and other horticulturalists put Cincinnati way ahead of Philadelphia, New York or Boston. In 1883 the directors of a London cemetery applied for information from Spring Grove, because it was, they wrote, the world's finest. And at the Paris International Exposition in 1900, Spring Grove won a gold medal as the United States' best landscape design. Doug Graf was not exaggerating when he claimed Spring Grove is world class.

But Strauch's name is largely forgotten, while Frederick Law Olmsted's remains well known and esteemed. Linde suggests that Strauch was too busy designing to document "his reputation for posterity." But perhaps also, as sightseers and promenaders were lured out of cemeteries and into parks, people lost interest in cemeteries; in the twentieth century, they lost—or suppressed— interest in death. Parks, and then landscaped suburbs, became the wave of the future.

▶ SPRING GROVE

Access: The northern end of Clifton Avenue comes to a T junction at Spring Grove Avenue; turn left/west to reach the cemetery. Alternatively, from I-75 take exit 6, Mitchell Avenue; take Mitchell north to Spring Grove Avenue; turn left. In Spring Grove Cemetery's modern Administration Center (513/681-6680) free maps and also walking-tour brochures by Blanche Linden-Ward are available. From the cemetery turn left/north on Spring Grove to Ivorydale.

SPRING GROVE CEMETERY
ADMINISTRATION BUILDING AND GATEHOUSE, 1867

James Keys Wilson, Cincinnati
4521 Spring Grove Avenue
Now office buildings

James Keys Wilson designed the two buildings at Spring Grove's entrance: a gatehouse, where ladies waited for carriages, on the left/west and an administration building on the right. One small and the other large, both Victorian Eclectic in a mix of smooth- and rough-cut sandstone, the two structures work well together. The one-room gate house has a mansard roof, a bay with windows, a porch with gargoyles, and a chimney that bulges at the top. The larger building has, besides a bevy of gables and a full complement of ornamented stone work, a tower with an open belfry. Originally it housed offices, a board room, and a waiting room that could function as a chapel. Today the sometime-chapel, not normally accessible to

▶ Spring Grove Administration Building

the public, is an employee lunch room with folding tables on the marble floor and spectacular woodwork that's partly obscured by dropped ceiling fixtures overhead. Just beyond the gate house to the west is the Norman Chapel, 1880, by Samuel Hannaford. The cemetery's main road leads from Spring Grove Avenue to an enticing low elliptical arch built as a railroad bridge. Trains no longer pass over it, but the row of evergreens that designer Adolph Strauch planned for screening the tracks is still there. The burial grounds lie beyond the arch. Most of Cincinnati's leading architects designed memorials or buildings at Spring Grove. Monuments of special interest, all on the cemetery map, are the Baroque Burnet mausoleum, 1865, by Charles Rule of Cincinnati; the Fleischmann mausoleum, 1913, a "small Parthenon"; and the Dexter Chapel, 1869, an imposing Gothic chapel complete with flying buttresses and some missing pinnacles, by James Keys Wilson. Liz Scheurer, an art consultant who has studied cemetery sculpture, says the Dexter Chapel was designed to have an organ and an elevator, though never installed. Missing pinnacles are not its only problem, she adds. The stone roof was so heavy that the chapel needed repairs from the day it was finished.

IVORYDALE, 1885

Solon Spencer Beman, Chicago
5209 Spring Green Avenue, St. Bernard
Procter & Gamble factory

For making its soaps Procter & Gamble built itself a factory complex called Ivorydale; though named for soap, it sounds like a never-never land. This is where nine-cents-an-hour soap boilers stirred kettles of Ivory, the soap that floated P&G into national markets. To check for doneness, the soapboilers tasted each batch. Ivorydale, the complex's flagship, has a fine, massive tower ascending between stepped gables. Though some facades on adjacent structures have been altered, most of those visible from the street are a handsome mixture of limestone and brick. Just before this project, architect Solon Spencer Beman had designed the famous (and later notorious) company town of Pullman, Illinois.

Mount Adams and Eden Park

Mount Adams, just northeast of downtown, is Cincinnati's highest hill, overlooking the city, the Ohio River, and Kentucky. To the north it has Eden Park, which Spring Grove landscape designer Adolph Strauch designed for Nicholas Longworth's erstwhile vineyard; it's also the site now of the Cincinnati Art Museum. To the south it has a mile-square city neighborhood with narrow streets and so many hills that sidewalks sometimes turn into stairs. ¶ John Clubbe re-

▶ THE VIEW CITYWARD FROM MOUNT ADAMS

minds us that if it does not have the architectural distinction of Beacon Hill, it does have a more dramatic site. It is, he says, Cincinnati's artistic heart, its Montmartre. ¶ In its post-vineyard days, it was home to limestone quarries that saw the hilltop considerably reduced even as it gave rise to the buildings down below. Historically, because nobody who was anybody wanted to have to climb such a hill to get home, this was a working-class neighborhood, its wonderful natural location over the city lying undiscovered by the real estate interests until the 1960s. ¶ When rehabbers began finding bargains in old housing with a view, they were unrestrained by design review boards, as all the siding and decks in the sky show. But this too is Cincinnati, so some of the vernacular architecture is good and hasn't had the charm altered out of it. Besides, at places like Carney and Pavilion Streets, you'll see what those great views are all about. ¶ Today, it is the most expensive location in the area and, as writer John Fleischman pointed out, an icon for Cincinnati. It is, he said, "the alternative to the standard American Dream of a three-bedroom ranch in the suburbs."

Access: From downtown take Central Parkway east; it merges with U.S. 42/Reading Road, which intersects shortly with Elsinore Place. Turn right/east, over I-71 to Gilbert Avenue where Elsinore is at the corner, at the foot of Mount Adams.

ELSINORE, 1883
Charles Hannaford, Cincinnati
Gilbert Avenue at Elsinore Place,
NRHP
Water works valve house

The superintendent of the Water Works went to see *Hamlet* and was so impressed by the Elsinore set that he had architect Charles Hannaford copy it to house a water valve. It must have been a wonderful set. Built of rough-cut stone in Romanesque Revival, this little valve castle has a round tower, a square tower and an arch that, viewed from the west, frames a stone stairway that winds up the wooded hillside to the Art Museum. It was also intended to be one of the main entrances into Eden Park.

▶ ELSINORE

CINCINNATI ART MUSEUM AND ART ACADEMY OF CINCINNATI, 1886, 1907, 1930, 1965, 1993

James W. McLaughlin; D.H. Burnham & Company, Chicago; Garber & Woodward; Potter, Tyler, Martin & Roth; Glaser Associates; all Cincinnati except Burnham
953 Eden Park Drive
Art museum, open daily except Mon, 513/721-5204

If you're a city famous for hogs, how do you upgrade your image? In 1877 a group of women decided Cincinnati needed an art museum. They were women who knew whom to ask for money, so that before a decade was out, 5,000 people could show up for the 1886 dedication of the Cincinnati Art Museum, a new Richardsonian Romanesque building designed by James W. McLaughlin. The following year,

the museum was joined by another structure in the same style and by the same architect, the Art Academy, set a little to the rear. In later decades, as the collections grew and Richardsonian Romanesque went out of fashion, other buildings were constructed, ultimately engulfing the original museum and connecting it to the Academy. But since the

▶ ART MUSEUM AND INTERIOR

original was never demolished, rediscovering McLaughlin becomes a sport, an architectural scavenger hunt. The best place to see McLaughlin's work is in the Art Academy's facade, which you'll pass while driving to the parking lot. It's mostly rough-cut limestone, with a fine round-arched entry in contrasting darker stone. Other McLaughlin is trickier. From a distance, it's possible to see a Richardsonian Romanesque tower looming out of the complex, and a dome roof. And inside, after a 1990s renovation, McLaughlin's front entry

reappeared, though in the middle of the museum. So it is that, on the second floor in gallery 214, you can have the top of a Richardsonian arch in your face. The museum also did well by Daniel Burnham, who designed what is now the Neoclassical entrance, with a fittingly grand porch of Greek Doric columns. An architectural highlight inside is the courtyard, which Garber & Woodward did. It's lovely by itself, and its enclosing walls offer a history of museum styles. A native of Cincinnati, James W. McLaughlin (1834-1923) apprenticed with James Keys Wilson and began practicing in 1856, only a few years before Immaculata was built He became the city's leading architect, until he lost out to Samuel Hannaford on the Cincinnati Music Hall design. Hannaford and McLaughlin were only a year apart in age, but many more of Hannaford's buildings remain today. McLaughlin's big projects were razed or obscured, like the Art Museum or his downtown Shillito (later Lazarus) department store.

From Elsinore, take Gilbert up the hill to next street, Eden Park Drive, and turn left into Eden Park. Spring House and Mirror Lake are on left; There, Eden Park Drive forks left, Art Museum Drive forks right; Continue on around to Art Museum.

Access: To get to Rookwood Pottery from Art Museum, go right onto Art Museum Drive which bends quickly to left and becomes Ida Street. Cross Ida Street Bridge, and the Pottery is on your right, overlooking the city. To find Immaculata Church, pick up Celestial Street at Rookwood, jog left on Jerome to St. Gregory, and immediately right on Pavilion to the church. This part of Mount Adams is very compact; if you are able to walk uphill at all, park anywhere and walk.

ROOKWOOD POTTERY, NOW CELESTIAL/ROOKWOOD POTTERY, 1891

H. Neill Wilson, Cincinnati, and Rookwood manager William Watts Taylor; Elzner & Anderson
1077 Celestial Street, NRHP
Complex of offices, restaurant

The nation's most famous art pottery, Rookwood Pottery was founded in Cincinnati in 1880 by Maria Longworth Nichols. Though ten years later she married Bellamy Storer and became less active, Rookwood Pottery flourished more and more until the Depression. The architectural division, established in 1902, embellished buildings all over Cincinnati. Examples in this guide include the Gidding-Jenny storefront on Fourth Street, the ice cream shop at Cincinnati Union Terminal, Hughes High School, the arches at Dixie Terminal. Rookwood occupied this complex of half-timbered buildings on Celestial Street. Though the structures have been stripped down and altered, you can still see the fan-shaped patterns that were molded by hand in the stucco, for Rookwood Pottery was part of the Arts and Crafts movement, which believed in hands-on craft. A building with kilns, built when Rookwood had 50 artists on staff, now houses a restaurant.

▶ ROOKWOOD POTTERY

CHURCH OF THE IMMACULATE CONCEPTION, OR IMMACULATA, NOW HOLY CROSS-IMMACULATA CHURCH, 1859

James W. McLaughlin and Louis Picket, Cincinnati
30 Guido Street at Pavilion, NRHP
Roman Catholic church; 513/721-6544

Immaculata Church has a simple Gothic Revival gable-front facade and a tower. What makes it spectacular is its hilltop site at the head of stairs that pilgrims climb every Good Friday. The 150 steps that lead to the church's front door ascend from the street below, St. Gregory. From Columbia Parkway, it's 356. In a tradition that dates from 1860, pilgrims, whose numbers were estimated at 8,000 to 12,000 in 1998, offer a prayer at each step. It was constructed of rough-cut limestone from Mount Adams itself. The vaulted interior is lovely, with apse paintings by ecclesiastical artist Johann Schmidt of Covington, Cincinnati painter Frank Duveneck's teacher. In 1910, when Mount Adams must have been overcrowded with 11,000 people, it was what writer John Fleischman called a "blue-collar Catholic principality," supporting two parishes, a German one at Immaculata and the Irish Holy Cross at the nearby monastery. In 1970 the two combined, a merger not consummated until a posse abducted the full-size statue of St. Patrick's from Holy Cross and carried it into Immaculata as a mass was ending. Everyone stood up and applauded.

Access: From Immaculata, retrace your steps around brow of Mount Adams to Art Museum Drive, and to Spring House. There, take Eden Park Drive around Mirror Lake, and past the Krohn Conservatory. Water Tower is at left.

SPRING HOUSE GAZEBO, 1904

Cornelius M. Foster, Cincinnati

Set next to a former reservoir, now Mirror Lake, the Spring House Gazebo's main purpose is to sit there looking cute. Which it does. Its secondary purpose is to provide a roof in case of rain. The exotic "Moorish" gazebo has eight sides and 16 scalloped arches under a red tile roof. Iron posts support the arches; a little green onion dome tops the roof. Once upon a time, there was a spring at this site; it became contaminated and was sealed in 1912.

WATER TOWER, 1894

Samuel Hannaford & Sons, Cincinnati
NRHP

Near the top this Water Tower has a distinctive band of brick and stone checkerboarding, which you'll see looming over the trees as you drive around the park. When this city built water facilities, they could be happily picturesque, as Elsinore and this tower show. But it's dismaying to learn that at the turn of the century, when the Cox political machine was running Cincinnati, the city was slow to provide the clean water supply that might have prevented children dying from typhoid. No longer used for water, this Romanesque Revival tower is 172 feet high. Until 1914 an elevator took people to the top for an overview.

▶ WALNUT HILLS

Walnut Hills and East Walnut Hills

Walnut Hills and East Walnut Hills are a wonderful area for buildings—a dormer here, a turret there, a splendid spire; delicious details seem to be everywhere. Between them, Walnut Hills and East Walnut Hills house both the very poor and the very rich. Blighted areas, which developed after Walnut Hills became a refuge for people displaced by urban renewal, still remain; east of Woodburn Avenue, the area looks more prosperous, and some enclaves are downright posh.

As for the boundary between Walnut Hills and East Walnut Hills, if you ask ten people where it is, you'll hear ten answers. So promises Mary Ann Olding, who was bothered by this when she first moved to Cincinnati in 1985, but has long since stopped worrying about it.

Access: This tour starts on East McMillan Avenue, just west of southbound I-71 exit 3, Taft Road. From I-71 go west on Taft; turn south on Highland Avenue and then turn left onto McMillan, which is one way eastbound.

GRUEN WATCH COMPANY, NOW UNION INSTITUTE, 1917

Guy C. Burroughs and John Henri Deeken, Cincinnati
401 East McMillan Street at Iowa Avenue, NRHP
Union Institute classrooms and offices

What an enchanting place to work. As its headquarters, the Gruen Watch
Company built an immense half-timbered Tudor Revival building that with
its hooded gables, decorative brickwork, and turrets looks like an immense,
romantic house. There's even a tower whose roof is shaped like an octagonal
witch's hat; to see it, turn right down adjacent Iowa Avenue and look back.
Gruen had plants all over the world; this international headquarters had
assembly and repair facilities. Though it was a major producer before World
War II, Gruen did even better after the war by specializing in fine watches.
Ultimately the company lost its manager, squandered its resources arguing,
moved to New York and was out of business by the late 1970s. The sign
with the company name for this place is still next to the driveway: Time Hill.
In the late 1990s Union Institute, a multi-state university for adults,
rehabbed the former Gruen building. Mary Ann Olding, a faculty member,
researched the original lobby so that it could be reconstructed.

GRUEN WATCH MAKERS GUILD, (EAST VIEW) TIME HILL, CINCINNATI, O., U. S. A.

BEAU BRUMMEL TIES, NOW UNION INSTITUTE, 1921

Elzner & Anderson, Cincinnati
440 East McMillan Street, NRHP
Union Institute headquarters, classrooms, offices

Just across the street from Gruen, an old tie factory has a distinctive tower.
Built for Procter & Collier Advertising but associated more with longtime
occupant Beau Brummel Ties, the building was rehabbed in 1989 as Union
Institute headquarters.

Access: Continue east on McMillan; at Victory Parkway turn right/ south. The second turn, at the Y intersection on the left, is Francis Lane; turn left/east onto Francis; then turn immediately onto Edgecliff Road which promptly offers a turn onto Edgecliff Point. (This may sound harder than it is.) Park Avenue parallels Victory Parkway a block to the west, joins it when Victory curves.

LAWRENCE MAXWELL HOUSE, NOW MAXWELTON, 1887

Burnham & Root, Chicago
2020 Edgecliff Point
Private house owned by high-rise apartment

The block-long street of Edgecliff Point is worth seeing for interesting houses, an Ohio River overlook, and one of the few Ohio examples of a building by Burnham & Root before the early death of John Root, the partnership's principal designer. The Richardsonian Romanesque house is of pale rough-cut stone with matching brick for trim.

MILLS ROW, C. 1880

2201-2209 Park Avenue at Victory Parkway, NRHP
Apartment house

This fanciful row is just west of Victory Parkway and readily visible from it. It's five attached red-brick houses, each with its own porch, and Second Empire mansard roofs at the third floor. The middle house has a tower with convex and concave segments; the two end houses have third-floor porches under large, exaggerated dormer roofs. The whole row is apartments now.

Access: Return north on Victory Parkway half a block to Cypress; turn right/east and continue to Upland Place; Swiss Chalet is across the street just below Cypress. Upland also connects with McMillan at its north end.

ALFRED DAY FISHER SWISS CHALET, 1892

Lucien F. Plympton, Cincinnati
2214 Upland Place
Private house

As Swiss Chalets go, this one is definitive—amazingly, all the front woodwork really was cut in Switzerland. It has the fine detail and many colors of folk embroidery. Seven-foot eaves are supported by carved brackets whose edges are painted white; in shadow the edge becomes a weird, undulating white line that seems to float by itself. Two-and-a-half stories high in front, the house is built on a slope so that the back has four-and-a-half stories. Architect Lucien Plympton (1856-1938) is remembered mostly for chalets, though Walter Langsam points out that Plympton's own house, a few doors from the Fisher Chalet at 2200 Upland Place, was a Tudor Revival with Arts and Crafts features.

Access: Return to Victory Parkway by turning south on Upland and then right/west on Cypress, and then turn north; as road turns bear right/east onto Madison Road. The Woodburn Avenue intersection with San Marco Flats comes almost immediately. Continue about half a mile on Madison to Baker Place; turn right/south.

SAN MARCO FLATS, C. 1893

Boll & Taylor, Cincinnati
1601 Madison Road at Woodburn, Madison and Woodburn HD
Apartments for elderly and disabled

This neighborhood has gaps among the buildings, but fortunately the San Marco Flats building still overlooks this intersection. Six-and-a-half stories tall, it faces two streets with a hinge-like round bay and turret at the corner. Red brick with stone trim, it has a mansard roof. Doug Graf likes it a lot as a massive background building, a common type in 1893. "So good," he says. "So urban." Across the street is St. Francis de Sales Church, 1879, which has a 230-foot tower.

DINSMORE HOUSE, 1912

Matthew H. Burton and George S. Werner, Cincinnati
2777 Baker Place near Madison Road
Private house

The first place I saw this wonderful house was in Walter E. Langsam's book on Cincinnati houses; he called it "belated Art Nouveau and precocious Art Deco." Its curved gables and swooping parapets are all the more conspicuous because they're edged in white, which contrasts with the gray stucco walls; roofs are red tile. Doug Graf pointed out that the gables have different personalities: the right one is gothicized and the left one, classical. To me, the house looks like a Charles Burchfield painting.

Hyde Park and Mount Lookout

These in-city residential neighborhoods both have commercial hubs. Hyde Park Square runs along Erie Avenue between Edwards Road and Michigan Avenue; a parkway and fountain give it focus. To the southeast, the less formal Mount Lookout Square is at the intersection of Delta and Linwood Avenues.

Access: From Baker Place continue east-northeast on Madison Road past Observatory Road; Withrow High School is on the west side of the road opposite Erie Avenue.

▶ WITHROW HIGH SCHOOL

EAST SIDE HIGH SCHOOL, NOW WITHROW HIGH SCHOOL, 1919
Garber & Woodward, Cincinnati
2488 Madison Road at Dana Avenue, NRHP
High school

In the beginning, everyone thought of Withrow High School as one of America's most beautiful schools. It's still beautiful. Georgian Revival, red-brick, it has columns, cupolas and balustrades. The best feature is its siting on its treed lawns: the building forms an arc facing a tall, freestanding clock tower that's on an axis with Erie Avenue; it's visible from Hyde Park Square. A closer look at Withrow takes away some of the grandeur. Brick stairs are missing mortar; Rookwood drinking fountains don't work. "Things," says Principal Dennis Matthews, "go lacking after the years." The 2,100 students here represent three groups. For some, it's the neighborhood school; for others, it's where they're sent if kicked out elsewhere; and for the third group, it's an international magnet school. All of them can thank the Withrow Alumni Association for giving the school some attention. First, under an alumna named Marlene Holwadel, the group opened an office in the building in 1995. The alumni raised money and paid for tree trimming, lawn maintenance, and repair to the tower and the bridge leading to it. They paid for trash cans and for painting auditorium seats. "Cleaning up is not everything," Holwadel said, "but it's a start. People act like things look." She has since died, but her cohort and former classmate, Bob McKeever, '50, is still manning the office. He's also spearheading a drive to raise money for a gym and activity center— Withrow is Ohio's only Division I school without a regulation basketball court. Alumnus and Cincinnati tycoon Richard Lindner pledged $1 million in 1998; in early 2000 the next $5 million was in sight.

**Access: Drive east on Erie to see Hyde Park Square; then turn right/
south on Michigan Avenue and drive one block to Observatory
Avenue; turn left/east. The Stone House is east of Kilgour Lane;
several blocks east of Delta, Observatory Place is on the left/north.
Then continue east on Observatory, which eventually enters Ault Park.**

GEORGE N. STONE HOUSE, C. 1880

Samuel Hannaford, Cincinnati
3025 Observatory Avenue at Kilgour Lane
Private house

What a fine tall house this is, in spiffy condition, painted in contrasting
colors so you can't miss what's going on. It's a Stick Style, two-and-a-half
stories, with a mansard roof, a tower in front and lots of gables.
George N. Stone came to Cincinnati and kept busy with a gambling house
and horse racing before he settled down in the telephone business. Perhaps
in 1878 telephones were just another gamble

UNIVERSITY OF CINCINNATI OBSERVATORY, 1873, AND O.M. MITCHEL BUILDING, 1904, NOW CINCINNATI OBSERVATORY CENTER

Samuel Hannaford, 1873, and Samuel Hannaford & Sons, 1904 and 1912,
Cincinnati
3489 Observatory Place, NHL, NRHP/Observatory HD, Hannaford TR
Buildings being developed as private museum and educational facility,
513/321-5186

The Observatory has a wonderful site: a grassy hilltop at the end of
Observatory Place. The red-brick building has classical forms—an anomaly
in 1873—and a bulbous metal observatory dome that seems to spring from
the front porch pediment. Inside the side rooms have 20-foot ceilings, while
the round section in the middle has two levels, above for the telescope and
below, originally, for books. The smaller 1904 O.M. Mitchel building,
which also has a telescope and dome, was originally all round; the front
section was added in 1912. At the beginning of 1999 a nonprofit group,

▶ THE OBSERVATORY

▶ AULT PARK PAVILION

Cincinnati Observatory Center, started leasing the site. The first year they expected to spend almost $300,000 on stabilizing the buildings, the larger one for a museum and the smaller one, for astronomy programs. The historic telescopes, says Paul Nohr, previously site coordinator for the University of Cincinnati, no longer offer cutting-edge research possibilities. Today all the best measurements are done in space.

AULT PARK PAVILION, 1930

Fechheimer & Ihorst, Cincinnati
Park building

In an uncommon combination, Ault Park Pavilion mixes an elegant, formal Italian Renaissance design with rough-cut stone. The pavilion is on a hilltop, approached by two grand stairways with Cascade Fountain descending between them. The building has an open central arcade linking two enclosed wings. The roof has multi-level terraces edged by balustrades; best view is from up there. Originally bands played here for dancing on summer evenings.

Access: Return to Observatory Avenue and go back to Delta Avenue; turn left/south, continuing on Delta through Mount Lookout Square to Kroger Avenue; turn left/east; continue to Stanley Avenue; turn right/ south to Vineyard Place; turn left/east to St. Ursula Villa.

RICHARD LEBLOND HOUSE, NOW ST. URSULA VILLA, 1925

George W. Rapp, Rapp, Zettel & Rapp, Cincinnati
3660 Vineyard Place
Private Catholic elementary school; not accessible to visitors

After their children had grown up and moved away, manufacturer Richard LeBlond and his wife Loretta built themselves this 40-room Tudor Revival house with redwood half-timbering. Ultimately the LeBlonds willed it to the Catholic archdiocese, and it was converted into an elementary school. Thus today the wine cellar has shelves stocked with colored paper and the paneled diningroom is furnished with tiny tables and chairs.

The East End (also an alternative route to Mariemont)

—To reach the East End from Vineyard Place, turn right/south onto Tusculum Avenue and wind downhill. After crossing Columbia Parkway, turn left on Eastern Avenue. Since World War II Cincinnati's East End has been mostly a poor industrial area. But it too has some architectural nuggets. First, both above and below Eastern Avenue (which parallels Columbia Parkway) the Victorian houses on and around Tusculum Avenue have had multi-colored paint jobs. Secondly, McKinley School, 1878 and 1919, 3905 Eastern Avenue at Tennyson, by Bausmith & Drainie, presents its 1919 side to the street: a Tudor facade with terra-cotta shields, a student, griffins. No doubt because it's neglected, the building has its original windows, handsomer than the usual replacements. Third, past Linwood Avenue still farther upriver, is the center of Linwood, a well-to-do suburb Cincinnati annexed in 1896. The Linwood Public School, 1929, is at 4900 Eastern Avenue. Designed by Cincinnati

▶ McKinley School

architects Fechheimer & Ihorst, it has a prominent square tower and is fronted majestically by a pair of stairways leading uphill to the school. The old Linwood Village Hall, 1875, has been a church since 1904. At 4928 Eastern Avenue, it has an open belfry. Linwood lost many of its best houses to the 1962 Columbia Parkway extension, which Eastern Avenue joins after Linwood.

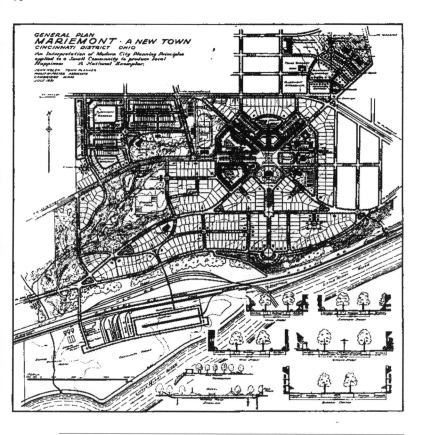

Access: From downtown take Columbia Parkway/U.S. 50 east to Mariemont. From I-71 southbound take exit 9 and drive south on Red Bank Expressway, which intersects Columbia Parkway just west of Mariemont.

Mariemont

In the 1920s Mariemont was planned and designed as an ideal community. For its many admirers, that's just what it is today. ¶ When Thomas J. Emery died in 1904, he left an enormous fortune, founded on candles and ballooned on real estate, to his wife, Mary Emery. Mrs. Emery had already lost her two grown sons, so now at 60 she was completely alone and incredibly rich. She could have done anything. But

what she decided to do, was build a model town
as a living memorial to her husband. It was such
an extraordinary decision that, as the creation of
one individual, the resulting town, complete with
shops, utilities and services, is unique. ¶ About
1910, she confided her hopes to her amanuensis
and surrogate son, Charles J. Livingood, a
Harvard classmate of Sheldon Emery. He was
Mrs. Emery's estate manager and "the majordomo
of her life." So says Millard Rogers, who's been
writing two books, one about Mary Emery and
the other about the origins of Mariemont. With
Livingood administering her philanthropies, Mrs.
Emery gave away millions, including an art collection and a wing at the Cincinnati Art Museum. ¶ Mariemont, says Rogers, who is also the
retired director of the Art Museum, "wouldn't
have happened without her wealth, but it was
Livingood's ideas and vision." Livingood honed
his vision on trips to Europe—he looked especially at English villages—and by visiting other

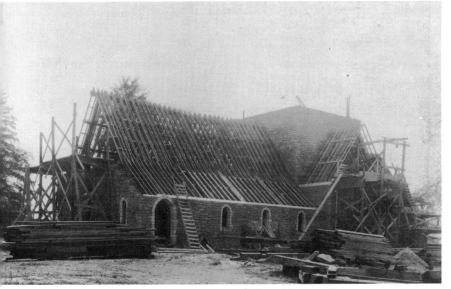

▶ EMERY MEMORIAL CHURCH

planned commu-
nities. In 1915
he quietly began
acquiring 400
acres of farmland
northeast of
Cincinnati along
the Little Miami
River. The last
parcel was
bought in 1922,
at an inflated
cost. ¶ Architec-
turally what is
most interesting

▶ EMERY MEMORIAL CHURCH

about Mariemont is the plan. Even before all the
land was in hand, Livingood called in John Nolen
of Cambridge, Massachusetts. Nolen was the
country's foremost planner, known for Kingsport,
Tennesee and Naples, Florida. He gave
Mariemont his trademark radial street plan and
vistas. He straightened out U.S. 50, which had
jogged south here; he divided the traffic lanes in
the Town Center and just to the east he preserved
a beech woods in the median. South of the Town
Center, he planned the axial vista and bluff overlook. ¶ Then Livingood, a man with the ideal
name for someone working on a model town,
chose the 25 architects—all from New York,
Philadelphia, Boston or Cincinnati. "Livingood
was an Anglophile," says Rogers. "He saw
Mariemont as a quaint English town, and he
made all the decisions." He ordered village cul-
de-sacs based on garden-city developments in

▶ RECREATION BUILDING

England. These are Mariemont's second most interesting architectural feature. ¶ But Mrs. Emery was the one who chose the name, Mariemont, pronounced Merrymont, which was also the name of her estate at Newport, Rhode Island, where she spent half her time. She was in Cincinnati for the 1923 groundbreaking at Mariemont. At almost 80, 20 years a widow, Mrs. Emery wore a long black mourning dress while she wielded a silver spade in one hand and a bouquet in the other. Her nurse, looking like a cross female bouncer, stood alongside. During the next two years, 1924 and 1925, with Mrs. Emery's money paying for everything, a thousand people were at work building Mariemont. By 1926 the place was impressive enough to merit 44 pages of pictures, floorplans and text in *Architecture* magazine. ¶ Mrs. Emery envisioned Mariemont as, in part, good housing for low-income families—low income white families. "And the children?," she wrote. "Are their faces a bit ruddier? Are their legs a little sturdier? Do they play and laugh a lot louder in Mariemont? Then I am content." From the beginning, the village had amenities such as parks, shops and a

hotel, underground utility lines, a school and a
fire department. It also had an industrial park: an
appendix of land to the west accessible by road
only from the adjacent town of Fairfax. Some of
Mariemont's original features, like the golf course
that flooded too much, were abandoned. And
some of the original plans were never executed,
like the cluster of tiny retirement cottages that
Mrs. Emery especially wanted. ¶ When Mrs.
Emery died in late 1927, the fountain of money
stopped; only one major construction project, the
Recreation Building, began after her death. Ultimately her investment in the town was transferred to a charitable foundation, the Thomas J.
Emery Memorial, which had some Mariemont
holdings into the 1960s. Most of Mariemont's
houses were built after World War II, with building commissioner Charles Cellarius functioning
as architectural czar. He abandoned the English
village concept and permitted any two-story
house in a conservative style; the results are unex-
ceptional. ¶ An incorporated village since 1941,
Mariemont today is small (3,000), white, and
well-to-do. It fiercely protects its 1920s neighborhoods and cul-de-sacs, which are all in the
National Register's Mariemont Historic District.
An Architectural Review Board passes on all
proposed exterior changes, including paint colors
and replacement garage doors. Yes, says the
Review Board head, Fred Rutherford, the police
have been sent to stop someone painting the
wrong color. But, he adds, historic properties
now are 98 percent unchanged on the outside,
except for air conditioning necessary to attract

renters. ¶ Overall today's Mariemont is attractive and likely more prosperous than Mary Emery envisioned. But it's clear that basically, she was right—a town *is* an effective memorial. Largely because of Mariemont, Mary and Thomas J. Emery are remembered.

Mariemont: A Walking Tour (Car Optional)—

The Mariemont Town Center straddles Wooster Pike/ U.S. 50; four roads extend diagonally from the square. The three-story Mariemont Inn, half-timbered and brick, has the square's northwest corner; a new (1990s) shop and office complex just to the west was done in the same style. To the east of Town Center a median and a triangular park are both in woods that planner John Nolen deliberately preserved when the road was built. Turn south at East Street, then right/northwest on Crystal Spring. The houses in Sheldon Close, the cul-de-sac on the left, were designed by Grosvenor Atterbury, New York, in the 1920s. At the corner turn left to Center Avenue's view south through an allée to the Concourse two blocks away. Planned by Nolen and Mariemont's most attractive original feature, the Concourse has a curved pergola by Phillip W. Foster of Cambridge, Massachusetts, and offers a view from the bluff over the Little Miami Valley. Return to Miami Road and see Albert Place. To see more in Mariemont: The Mariemont Preservation Foundation publishes "A Tour of Mariemont" available for 50 cents at the Mariemont Inn or at the MPF office at 3919 Plainville Road (rear; follow brick walk); 513/272-1166. The Historic District, including these sites, is on the National Register.

ALBERT PLACE, 1924

Robert R. McGoodwin, Philadelphia
1-10 Albert Place and 3825 and 3845 Miami Road

The first residential group to be finished, Albert Place has 12 six-room detached and semi-detached houses in white-painted brick. They're arranged in a U with two extra houses at the street end. The road and sidewalk in front both form Us. In back an alley that forms an irregular U serves the houses and their garages. Walk north on West Avenue to Wooster Pike, cross the street and turn left/west past the school to Dale Park; see Memorial Church.

THOMAS J. EMERY MEMORIAL CHURCH, NOW MEMORIAL CHAPEL, 1926

Louis E. Jallade, New York
Cherry Lane
Mariemont Community Church chapel

Writer John Fleischman, a Cincinnatian who has seen dozens of Anglo Norman Gothic parish churches in England, says the Memorial Church is such a good example that it's "eerie. The only thing it doesn't have is the smell." Even the pointed spire later added to Anglo Norman Gothic churches is authentic, he says. As for the stone roof, it's genuinely old. It was taken from an abbey tithe barn—where the abbey stored grain tithes that tenants brought in—built in England about 1300. Then it was shipped to Cincinnati and deliberately rebuilt with the sag. The Memorial Church was

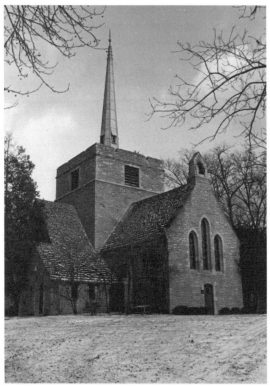

the first building started in Mariemont, and the one of most interest to town founder and benefactor Mary Emery. Mariemont's original shopping district was at the corner of Cherry Lane and Chestnut, where stores have now become offices. Go east along Chestnut Street to see apartment buildings. The Parish Center tower is at the end of Chestnut Street on Plainville Road.

▶ EMERY MEMORIAL CHURCH

RECREATION BUILDING, NOW PARISH CENTER, 1930

George B. deGersdorff, New York
3908 Plainville Road
The nondenominational Protestant Mariemont Community Church uses the
Parish Center for offices, Sunday school, and a weekly service; 513/271-4376

This Mediterranean structure is dominated by a tall brick clock and bell
tower next to an arcaded entry porch. It looks like a row of attached stucco
and brick houses along an Italian village street.

Cincinnati - Northern Suburbs

This is a tour to see some exceptional buildings,
of course, but also to see two examples of how
developers laid out nineteenth-century towns to
attract affluent residents. Glendale, Wyoming,
Hartwell, and Carthage all began as railroad
suburbs—suddenly, the advent of train service
put them within commuting distance and inspired ambitious development plans. Glendale's
lovely street layout was a pioneering first nationally. Hartwell had the sense to copy Glendale,
though in a less sophisticated way. ¶ For the
architectural tourist, these four communities are
easy to find, because they're all strung along one
road. The biggest obvious difference between the
four today is that the southern two, Hartwell and
Carthage, were annexed by Cincinnati in the
early twentieth century, and are less affluent than
Wyoming and Glendale.

Access: This tour is north to south here, but may be done the reverse
way. If approaching from the south and Ivorydale, continue north on
Spring Grove, which merges into Vine Street. Coming from the north,
take exit 42/42B from I-275 and go south on State Route 747, called
Congress Avenue in Glendale. See the Church of the New Jerusalem
on Congress Avenue and then turn left/east on Fountain Avenue.
After exploring Fountain Avenue return to Congress Avenue/747 and
turn left/south.

CHURCH OF THE NEW JERUSALEM, 1861

Peter Mullett
845 Congress Avenue
Swedenborgian church; 513/772-1478

The Church of the New Jerusalem is a small frame Gothic Revival church, laid out in a cross so that it has four gable ends and, above the point of the crossing, a spire. Siding is vertical board and batten. The sanctuary interior is simple, with dark woodwork in pews, windows, and the arch and railing in front of the altar. The pastor, Rev. Patrick Rose, says that only about 25 people attend the twice-monthly Sunday services. Small or no, the congregation built an addition to the church's south side in the 1980s. Based on the religious teachings of a Swedish scientist named Emanuel Swedenborg, Swedenborgianism is a Protestant church that was founded in England in 1792. Though this church is usually attributed to Peter Mullett, Walter Langsam thinks that it's probably an early work of Alfred B. Mullett (1834-1890), who grew up to be an influential supervising architect for the U.S. Treasury. He designed 40 public buildings, including the massive and elaborate Second Empire Old Executive Office Building next to the White House in Washington—it's hard to imagine anything more different from this exquisitely simple church. Alfred Mullett's family came to the Glendale area from England when he was ten. As an architect, he started out in Isaiah Rogers's Cincinnati office and became a partner there in 1861.

FOUNTAIN AVENUE/GLENDALE PLAT, 1851

National Register's Glendale Historic District is also a National Historic Landmark

Glendale is a place that should be famous for its street plan, its lovely curving roads that follow the topography. The romantic suburbs of the future would all be platted this way; Glendale was the first. But unlike Llewellyn Park in New Jersey and Riverside in Illinois, laid out in 1852 and 1868, respectively, Glendale doesn't make the history books. That could be because Robert C. Phillips, a Cincinnati civil engineer who platted the town, was not known for town planning, nor did he become so with Glendale—he was a historical sidetrack. John Clubbe calls Phillips a pioneer, though one with a spiritual debt to landscape architect Andrew Jackson Downing. In 1849 and 1850 Downing publishing two articles on designing country villages. Those articles, avers Clubbe, "read like a blueprint for Glendale." Another source of inspiration for Phillips may have been the curvilinear platting that Howard Daniels had designed for Spring Grove in 1846-1848. I wonder if it's possible that Daniels himself might have laid out Glendale, and Phillips, executed it. The first train that went all the way to Glendale ran in September 1851; that was also the year Phillips platted 200 acres, which he laid out in irregularly shaped lots ranging from one to 20 acres in size. Fountain Avenue, the diagonal spine, is the best single road to see. It follows a wavy path, wooded, lined by fine old houses set back from the road; in the middle is a diminutive park. Another four streets curl away from that park, so it's easy to see why, when Sidney D. Maxwell wrote about Cincinnati suburbs in 1870, he complained that Glendale was confusing.

▶ THE GLENDALE PLAT

FIRST PRESBYTERIAN CHURCH, 1873

A.C. Nash, Cincinnati
155 East Fountain Avenue
Church

Here's an A.C. Nash Gothic Revival church in brick. The earlier church, 1860, is next door. It needed those buttresses because of the steep roof.

Access: At Glendale's southern boundary the main north-south road becomes Springfield Pike/State Route 4. Take it south to Wyoming; to see historic streets, turn left/east on Wyoming Avenue, then right/ south on Burns Avenue. See the Wyoming Baptist Church and the house at 30 Burns; then return to Springfield by Mills Avenue.

WYOMING BAPTIST CHURCH, 1882

A.C. Nash, Cincinnati
164 Burns Avenue at Waverly, NRHP/Village HD, Wyoming MRA
Baptist church; pastor will show interior; 513/821-8430

What an impressive building the Wyoming Baptist Church is, with its tower's height mostly in its steep roof. The white frame structure is such a good example of Stick Style that Stephen Gordon chose it as an example for his book, *How to Complete the Ohio Historic Inventory.* The sanctuary has a beamed dark-wood ceiling. A round window over the altar, with a scene depicting Christ as a shepherd, was covered up in a 1950s renovation and uncovered in the early 1990s. The window opposite that one, in the large gable nearest the street, has a Star of David, which the Rev. Charles Fox, the minister, finds a little surprising. He also finds it hard to believe that the neighborhood's spacious Victorian houses all started with outhouses. That is indeed a big leap in comprehending daily life, historically. The architect who liked elongated tower roofs was Albert C. Nash (1826-1890), who practiced in Cincinnati and twice served as president of the local A.I.A. chapter. Another of his designs was Trinity Episcopal Church in Hamilton (see also; Vol. II).

▶ WYOMING BAPTIST

30 BURNS AVENUE, 1895

NRHP/Village HD
Private house

As a drive along Burns and then Mills shows, Wyoming is deservedly known for its nineteenth-century houses. This Shingle Style house's facade has two dominant features that overlap in the middle: a big entry arch and an octagonal tower with a convex roof.

Access: From Wyoming continue south on Springfield, which becomes Vine Street in Cincinnati. South of Galbraith Road, turn left/east on Parkway Avenue, which leads to the center of Hartwell. To reach Carthage, the next neighborhood south, return to Vine Street.

HARTWELL PLAT, 1867

Along with its mix of big and small houses, this Cincinnati neighborhood has an ambitious street plan with curling roads radiating from a central green. To see, follow Woodbine north and south. Though Hartwell is said to have been based on Glendale, the plan isn't a copy; perhaps it was simply inspired. The developer, the Hamilton County Home Building Association, named Hartwell for a railroad executive and platted it with a view to attracting well-to-do commuters; churches in the central green showed the kind of people they wanted. So does a house like the nice white frame at 135 Parkway.

▶ THE HARTWELL PLAT

FIREHOUSE OF ENGINE COMPANY NO. 48, NOW CARTHAGE MEDICAL CENTER, 1912

Harry Hake, Cincinnati
7019 Vine Street just north of 70th Street
Private medical offices

Here's a small facade with an immense arch that's outlined delectably in terra cotta. Once upon a time the arch was for fire trucks coming and going; the building was designed to look like just another bungalow in a residential neighborhood. Two side doors and the central one have been filled in with walls and windows; but the terra-cotta trim and red tile roof remain.

▶ THE ARCADE

Cleveland

In less than a day in Cleveland, you can see more sumptuous interiors than you'll find in all the rest of the state put together. You can dazzle your eyes with marble wainscoting and marble columns, vaulted and coffered ceilings or, if you prefer, high, dark wooden ceilings with great beams. Located in the likes of banks, court-houses, and churches, virtually all these spaces are accessible to the public. ¶ In their number, they reveal a Cleveland peculiarity: it is not unusual here that a building's inside is more interesting than the outside. To that, the Terminal Tower is an exception. Its exterior became the symbol of the region. ¶ Steven Litt, architecture critic at the *Plain Dealer*, offers a thumbnail assessment of Cleveland's architec-ture: it is and always has been conservative. He ticks off on his fingers the once avant garde architects who never worked in Cleveland: Louis Sullivan, Frank Lloyd Wright, Eliel

Saarinen, Mies van der Rohe. Marcel Breuer and I.M. Pei did do Cleveland buildings, but toward the end of their careers rather than while they were still radical. What Cleveland does have, says Litt, is "good, traditional urbanism in the Beaux Arts vein, good street car suburbs, and fine neighborhood architecture—neo-Tudor, neo-Georgian." ¶ What Cleveland also has is Steven Litt, Ohio's only writer whose byline reads "architecture critic." Litt also covers art for the newspaper, but architecture takes most of his time. ¶ Admittedly, there are a couple possible exceptions to Cleveland's customary shunning of the avant garde. One is the 1950 Park Synagogue in Cleveland Heights. It's an exception that proves the rule, for Rabbi Armond Cohen, the individual who brought in German expressionist architect Eric Mendelsohn, is a native New Yorker. ¶ Another is under construction: Case Western Reserve University's new Peter B. Lewis Building for the Weatherhead School of Management. It was designed by Los Angeles architect Frank O. Gehry and promises to be in the best Gehry mode, with a mix of curving brick walls for structure and immense, waving ribbons of shiny stainless steel for art. Litt is delighted, for Gehry is more celebrated than ever, and an architecture critic likes to have some high-hype stuff on his beat. But the fact is, even Gehry is no longer the radical he was. ¶ The new business school was made possible by a Cleveland businessman who'd been trying for years to build a house or a skyscraper with Gehry. He was Peter Lewis, head of Progressive, an insurance company, who was contributing $24 million toward the $40 million project. Expected completion date: 2001. ¶ For this guide Cleveland is divided into Downtown, East Side and University Circle, Lakeview Cemetery and the Heights, Ohio City and Tremont Neighborhoods, and Lakewood, in that order. *To see more in Cleveland*—The Cleveland Chapter of the American Institute of Architects publishes an illustrated *Guide to Cleveland Architecture*. Issued in 1997, the second edition is available at Cleveland bookstores or directly from AIA Cleveland, 216/771-3218.

Access: Cleveland is at the junction of I-71, I-77, and I-90, as well as the State Route 2 Shoreway. From all, downtown exits, such as Ontario Street or East 9th Street, are marked.

Downtown
Public Square, NRHP, and Southeast Downtown

Downtown Cleveland has two planned public spaces, one cited in architectural books (see the Mall below), and another that should be. The successful one is Public Square, ten acres that the founding father, General Moses Cleaveland, paced out himself. Cleaveland was in Ohio in 1776 to map the state's northeast corner, which was a Connecticut colony of sorts, the Western Reserve. After laying out five-mile-square townships (the norm elsewhere is six miles), Cleaveland arrived at the Cuyahoga River, where he founded the town that took his name, though ultimately without the first *a*. After expressing the hope that his town might grow "as large as Old Windham" in Connecticut, Cleaveland went back to New England. The square that he left was a typical feature of New England-style country villages. This one evolved successfully into an urban hub that is probably Ohio's best. That's not to say it's at its peak today. Retail facing the square has ebbed; the wall of surrounding buildings has a gap on the west; and sidewalks are not necessarily crowded with fashionable people.

Access: Downtown Cleveland's central Public Square is divided into quadrants by Ontario Street and Superior Avenue. Streets go north-south and avenues, east-west, paralleling the lake shore. Except for Ontario, streets are numbered, counting in two directions, so Cleveland has, for example, both East 6th and West 6th Streets, a curiosity that may be confusing. Of avenues, for our purposes Lakeside is northernmost, followed in order by Superior, Euclid, and Prospect. Below Prospect Huron Road, an anomaly, runs east-west, and then bends north at the river. This downtown tour may be done by foot but might well be divided between, say, a morning and an afternoon, on a weekday if possible, because opulent interiors are accessible. Buildings here are grouped thematically and may be toured in this order. However, after the Federal Reserve Bank, it is shorter and easier to continue west on Superior to the Library and Federal Building before finishing the Banks tour on Public Square. The Greater Cleveland CVB runs an Information Center that provides free downtown walking maps including all sites listed here, and more, as well as a University Circle map. Center is located in the Terminal Tower lobby and is open daily; for hours, call 216/621-7981.

TERMINAL TOWER, 1928

Graham, Anderson, Probst & White, Chicago
Public Square, southwest corner, NRHP
Office building in complex now called Tower City Center, with adjacent store, hotel, and shopping center; 42nd-floor observation deck open year round weekends, 216/621-7981

The Terminal Tower complex was the world's largest multi-building, multi-use project; it predated Rockefeller Center and incorporated more facilities. "As a megabuilding," says Ohio State's Douglas Graf, "it's unparalleled." He puts it on his short list of Ohio masterpieces. Terminal Tower succeeds above all because for ordinary people, it became an image for a region. So

▶ UNDER CONSTRUCTION IN 1927, ETCHING BY LOUIS ROSENBERG

avers Walter Leedy, architectural historian and Cleveland State University art professor. "How many buildings try to create an image for a city and fail?" says Leedy, who has a populist approach to architecture. "This building has the most meaning for Clevelanders. People talk about taking the train and eating at Harvey's. Every day thousands of people walked through that space. They would come in on a train, walk up the steep ramps, and then suddenly Public Square burst upon them." Two brothers built the whole Terminal Tower complex, though their original intention was merely to

develop suburban Shaker Heights. Oris P. and Mantis J. Van Sweringen's projects did have a way of ballooning. What became Terminal Tower was conceived initially as a downtown station for interurban trains to Shaker Heights. Then in 1916, to acquire the right-of-way for that interurban, the Van Sweringens bought the Nickel Plate Railroad; 13 years later they owned a $3 billion transcontinental rail system. And by then, the interurban rail terminal had grown to include a union terminal and the Terminal Tower complex itself. The Van Sweringens gave Cleveland a skyline second only to those of New York and Chicago, writes historian John R. Stilgoe; they were credited with making Cleveland into a real city. The Depression brought it all to an end for the Van Sweringens. It bankrupted them, and both died in the mid-1930s. But Terminal Tower, their monument on Public Square, is still going on. The tower itself is a 52-story skyscraper on 20-story piers anchored on bedrock. Set on the diagonal at the southwest corner of Public Square, it is the pivot of an L whose arms are a

▶ TERMINAL TOWER, FROM THE FLATS

department store and a hotel; the union terminal and interurban station were below to the rear. Sixty years later, long abandoned by railroads and serving only local transit, the railroad station was remodeled into Tower City shopping mall. In back the complex has three Art Deco skyscrapers and a former post office; two new high rises, the Ritz Hotel, 1990, and the Skylight Office Tower, 1991, flank the shopping mall. Critics have made much of Terminal Tower being out-of-style when it was built; it echoes McKim, Mead, and White's Neoclassical New York Municipal Building, completed a dozen years earlier. But Walter Leedy says the use of the dated Neoclassical style was deliberate. For the Terminal Tower to make money, it had to be monumental, Leedy says. And therefore it had to be Neoclassical.

THE MAY COMPANY, 1914, TWO-STORY ADDITION, 1931

D.H. Burnham & Co., Chicago
150 Euclid Avenue, NRHP
Former department store; in 1997 four stories in use as bank offices
Front and rear, the May Company building has terra cotta facing and three-part Chicago Style windows. The eight-story structure had 17 acres of floor space—it was the largest in Ohio.

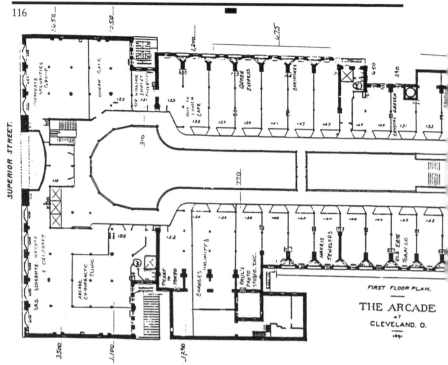

FIRST FLOOR PLAN.

THE ARCADE
AT
CLEVELAND. O.
1891

THE ARCADE, NOW HYATT REGENCY CLEVELAND AT THE ARCADE, 1890, 2001

John M. Eisenmann and George H. Smith, Cleveland
401 Euclid Avenue between Euclid and Superior Avenues, NHL, NRHP
Hotel and retail shops

The Arcade has a great interior—for the late architectural historian Eric Johannesen, author of the classic *Cleveland Architecture 1876-1976*, it was "the most breathtaking" interior in Cleveland. It's unique in the world: a 300-foot long shopping and office arcade lined all around by four levels of balconies fronted with cast iron railings. Overhead—100 feet overhead at the highest point—arched trusses support a glass ceiling of two-by-

▶ SUPERIOR AVENUE ENTRANCE

four-foot panes. The Arcade is not a static place. Near Euclid Avenue it turns; near Superior, it gains a lower floor to accommodate a difference in street elevations. At both ends it has nine-story red brick and sandstone office buildings facing the street, with the original Romanesque entry arch still intact at Superior. This grand, up-to-date production was a local project, with local designers working for local investors, though here the locals included John D. Rockefeller and John L. Severance from Standard Oil and electrical inventor Charles Brush. The structural concept was that of John Eisenmann, an engineering professor at Case School of Applied

Sciences, who transmitted the thrust of the ceiling arches to load-bearing masonry walls. The concept was so innovative that no local construction company would take on the job; the builder who came to the rescue was the Detroit Bridge Company, experienced in iron trusses. Eisenmann's name comes up again later. In 1904 he produced Cleveland's building code, which became the model for other cities. He also designed the Ohio flag. In 1977 Harvey G. Oppmann was a 31-year old real estate man who liked old buildings. After he outbid a developer who proposed razing the Arcade to put up a new building, no local bank would give him a loan. Oppmann found his money at California's Bank of America—bankers there were dazzled by the pictures—and for years he owned the building with two California partners. They spruced it up, replacing 3,600 panes of glass, polishing brass, restoring signage. To lure the tenants he wanted, Oppmann himself opened a French bakery and a poster shop, both so successful that they soon sold.

What Oppmann never expected, was that 20 years, he'd have to be rethinking the Arcade. The city's legal and financial hub was no longer at East 9th and Euclid, and retail was down in the area. So in 1999 Oppmann sold the building, and Hyatt hotels started converting the Arcade into a 293-room Hyatt Regency, with rooms in the nine-story buildings at the ends and on the top three Arcade levels. The $60 million financing package had support from the city, the county, and private foundations. The hotel opened in 2001, with its main entrance on Superior and retail space looking for tenants. The year before, a smaller arcade in the neighborhood, the Colonial, also reopened as a hotel, a Residence Inn at 527 Prospect Avenue.

Access: Opposite Arcade take East 4th Street down past Prospect to Huron; turn left for Ameritech. To see Jacobs Field go right on East 9th; afterward turn around and walk back to Huron; turn right; road connects with Euclid near Playhouse Square.

OHIO BELL TELEPHONE BUILDING, NOW AMERITECH, 1927

Hubbell & Benes, Cleveland
750 Huron Avenue, NRHP/Lower Prospect-Huron HD
Office building

The telephone company built Cleveland's best Art Deco skyscraper and one of Ohio's earliest. Eleven years earlier, architects Hubbell & Benes had done the Neoclassical Art Museum. Eric Johannesen observed that "nearly every Cleveland building of ten stories or more was commissioned from an out-of-town architect." To judge by this exception, that may have been unfortunate. Lobby, accessible during business hours, has fine Art Deco detailing.

JACOBS FIELD, 1994

Hellmuth, Obata & Kassabaum Sports Group, St. Louis
2401 Ontario Street
Cleveland Indians baseball stadium

Glass, steel and brick, Cleveland's asymmetrical new stadium has been acclaimed for bringing old-fashioned charm back to the ball park. At least between games, it's possible to look in and see the playing field from the parking garage to the north, accessible from East Ninth Street.

Playhouse Square, NRHP

The Cleveland Theater District includes five theaters straddling Euclid Avenue just east of East 14th Street; all five opened in 1921 and 1922, for legitimate theater, movies, and vaudeville. It's a remarkable concentration, and

▶ STATE THEATRE INTERIOR

with the reopening of the Allen in 1998 mustered enough glittering marquees to give Euclid Avenue some nighttime razzle dazzle. ¶ As of 2000, all five were under the same ownership. Playhouse Square Center originally referred to the four interconnected theaters, on the north side of Euclid. The four closed in the late 1960s, when three were to be razed for parking (doesn't this seem zany—parking for what?). Rescue forces fortunately intervened, and three of them reopened in the 1980s. Across the street the Hanna Theatre, a legitimate stage designed by New York architect Charles Platt, closed in the 1980s. In 2000, Playhouse Square Center bought the Hanna and reopened the theater in a cabaret format. ¶ Architecturally, Playhouse Square's two best theaters are the State and the Palace. The 3,200-seat State, 1921, designed by Thomas W.

Lamb of New York, has an awesome 320-foot lobby extending from Euclid to the auditorium; it actually runs between the two adjacent theaters, the Ohio and the Palace. Besides length, the lobby has murals and fluted mahogany pillars. The 2,800-seat Palace, 1922, designed by Chicago's Rapp & Rapp, was the only one in this cluster never scheduled to be torn down; it alone has its original chandeliers. With marble on the walls and a spectacular lobby with two grand staircases, it was also the most opulent to begin with.

¶ Outer lobbies are accessible weekdays; for seeing all interiors and auditoriums, Playhouse Square offers free public tours the first full weekend every month, 10-noon, starting in State Theatre lobby; private tours may be arranged for a fee; call 216/771-4444, ext. 3251.

Banks and Banking Halls

Cleveland's banking halls offer one of Ohio's best architectural tours. The first time I did any touring

▶ HUNTINGTON BANK BUILDING

in Cleveland, in the late 1980s, I saw the banking halls near Euclid and couldn't believe all the splendor. Though one of those is now closed, the tour includes one I missed that time, the fabulous hall in the old Society Bank on Public Square.

▶ Huntington Bank Building

UNION TRUST COMPANY, NOW HUNTINGTON NATIONAL BANK, 1924, RESTORATION, 1975

Graham, Anderson, Probst & White, Chicago; restoration by Dalton, van Dijk, Johnson & Partners, Cleveland
917 Euclid Avenue at East 9th Street, northeast corner
Lobby, accessible from Euclid, East 9th and Chester, open during business hours

This is the world's largest banking hall—sheer swagger in stone. It's like an L-shaped basilica, complete with colonnades of fluted marble Corinthian columns and side aisles beyond them. Ceilings are glazed barrel vaults 72 feet high; the dome over the rotunda between the two wings is 84 feet high. Together, the two wings traverse over 500 feet; the one that runs west to east is 310 feet, the length of the proverbial football field. Murals in the arcs were by Jules Guerin of New York. Fortunately, in the mid-1970s, an award-winning renovation removed dropped ceilings. The building was originally the world's second largest in area; an amazing 136,000 people toured on opening day in 1924.

CLEVELAND TRUST COMPANY, NOW CLEVELAND TRUST ROTUNDA BUILDING, 1908

George B. Post & Sons, New York
900 Euclid Avenue, at East 9th Street, southeast corner NRHP
Closed

This bank shows just how grand a Beaux Arts building could be. Perhaps the odd site—the corner is an acute angle—challenged the architect to design

▶ OLD NATIONAL CITY BANK

something really special. Formal facades face both Euclid and East 9th, while between them an inward curving bay with a pair of columns faces the corner. A round dome rises above. The ground floor has rusticated, or heavily grooved stone with round-arched openings and heavy, ornate doors that look capable of securing the king's own gold. Inside there's one of Cleveland's most spectacular interiors: a rotunda under the dome. Eighty-five feet high and 61 feet across, the rotunda is enclosed by a colonnade fronting two balconies; the ceiling has exquisite stained glass. (Alas, this rotunda isn't open to the public at present. At least, it is still there.) Originally bank offices were in parts of the building off the rotunda. Just south on 9th is a 29-story tower added in 1971, designed by Marcel Breuer and Hamilton Smith, New York. A twin was planned for the Euclid side, but never built.

GUARDIAN SAVINGS AND TRUST, NOW
NATIONAL CITY BANK, 1915
Banking room by Walker & Weeks, Cleveland
623 Euclid Avenue
Bank open during business hours

Clevelanders fill in their deposit slips on marble tables and wait for a teller under high coffered ceilings in rooms defined by colonnades. This three-story banking room has pink marble on the walls. The structure was originally the

New England Building, 1895, by Boston's Shepley, Rutan & Coolidge.
Walker & Weeks did the banking room and its colonnaded entry. In the late
1990s, the top floors of the
one-time New England
Building were converted into
a 150-room Holiday Inn
Express.

**Access: Continue west
on Euclid to the corner,
East 6th, and turn right to
Superior and Federal
Reserve Bank. Street
bends, with a catch-your-
breath glimpse of City
Hall at the far end.**

FEDERAL RESERVE BANK, 1923

> OLD NATIONAL CITY INTERIOR

*Walker & Weeks, Cleveland;
1997 addition, Hellmuth,
Obata & Kassabaum, St. Louis; 1998 renovation, van Dijk Pace Westlake,
Cleveland
1455 East 6th Street at Superior Avenue, northeast corner, NRHP
Regional Federal Reserve Bank; lobby open during business hours; tours by
prearrangement, 216/579-2102*

While the Huntington has swagger, the Federal Reserve's banking hall
wallows in opulence—entering it has been compared to walking into a bar of
gold. The lobby ceilings are coffered and gilded vaults and walls are gold

> FEDERAL RESERVE

marble; for visual
contrast ornamental
black wrought iron grills
front the arches along
the hall. Since the
Federal Reserve is a bank
for banks, the lobby
doesn't draw a string of
customers; its visual
delights are mostly for
sightseers. The bank's
elegant exterior is also
exceptional. Second
Renaissance Revival in
style, it has twelve
stories all in pink stone:
marble for the upper
floors, granite for the
rusticated ground-floor
base. Just above the
base, a continuous
balustrade girds the

▶ KEY TOWER, WITH OLD SOCIETY BANK AT LEFT

building, projecting only slightly. The bank was built around its vault, housed in a two-story structure that was completed first. A renovation was finished in 1998, the year after a pink marble addition to the rear, the Operations Center Annex, opened. Walter Leedy thought the Reserve's addition more successful than the library's contemporary one across the street. The bank expansion was, he joked, "very expensive—they have unlimited resources you know." The 1923 Federal Reserve has had many admirers; one called it one of Walker & Week's "major triumphs;" another, their bank "masterpiece"—and this was a firm that did 60 banks just in Ohio. For Eric Johannesen, who spent 17 years as preservation officer at the Western Reserve Historical Society in Cleveland, Walker & Weeks was the local firm that best represented "the spirit of the twenties." For the five decades beginning with the 1880s, Johannesen nominated a Cleveland architect or firm that he thought best summed up the decade: Frank Cudell of Cudell & Richardson in the 1880s, Charles Schweinfurth in the 1890s, J. Milton Dyer in the 1900s decade, and Hubbell & Benes in the 1910s. This guide includes examples of the work of all five. Though six years apart in age, Frank R. Walker (1877-1949) and Harry E. Weeks (1871-1935) had a lot in common. Natives of Massachusetts, both studied architecture at MIT and in 1905 moved to Cleveland, where they worked in J. Milton Dyer's office. In 1911 they set up their own firm, which became the largest in Ohio.

Walker was a big, agreeable man, strong in design. Weeks was quieter, smaller in stature, more interested in structure. Johannesen did a catalogue and survey of Walker & Weeks. Published posthumously in 1999, the book is the only comprehensive study of an Ohio architectural firm.

SOCIETY TOWER, NOW KEY TOWER, 1992

Cesar Pelli & Associates, New Haven, Connecticut
127 Public Square
Bank building

If you enter Key Tower's lobby from the older Society building next door, you may feel a letdown, for this modern skyscraper's strongest virtues are on the outside. At 948 feet in height, it is Ohio's tallest building. A stainless-steel pyramid at the summit is topped with a 60-foot steel pylon that's included in the height tabulation. With the pylon, says Cleveland architect Robert C. Gaede, Key Tower went from 24th to 18th tallest nationally. The pattern of shallow setbacks varies on Key Tower's adjacent facades; window columns are slightly recessed, with continuous steel ribbons dividing windows vertically into pairs; exterior facing is a polished rose granite. At different times the building catches the light in varying ways, so that sometimes it looks quiet, while at other times it's dazzling. Another thing about Key Tower. It faces the Mall.

▶ SOCIETY FOR SAVINGS BUILDING

SOCIETY FOR SAVINGS BUILDING, NOW KEYBANK, 1890

Burnham and Root, Chicago
127 Public Square, north side of
square at Ontario Street, NRHP
Bank; lobby open during business
hours

This red sandstone bank was one of the last buildings by Chicago architect John Wellborn Root, who died relatively young; it was said to be a favorite of his. It was built as a Medieval fortress, with Gothic, Romanesque, and Renaissance features, including round turrets at the top corners and squat round granite pillars between the Gothic windows on the ground floor. Though the ten-story building has a steel frame, its stone walls are up to five feet thick. A central light court, an original feature, has been completely filled in with offices. This building has a superb banking hall, built earlier than the others downtown. The room is swathed in rich, multi-colored papers; murals were painted by an English associate of William Morris, Walter Crane. A stained glass skylight is in the center of the ceiling. Enter the room from the Public Square side, which will take you past an ornate black lamp at the corner of the building. The story is that inventor Charles Brush originally fitted it with an electric arc lamp; later an incandescent light was installed.

FIRST PRESBYTERIAN CHURCH, NOW OLD STONE CHURCH, 1858, 1884

Charles Heard and Simeon Porter, Cleveland
91 Public Square, NRHP
Church; to see interior enter around the corner at 1380 Ontario; 216/241-6145

Gutted by fire in 1857 and 1884, the Old Stone Church has been much remodeled. At Public Square, it holds its own among heavyweights.

CLEVELAND MALL, NRHP

Cleveland Mall represents an era when the city was nationally significant. Mayor Tom L. Johnson, elected three times starting in 1901, was a great reformer, a Mall proponent, and the leader under whom Cleveland was called the "best governed city in America." Cleveland was also in the cultural forefront. Although many cities ultimately talked about grouping public buildings in the way demonstrated at Chicago's 1893 Columbian Exposition, Cleveland was the first to do so; its Mall swept away slums and became the largest planned public area outside Washington, D.C. So today the Mall is a big area—500 by 1,500 feet—partly landscaped, partly paved, extending

▶ SOUTH END OF MALL; LIBRARY, BP BUILDING, AND FEDERAL BUILDING

from Lakeside Avenue south to Rockwell Avenue. At least four of the Beaux Arts buildings associated with it are very good. And although it never seems crowded, the Mall doesn't flunk the people test: pedestrians use it as a short cut, and on summer days people are sitting near the fountain. Even so, compared to Public Square, the Mall is easy to overlook. As Doug Graf observes, the Mall "is a little boring." Graf isn't the first to discern that. It turns out that one of its designers, Daniel Burnham, also found the Mall dull, so he rationalized it as "repose" in an urban setting. This insight comes from Walter Leedy, who explains that the excess calm was the result of the Mall's not being on the busy arteries of Superior and Ontario—an impossibility because of existing real estate holdings, including the Federal Building site. That's not the Mall's only problem. It's not possible to see its four especially good Beaux Arts buildings all at once, so their impact is diffused. And not one of the four faces into the Mall. To the north City Hall and the old courthouse, intentionally paired, are off to the sides, facing down East 6th and Ontario Streets, respectively. To the south the Old Federal Building and its pair, the Library, turn their backs to the Mall. So do the less spectacular buildings along the Mall's east side. Key Tower hardly qualifies as part of the Beaux Arts scheme, but it, at least, faces into the Mall.

FEDERAL BUILDING, 1910

Arnold W. Brunner,
New York
201 Superior Avenue,
NRHP/Cleveland Mall HD
Federal courts building; open
weekdays

This is really the Old Federal Building. Its

▶ FEDERAL BUILDING INTERIOR

construction was unusually painstaking, for part of the building was erected beforehand in temporary materials, to test the scale in relation to the Mall behind it. Having passed the test, the whole building ultimately appeared in gray granite. It has five stories, rusticated ground-floor stonework, and a partly attached Corinthian colonnade from second through fourth floors. On the front corners of the building, two stone eagles with 20-foot wingspreads are forever poised to fly away. In spite of the security procedures on entering (surrendering cameras, tape recorders, and weapons during one's visit) the interior should not be missed. The long front hall, 30 feet deep and 30 feet high, has a series of elliptical arches overhead; everything is in marble. The third floor has two good courtrooms, 301 and 342. Both have marble pilasters and wainscoting, coffered ceilings, painted murals, and acoustic panels on the walls.

▶ CUYAHOGA COUNTY COURTHOUSE

CLEVELAND PUBLIC LIBRARY, 1925; LOUIS STOKES WING, 1997

Walker & Weeks, Cleveland; addition by Hardy Holzman Pfeiffer Associates, New York
325 Superior Avenue, NRHP/Cleveland Mall HD
Library open daily except Sunday; 216/623-2800

The Library was the last of the Mall's four original Beaux Arts worthies—it had to wait for the new City Hall to be completed, in 1916, so as to free up its old site for the Library. Another nine years—encompassing World War I—elapsed before the Library also was finished. Perhaps to make up for the lost time, it emerged covered in white Georgia marble rather than granite like its three predecessors. In dimensions, rusticated first floor, balustrades at the roof, and colonnades, the Library was matched with the Federal Building. The interior had a three-story reference room, a pair of grand staircases, and white marble on the basement restroom walls. In May 1999 the Library reopened after a renovation whose results were disappointing; the ubiquitous zigzag light fixtures seem to thumb their nose at a still mostly Beaux Arts venue. An underground passage links the Library with its 1997 addition, the Louis Stokes Wing, a 10-story oval glass building with squared-off, rough-cut stone towers at the four corners.

CUYAHOGA COUNTY COURTHOUSE, 1912

Lehman & Schmitt, Cleveland
1 Lakeside Avenue, NRHP/Cleveland Mall HD
Courthouse open weekdays

▶ CUYAHOGA COURTHOUSE

This too is now an *Old* Courthouse; it's visible from a distance at the north end of Ontario Street. This building and its Lakeside Avenue pair, City Hall, are larger than the Federal Building and the Library, but they also have the Beaux Arts look, with rusticated bases and columns above. The Courthouse's stunning interior, designed partly by Charles Schweinfurth, features a large central hall with ceiling vaults, coffers, second-story balustrades in the arches; it has Tennessee and Georgia marble on the floors, and Colorado marble on the walls. On the east side see especially the carved marble stairway, turning and bending like a ballerina. A stained glass window depicting Justice overlooks the stairway; Schweinfurth designed it to catch the morning light. The second floor has two courtrooms of interest, Probate and Appeals, both altered; but Appeals retains more woodwork and an exceptional beamed and coffered ceiling. Both rooms have a pair of small balconies high in the wall.

CLEVELAND CITY HALL, 1916

J. Milton Dyer, Cleveland
601 Lakeside Avenue, NRHP/Cleveland Mall HD
City hall open weekdays, 216/664-2000

Located at the north end of East 6th Street, City Hall has a fine central hall, with colonnades and a barrel-vaulted ceiling. Be sure to see the grand three-story Council Chambers on the second floor: dark oak paneling, coffered ceilings. When I visited Robert D. Keiser, secretary of the city's Cleveland Landmarks Commission, in City Hall's Room 519, I found him in an aerie whose windows peeped out between balusters at the roof's edge. The commission's files on Cleveland buildings are surrounded by one of their own.

Rock and Roll and the Warehouse District

ROCK AND ROLL HALL OF FAME AND MUSEUM, 1995

I.M. Pei of Pei Cobb Freed & Partners, New York
1 Key Plaza
Museum open daily year round except Thanksgiving and Christmas; fee; 216/515-8444

"Star power" was the reason for choosing renowned architect I.M. Pei to design the Rock and Roll Hall of Fame and Museum. So says Steven Litt, the *Plain Dealer's* architecture critic, who pronounces the result a success: "a beautiful piece of sculpture." The star power worked. The first year, a million people came. More than any other architect working in the United States in 1986, Pei offered just what rock and roll needed—class and respectability. His credentials were high-culture icons, like Boston's Kennedy Library and the Louvre, which was building his pyramids in Paris. But at almost 70, Pei wasn't so sure about rock and roll—what he remembered about it was telling his kids to turn it down. So Hall of Fame organizers took him on a tour of persuasion if not conversion. It included New Orleans and Graceland, Elvis Presley's Memphis home— Cleveland's claim to rock isn't based on originating the music, but on launching the hype. It was here that in the early 1950s disk jockey Alan Freed first popularized the term "rock 'n' roll"—his name for black blues music for white audiences and musicians. Pei helped

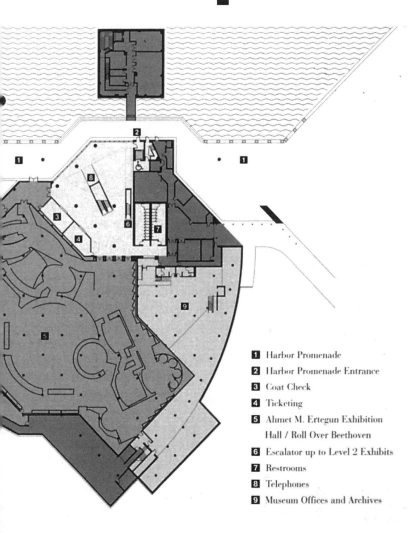

1 Harbor Promenade
2 Harbor Promenade Entrance
3 Coat Check
4 Ticketing
5 Ahmet M. Ertegun Exhibition
   Hall / Roll Over Beethoven
6 Escalator up to Level 2 Exhibits
7 Restrooms
8 Telephones
9 Museum Offices and Archives

pick the first site next to Tower City, overlooking the Cuyahoga River; the design showed exhibit rooms descending a steep slope. Politics and money ultimately moved the project to the lakefront, where major exhibit spaces went to an underground level below the Hall of Fame's plaza. Construction didn't begin until 1993. The front of the building is a 115-foot high triangular glass wall, pyramid-like, canted back so that it rises at a relatively sharp 50-degree angle. Though it looks akin to the Louvre's glass pyramids, Pei calls it a "tent". It abuts a rectangular white tower behind and above it. The white trapezoidal extension on the right is a cantilevered theater; the Hall of Fame itself was moved from high in the tower to the white cylinder on the left in 1997-98. Both the tower and a concrete support pole under the round wing are anchored underwater.

Access: Rock and Roll Hall of Fame is on East 9th Street extension north of I-90.

▶ THE BRADLEY BUILDING

ROOT AND MCBRIDE WAREHOUSE, NOW THE BRADLEY BUILDING, 1884, REHAB 1985

Cudell & Richardson, Cleveland
1220-1230 West 6th Street at Lakeside, NRHP
Residential and commercial building

Cleveland's Historic Warehouse District, in northwest downtown, has been the city's most striking rehab area; it's also the location of most recently developed downtown housing. The Bradley Building was the leader of the pack. Early in the 1980s it pioneered with seven apartments; now it has 38. In 1997 the district had a thousand housing units, with several hundred more in the pipeline. Red brick, seven stories, the Bradley has especially nice windows on its West 6th Street facade; in two and three-story groups, they rise up to fan lights—fan-shaped windows with radiating dividers. The architects, Scottish-born John N. Richardson (1837-1902) and German-born Frank E. Cudell (1844-1916) formed their Cleveland partnership in 1870. Because Cudell didn't emigrate until he was 22, Johannesen found continental influences in his work.

ROCKEFELLER BUILDING, 1905, 1910

Knox & Elliot, Cleveland
614 Superior Avenue at West 6th Street, NRHP
Office building

Built by John D. Rockefeller, this was Cleveland's first skyscraper with a
structural steel frame. Originally it had just the seven bays (each two
windows wide) from the corner, with the building's signature arch containing
an oculus—a round window—over the middle door. Several years later, four
more similar bays were added on the west. The building is a good example of
a Chicago Style building. Detailing on the Rockefeller's first three floors is
Sullivanesque, which refers to the curling-leaf ornamentation that Chicago
architect Louis Sullivan developed. One day I was standing on the sidewalk
studying it when Bob Gaede, whose office is a few doors away, came along,
looking dapper in a seersucker suit. I told him that I'd supposed the
ornamentation was terra cotta, but it looked like metal. Gaede confirmed
that it was indeed a rare example of metal ornament, cast iron in this case,
which is why it has to be repainted all the time. It reminded him of another
example of metal foliation, on Louis Sullivan's Chicago department store,
Carson Pirie Scott. Then he breezed off, walking briskly to his next
appointment. John D. Rockefeller, founder of Standard Oil and a Cleveland
resident, was "the world's first self-made millionaire." Rockefeller transferred
this building to his son, John D., Jr., who in 1920 sold it to Josiah Kirby, who
put his own name on it. That made the older John D. so angry that in 1923
he bought the building back at an inflated price, in order to reinstate the
Rockefeller name. When the Rockefellers sold it again in 1936, the contract
stipulated that the new owner keep the old name.

PERRY-PAYNE BUILDING, 1889, 1996

Cudell & Richardson, Cleveland
740 Superior Avenue, NRHP
Commercial and residential building

The Perry-Payne Building started out with an interior light court, or atrium,
long since filled in with floor space. The 1996 rehab here gave the
Warehouse District another 92 apartments.

East Side and Euclid Avenue

For the architectural tourist, this is
Schweinfurth Country. It's also the famed
Euclid Avenue, struggling back to life, though
not to its former grandeur. From downtown,
drive east on Euclid. Trinity Cathedral is at
East 22nd Street, south side.

TRINITY CATHEDRAL, CLEVELAND, O.   10690

▶ TRINITY CATHEDRAL

TRINITY CATHEDRAL, 1907

Charles F. Schweinfurth, Cleveland
Euclid Avenue at East 22nd Street, southeast corner, NRHP
Episcopal cathedral open weekdays; if Euclid Avenue door isn't open ring at back
door off Prospect Avenue parking lot; for office hours call 216/771-3630.
Descriptive flyers, including some on the stained glass windows, available in racks
in hall behind choir on east side

Rather than immense and soaring, Trinity Cathedral is solid and compact.
And, says Barbara Thomas emphatically, it is "not a replica of anything. But
it's a perfect example of English Perpendicular Gothic." Thomas, Trinity's
associate in Christian education and a sometime tour giver, says that for a
cathedral this one is small; it's sometimes called the "little gem." That it is a
cathedral is signified by the bishop's high, carved chair at the side in front. In
fact, Thomas says, the bishop usually sits in the center rather than in this
chair, so its most frequent occupants nowadays are children on tours.
Charles Schweinfurth began working on plans for this church in 1890, 11
years before construction actually began; many people consider Trinity his
masterpiece. Architectural historian Richard Campen told a story about the
architect and his principal patron, Samuel Mather. To save money, Trinity's
trustees approved the cathedral plans without the tower. Schweinfurth
objected; at the end of the meeting Mather offered to contribute the tower
himself, in memory of his father. Schweinfurth left the meeting, and the
bishop found him later in another room, crying tears of relief. Complete
with Gothic windows, buttresses, turrets, and the tower, Trinity dominates
its Euclid Avenue corner. Built of Indiana limestone, it is cruciform, or cross-
shaped, in plan. There's fabulous carving at the front of the church; note
especially the marble pulpit, the oak choir stalls and, behind the altar, the
reredos, a limestone screen inspired by one at England's Winchester
Cathedral. Of the 59 figures on the reredos, King Arthur is the one with
round disks over his knees, bottom row, third from the left. Pews were
removed from Trinity's nave in 1994 and replaced with chairs, for more
flexible seating.

Access: From downtown, drive east on Euclid. Trinity Cathedral is at East 22nd Street, south side; Mather Mansion a few blocks farther east, north side. Continue east, and at East 30th Street or East 36th turn right/south one block to Prospect Avenue.

MATHER MANSION, NOW PART OF CLEVELAND STATE UNIVERSITY, 1910

Charles F. Schweinfurth, Cleveland
2605 Euclid Avenue, NRHP
University building used for offices, including alumni association; accessible to the public weekdays

Samuel Mather's Tudor Revival house was one of the last mansions built on Euclid Avenue; it cost so much—over $1 million—that it's hard to imagine where the money went. Surely the bricks helped. They were dark red bricks shipped from New Hampshire, handmade and fired to look like crude early bricks. To go with crude bricks, architect Charles Schweinfurth ordered a sunken Italian garden, complete with statues and fountain. Built on a lot that extended from Euclid to Chester, the mansion was deeper than Trinity Cathedral and wider than its nave.

▶ MATHER MANSION

The trim with those bricks is Indiana limestone, seen in the beautifully carved second-floor bay window on the left front—Mrs. Mather's room— and in the more massive, more masculine bay on the right—Mr. Mather's room. The good news is that visitors usually have access to the inside of the house. They can wander through the entry hall (40 by 28 feet, oak paneling, marble floor), the front drawing room (gilt on the wood carving), the library, and the diningroom, with ten-foot fireplace and marble figure in a niche; and they can climb the ten-foot-wide carved oak stairway. Samuel Mather (1851-1931) was Cleveland's first citizen, renowned for integrity. Born rich, he made himself richer by founding his own business shipping iron ore. Once the president of Western Reserve University called on him to ask for $500,000. Mather said he guessed he could make the donation and asked his secretary to write the check. Came the secretary's reply: "Which bank, Mr. Mather?" Mather was slight in build and had a long bespectacled face; he didn't look like a tycoon who'd made so much money that he had multiple half-million-dollar checking accounts. He was an aesthete, the author of a book on Italian unification. He's remembered today not because he was rich, but because he was generous—he founded Case Western Reserve University's medical school and Cleveland's United Appeal. Another reason he's remembered is that he was Schweinfurth's leading patron. Besides the Euclid Avenue house, Schweinfurth did Shoreby in Bratenahl, now a private club, for Mather in 1890.

THE MOST BEAUTIFUL
STREET—Once upon a time, Euclid Avenue was a glorious place. In the 1860s Frederick Law Olmsted, co-designer of Central Park, pronounced it grander than New York's Fifth Avenue and "a thousand-fold more distinctively American." In 1893 Baedeker's guide called it "one of the most beautiful residence-streets in America."

Euclid Avenue's row of substantial houses began emerging in the mid-1830s; for over 60 years, it became only better. A succession of extensive lawns made vistas parklike, while houses, wrote author Jan Cigliano, were of high quality and varied styles. At the peak in the late 1890s, almost 260 houses lined the four miles between East 9th Street and East 90th.

But less than 15 years later, the street would be in an irreversible decline. Virtually all the great houses were demolished, a laying waste on such a scale that it was one of Ohio's worst architectural losses; perhaps, the worst. By the 1980s, much of Euclid Avenue was a rubble-strewn wasteland; today only six of the 260 houses remain.

Though the greatest loss was the ensemble, particular losses were significant too. Just next door to Samuel Mather's mansion was New York architect Stanford White's only Ohio house, a 1904 Georgian Revival razed for the freeway. It was one of 30 leveled for the highway.

The initial threat to the avenue, Cigliano says, was pressure for commercialization. Businesses wanted to be closer to the rich, and as they increasingly were, the neighborhood became less desirable. Though Euclid Avenue was home for the rich and powerful, they were too few to defend it; nor did they attract much sympathy. Inflated by commercial demand, property assessments led to exorbitant real-estate taxes. When residents petitioned for relief in the Depression, taxes for some were raised instead.

And there was no such thing as protective zoning. Euclid Avenue finally was zoned in 1929, but then retail, apartments, and heights up to 250 feet were permitted on all of it. By the 1930s Terminal Tower was shifting civic energy and commerce away from Euclid to Public Square. The forces against Euclid Avenue seemed so numerous and so inexorable that some residents, like Standard Oil founder J.D. Rockefeller and General Electric founder Charles Brush, ordered their houses demolished after their deaths. They couldn't bear to see the old manses subdivided into apartments.

Doug Graf describes it as an elemental loss. "It killed Cleveland," he says. He explains that a strong corridor between downtown and outlying areas is essential to the health of a city—a lifeline.

In recent years, the unexpected has happened: bit by bit Euclid Avenue's acres of desolation have begun disappearing. No Millionaire's Row has sprouted, but where almost nothing was, Cleveland State University has appeared with a whole new campus. At 36th Street, a large 1997 building, Applied Industrial Technologies, flaunts expanses of green glass under a white wheel in the sky. And starting in 1996 in the East 80s, a 92-unit housing development, Beacon Place at Church Square, was under construction, with a neotraditional layout and a row of town houses facing Euclid Avenue.

If the loss of Euclid Avenue killed Cleveland, the city may be coming back to life.

Access: Drive east on Prospect to Tavern Club and Row Houses at East 36th Street; continue to diner at 40th. At East 55th Street, turn left/north and return to Euclid.

TAVERN CLUB, 1905

J. Milton Dyer, Cleveland
3522 Prospect Avenue at East 36th Street, southwest corner, NRHP
Private club

The long and narrow Tavern Club is distinctive and romantic, straight out of a Medieval stage setting for *Die Meistersinger*. Four stories tall, brick and stone, the building has a steep two-story roof with picturesque steep-roofed dormers and large gables facing both Prospect and East 36th. The oversized roof was big enough to accommodate a third-floor squash court with 20-foot slate walls. Given the rest of the building, the plain brick wall on the west side comes as a letdown, but until the 1970s it was hidden by an apartment building. The Tavern Club is a men's club; though architect J. Milton Dyer was a member, but he won this assignment in a competition. The work of J. Milton Dyer (1870-1957), at its best in the 1900s decade, was progressive and original. He studied at the École des Beaux Arts in Paris and opened his Cleveland practice in 1900. Just six years later his buildings were considered so remarkable that *Architectural Record* did a 19-page article on them. But from 1916 Dyer faded from the scene, developing erratic work habits, and becoming unreliable. Then after decades of scarcely working at all, he reemerged in 1940 and did the Art Deco U.S. Coast Guard Station.

PROSPECT ROW HOUSES, 1873-1880

3645, 3649, 3651 and 3657 Prospect Avenue east of East 36th Street, NRHP
Private residences and offices

In a city that has lost so much residential architecture, that never did have many attached town houses, this little group of row houses is astonishing. Three stories with raised basements, they are kitty-corner from the Tavern Club.

RUTHIE AND MOE'S DINER, 1930s, 1952

4002 Prospect Avenue at East 40th Street
Restaurant; closed at least temporarily in 2001 after fire; 216/431-8063

In this neighborhood Steve Litt has a favorite architectural restaurant that he likes both for its good food and its eye appeal. Ruthie and Moe's Diner combines a 1930s diner, facing the corner, with an addition, a 1952 diner moved from Pennsylvania in 1995. Even with the addition, lunch attracts an overflow crowd.

▶ PROSPECT ROW HOUSES

SCHWEINFURTH'S HOUSE, 1894

Charles F. Schweinfurth, Cleveland
1951 East 75th Street, between Euclid and Chester Avenues, NRHP
Private house

The Charles Schweinfurth house, where Schweinfurth himself lived, is a little castle: a squarish box of rough-cut sandstone, crowned with a crenellated parapet. The door has a hesitant Gothic arch; the four asymmetrical windows on the facade are all different. The interior has Art Nouveau detailing. Architect R. Van Petten and designer Dale Smith, who bought the house in 1970, have won awards for their restoration work on it. Born in Auburn, New York, Schweinfurth (1856-1919) trained in the East; in the early 1870s, he may even have worked with architect H.H. Richardson in New York, and came to Cleveland at the behest of a client, Sylvester Everett, who specifically wanted a Richardsonian Romanesque house. Ultimately Schweinfurth did 18 homes, two churches, and two institutions on Euclid Avenue. In Rockefeller Park he did four beautiful arched stone bridges. Six feet tall, red haired, he was considerate of clients and demanding of subcontractors. Whether from a flying chip or a plasterer's revenge, he lost an eye after taking an ax to plaster work that he judged substandard.

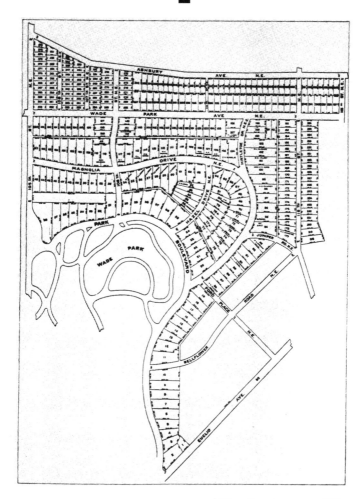

▶ WADE PARK ALLOTMENT, 1918

University Circle

University Circle, which takes its name from Case Western Reserve, is unique in Ohio: an elegant, urban place, with the lovely Wade Park as a focal point surrounded by great institutional buildings. Then off to the side, on Bellflower Road, is the campus of the former College for Women, with its own exceptional buildings.

▶ A SCHWEINFURTH BRIDGE

Access: From downtown (or Schweinforth's house) drive east on Chester Avenue. Turn left/north on East 101 Street. To see Temple, turn into parking lot on right. Alternatively, from I-90 near the lake exit at University Circle/Martin Luther King, Jr. Drive, and take the drive south about three miles to Chester Avenue. Turn right, then right/north on East 101 Street. Park as above. To see Epworth-Euclid Church, exit from other side of parking lot and cross East 105th Street onto Park Lane. Follow Park Lane around corner to church, which has adjacent parking lot.

THE TEMPLE-TIFERETH ISRAEL, 1924, 1958

Charles R. Greco, Boston; 1958 addition by Perkins and Will, Chicago
1855 Ansel Road at East 105th Street, Wade Park HD
Synagogue; for tours call Susan Koletsky, 216/831-3233

The Temple-Tifereth Israel looms over the street on its triangular site, to which it adapted improbably by being a heptagon, a seven-sided structure. It has high gray Indiana limestone walls and arcaded round-arched windows. But above all it has gold domes—an immense central one and two smaller ones on towers flanking the main entrance. The style is called Neo-Byzantine. The gold shingles on the dome roofs are ceramic tiles. The Temple seats 1,900 people on the raked main floor and in balconies on four of the seven sides. Though the inside diameter is 90 feet and the height, 88 feet, the room has an intimate quality; the current rabbi, Rev. Benjamin Kamin, has said that when speaking here, he feels as though he can make eye contact with everyone in the room. Interior surfaces play with colors, predominantly tan with brown and rust, and textures—for example, by juxtaposing polished marble columns and intricately decorated tiles. The carved walnut screen around the ark, where the Torah scrolls are kept, is beautiful. The choir sits behind the screen; the wall behind their seats is curved, to enhance acoustics. Starting in 1974, the Temple's Reform congregation moved most of its day-to-day operations to an eastern suburb, Beachwood, where the phone number above rings. The University Circle Temple is used for high holy days, for weddings and bar mitzvahs, and for community ceremonies, like CWRU law and medical school graduations. In the basement is the Temple Museum of Religious Art, a museum of Judaica founded in 1950 and overseen now by Susan Koletsky, who also gives tours. Unseen above but accessible by stairs, an enclosed corridor encircles the arcaded stained-glass sanctuary windows. Made by a Boston firm, the windows also were installed by a Boston man, Phil Kearney of Local #1181, who on November 21, 1924 signed his work on an adjacent pillar.

EPWORTH-EUCLID UNITED METHODIST CHURCH, 1928

Bertram Goodhue, New York; Walker & Weeks, Cleveland
East 107th Street at Chester Avenue, northeast corner, NRHP/Wade Park HD
Church; accessible through office weekdays during business hours

Seen from the opposite side of Wade Lagoon, Epworth-Euclid United Methodist Church looms over the trees: a massive brown granite tower topped by tapered roof and a spire. It's a singular silhouette, irreverently nicknamed the "oil can church" or "holy oil can." Architect Bertram

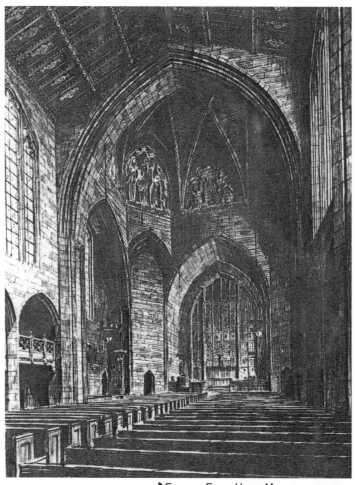

▶ Epworth-Euclid United Methodist interior

Goodhue, known for churches and the modernistic Nebraska State Capitol, worked on these plans before his death in 1924. Walker & Weeks saw the project to completion. In an era dominated by Beaux Arts designs, Goodhue was an independent-minded architect. This church is cruciform in plan, transepts are short, windows are Gothic. On site, the octagonal tower, supported by arches, is no less massive than it seems from a distance. The interior is mostly in dark woods, with some nice detailing. Johannesen, who thought the church's exterior more successful than its interior, observed

▶ The church and the Museum of Art

that both this church and the contemporary Temple rely on artificial lighting. In the mid 1920s, *that* was the cutting edge.

Access: From church turn south to Euclid Avenue, then left/east. To park and tour University Circle area on foot, including Severance and Museum, stay in left lane for turn north/left onto East Boulevard. Park on East or on Bellflower Road, the first right turn. CWRU buildings are on Bellflower.

SEVERANCE HALL, 1931

*Walker & Weeks, Cleveland
11001 Euclid Avenue at
East Boulevard, NRHP/
Wade Park HD
Cleveland Orchestra
auditorium; tours by
prearrangement; Richard
Worswick, 216/231-7300*

By site and by design, Severance Hall is a landmark. Its becolumned portico overlooks a major intersection where in the 1930s street cars deposited flocks of concert-goers. The crowds moved up the front stairs and passed into the great foyer. Entering the temple became part of the occasion. Severance Hall's exterior is classical and polygonal, of Indiana limestone with a rusticated, or deeply grooved sandstone base. The oval-shaped foyer, Art Deco and Egyptian Revival, is the interior's—nay, the building's—architectural high point. Two levels with stairways at both ends, the foyer is outlined by a colonnade in a variegated burgundy-colored jasper marble. The terrazzo floor pattern has three large round pastel lotus blossoms whose shapes are echoed in the chandeliers and golden ceiling overhead. For $2,700

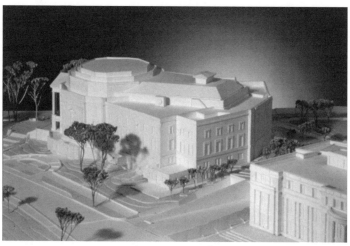

▶ SEVERANCE HALL MODEL

it's possible to rent the foyer for summer weddings. The 2,100-seat auditorium, called orchestra hall, is more sedate than the foyer, though it has a silver-leaf ceiling in a vine pattern said to have come from Elisabeth Severance's wedding dress. Her husband John was the hall's principal benefactor; when she died a few months after the ground breaking, he turned the project into a memorial to her. Ultimately he contributed $3 million of the total $7 million cost. In the late 1950s, because the orchestra's sound was dry, or muffled, conductor George Szell ordered changes to improve acoustics. Curtain and carpets came out, and a shell to reflect sounds was installed at the back of the stage. A new round of restoration and alterations, including an addition at the back of the building and a new restaurant, began in 1998 and was completed early in 2000.

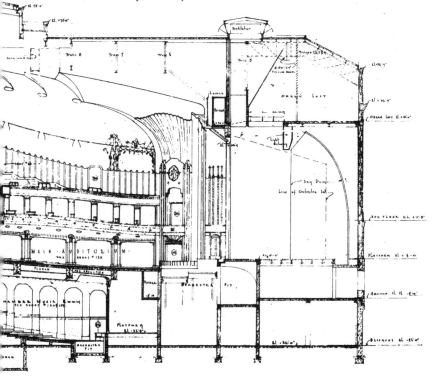

▶ Museum of Art

CLEVELAND MUSEUM OF ART, 1916, 1958, 1982

Hubbell & Benes, Cleveland; 1958 addition, Hays & Ruth, Cleveland; 1970
addition, Marcel Breuer & Hamilton P. Smith, New York; 1982 addition,
Dalton, van Dijk, Johnson & Partners, Cleveland
11150 East Boulevard, NRHP/Wade Park HD
Art museum open daily except Monday; 216/421-7340

See the Cleveland Museum of Art's great site on foot. The building faces
south toward the Wade Park lagoon and Euclid Avenue; walk around the
lagoon and walk up the stairs to the sidewalk to look back from Euclid. This
is one of Ohio's best architectural moments: a place that's been landscaped
into something beautiful. The museum building is fronted with a series of
descending spaces, starting with its own balustraded porch, followed by a
balustraded terrace, a formal garden with a fountain, and finally a lawn that
slopes down to the manmade lagoon. On the far side of the water a double
stairway leads up to Euclid Avenue, which is a quarter mile away from the
museum but at the same level, 24 feet above the lagoon. What makes all this
so good, says Walter Leedy, is the gradual transition from the formal museum
to the informal lagoon. Originally architects Hubbell & Benes envisioned
formal pools in front of the museum (Leedy has 7,000 Cleveland postcards,
including one to illustrate this), but the trustees resisted. Later the garden
with the fountain was built and, Leedy says, "the Olmsted Brothers reworked
the edge." The museum's site seems so perfect that it's hard to believe it
wasn't obvious from the beginning, but took years of fussing to settle. Then,
before construction started, the architects checked the building size with
white ink drawings on photographs and later, with on-site telephone poles
draped with bunting. The Neoclassical facade has a formal central porch
with pediment and Ionic columns, and the slightly projecting end pavilions

have pairs of recessed columns. All the wall between the central and end pavilions is plain and uninterrupted but not dull, partly because of good proportions and cornice, but also because of variations in the shade of the marble. It's the exact marble the architects wanted, but its use was in doubt until after construction started, because a family in the sandstone business was a major benefactor. The museum collection was modest, Leedy says, until 1958, when it came into a $33 million bequest from Leonard C. Hanna. Thus by 1970 it needed Marcel Breuer's large addition at the back, enclosing most of an earlier one. Breuer, a Hungarian and veteran of Germany's Bauhaus, where he developed a famous chair, in effect gave

Cleveland a second museum. His addition is massive, windowless and mostly rectilinear. The siding is horizontal bands of light and dark granite, which were attached to concrete sheets at the quarry to assure color

▶ MUSEUM OF ART

control. From the outside, at least in summer, it's hard to see both the addition and the original museum at once. Breuer said he enjoyed the "tensions" between old and new, but they don't really interact.

Case Western Reserve University: Old College for Women Campus

Basically the union of Case Institute of Technology and Western Reserve University, CWRU has a history of merging and dividing. The oldest component, Western Reserve College, moved to Cleveland from Hudson in 1882. Six years later the trustees separated men and women students and founded a separate College for Women. The campus built for that college, which has long since been absorbed back into the larger institution for both men and women, has several unusually interesting buildings on the south side of Bellflower Road.

Touring CWRU, old College for Women: All
campus buildings have signs giving their names.
The first one on the right is the sprawling, four-
story Guilford House, 1892, a former residence
hall now used for offices. Left of Guilford is
the red brick Tudor Revival Haydn Hall, 1902,
by Cleveland's Charles Schweinfurth. Clark
Hall, discussed below, is next to the left/north;
then Harkness Chapel, also by Schweinfurth, in
1902, now used for concerts; and at the corner
of Ford Drive, is Mather Memorial, discussed
below. The Weatherhead School of Management by Los Angeles architect Frank O. Gehry,
slated for completion in 2001, is across Bellflower from Mather Memorial. To find Mather
Gym, also below, take the walkway between
Haydn and Guilford. Behind the gym the
Kelvin Smith Library, 1996, is visible, as well as
a Philip Johnson sculpture, *Turning Point*, 1996.
Campus buildings are usually open and
accessible weekdays.

Clark Hall

CLARK HALL, 1892

Richard Morris Hunt, New York
NRHP/Mather College HD
CWRU classroom and office building

Clark was the College for Women's first building, so besides offices and classrooms, it had a library on the second floor and a gym on the third; visitors can see both if they're not in use. The large Gothic window (complete with tracery, or curved stone dividers) on the southwest wing was the library's. The gym upstairs is at the front of the building, lit by the front window and by windows in dormers at three levels. The library, now a classroom, has an oversized fireplace and a wooden ceiling whose beams extend down onto the walls, descending halfway to the floor. Clark is brick and sandstone outside. Before a recent cleaning, the pale-colored lintels over the windows had darkened into heavy eyebrows. Architect Richard Morris Hunt also did college buildings at places like Harvard, Yale, and Princeton; but today he is best remembered for mansions, which he was doing at Newport, Rhode Island, at the time he did Clark. His most famous mansion is Biltmore, 1895, George Vanderbilt's house in North Carolina.

MATHER MEMORIAL, 1912

Charles F. Schweinfurth, Cleveland
NRHP/Mather College HD
CWRU offices and classrooms

After Flora Stone Mather, a benefactor of the College for Women, died in

Mather Memorial Building

1909, her husband, Samuel, and children donated this building as a memorial to her. It's Tudor Revival, two stories in brick and stone, with crenellated parapets and a U-shaped footprint. At one corner there's a three-story all-stone gatehouse functioning as a pivot between two wings. The gatehouse appears broader on the street side than in the courtyard, where it has an intimate stage-like porch that students used for performances. Four octagonal turrets rise above the gatehouse corners. Where gargoyles might otherwise be these turrets have small winged angels. Given all the Cleveland buildings now named for them, it might seem that the Mathers indulged in self-aggrandizement on a spectacular scale. Not so, says Gladys Haddad, a CWRU professor who is writing a biography of Flora Stone Mather. The name went on after the Mathers died, assigned to Mather Memorial by a grieving family, and to other buildings by grateful institutions. Flora Mather inherited a fortune from her father, Amasa Stone. Following his example, she devoted much of her energy to giving it away; when she died three dozen institutions that she had helped paid tribute to her. Twenty-two years later her husband consented to the College for Women's taking a new name: Flora Stone Mather College. In her lifetime, says Haddad, Flora would never have allowed that: "She felt she could never take credit because she hadn't earned the money." Haddad also believes that Flora Mather's benefactions had an unexpected ripple effect. She inspired her husband, who otherwise might never have become the great philanthropist he was.

GYMNASIUM OF THE COLLEGE FOR WOMEN, NOW MATHER GYM, 1907

Hubbell & Benes, Cleveland
A CWRU gym, used for dance

This gym shows that some of Frank Lloyd Wright's ideas had reached Cleveland. The front section is a rectangular two-story block. Basilica-like, the two-story gym space extends back between one-story side aisles. The building is brick with a stone basement. All the way around trios of windows are set under the eaves. In the front the brackets under the eaves turn downward and become mullions dividing windows. Designers also of the Cleveland Museum of Art, Hubbell & Benes were clearly masters of different styles. A native of Prague, W. Dominick Benes (1857-1935) was brought to America as a child. After a four-year apprenticeship, he went to the Cleveland firm of Coburn and Barnum, where he stayed 20 years. Benjamin S. Hubbell (1867-1953) was a Kansan who studied architecture at Cornell and then also joined Coburn and Barnum. In 1897 Hubbell and Benes formed a partnership that lasted until 1935, when Benes died.

Mather Gymnasium

Access: Continue on East Boulevard to Hazel Drive, second right after Bellflower, and turn right/north to Magnolia Drive. Turn left to see Ferris House

---

JAMES FERRIS HOUSE, 1909

J. Milton Dyer, Cleveland
10924 Magnolia Drive, NRHP/Magnolia Wade Park HD
Private house

For another glimpse of J. Milton Dyer's work, look for this Arts and Craft house, with its roof brackets and tapered walls and porch columns.

▶ St. Mary Seminary

Access: Continue on Magnolia to next left to return to East Boulevard; turn right; take next right/north turn onto East 105th Street and drive north, passing several lights, to Superior Avenue. Turn left/west, cross over park and turn right/north immediately on Ansel Road; seminary is .2 mile north of Superior on right/east side of street. After seeing it, return by same route in reverse to University Circle or continue west on Superior to downtown.

ST. MARY SEMINARY, NOW HITCHCOCK CENTER FOR WOMEN, 1925

Franz Warner, Cleveland
1227 Ansel Road, .2 mile north of Superior Avenue
Private social service agency, residential facility; not open to the public; 216/421-0662

With Baroque touches in its Spanish Colonial Revival style, this former Catholic seminary provides the spice of diversity for a Cleveland architectural tour. The front facade has curved gables and statues in niches; under another curved gable, twisted columns flank a side entrance. The layout, Walter Leedy says, is Palladian: a high central pavilion has flanking wings and smaller end pavilions. The main door is set between two belfries; behind and above, an octagonal tower holds the library. This door leads to a chapel that bisects the long, rectangular complex and forms two arcaded courtyards; the footprint is like a squared off numeral eight. Materials are brown brick, decoratively laid, stone, and red tile on the roof. After declining enrollments led the seminary to transfer to another campus in 1991, a center offering a treatment program for chemically dependent women moved in. At the back, the site overlooks Rockefeller Park; in winter especially, the rear of the building is visible from Martin Luther King Drive.

Access: From University Circle drive east on Euclid Avenue to Lake View Cemetery, on right/south side just after East 123rd Street.

Lake View Cemetery

LAKE VIEW CEMETERY
12316 Euclid Avenue
Cemetery open daily. Maps available at office; signs direct visitors to Wade Chapel and Garfield Monument; 216/421-2665

Founded in 1869, Lake View is one of Ohio's great cemeteries, with a rolling terrain landscaped initially by Adolph Strauch of Cincinnati's Spring Grove Cemetery. Many celebrated names came to rest in Lake View, including John D. Rockefeller (his obelisk is in section ten on the cemetery map), Samuel Mather, Senator Marcus Hanna, and Mantis and Oris Van Sweringen. Then, too, there were Jeptha H. Wade, who donated Wade Park to the city and was a founder of Lake View, and President James Abram Garfield, whose memorials are featured here.

JEPTHA H. WADE MEMORIAL CHAPEL, 1902
Hubbell & Benes, Cleveland
NRHP
Open daily April through October

Wade Chapel is a small Neoclassical temple that Jeptha Wade II had built for his grandfather, who had seen the possibilities of the telegraph at a timely moment. Set between two lakes, the memorial has a site not unlike some that landscape designer Adolph Strauch laid out at Cincinnati's Spring

Grove. This chapel's most remarkable feature is its Art Nouveau interior by Louis Comfort Tiffany. Roger Sherman Schnoke, one of the attendants, can point out a lamp cut from a single block of alabaster, or the seamless front steps cut from one ten-ton piece of marble. He explains that Tiffany's studio did the marble and glass wall mosaics in New York and then shipped them here, and that the resurrection window is one of Tiffany's most famous works. Schnoke's a retired teacher who hasn't retired from teaching.

▶ Wade Memorial Chapel

JAMES A. GARFIELD MONUMENT, 1890

George Keller, Hartford, Connecticut
NRHP
Open daily April through November 19, Garfield's birthday

To visit the Garfield Monument is to revisit Victorian America. Before Walter Leedy began accumulating his Cleveland postcard collection, he had never imagined how popular this monument was when it was first built—it was Cleveland's favorite tourist attraction into the twentieth century. Today, Leedy muses, young Clevelanders are unlikely even to know where Lake View Cemetery is. Richardsonian Romanesque with some Gothic features, the Garfield Monument is a round tower with a conical roof. For its height, 180 feet including the roof, the tower is a relatively fat 50 feet in diameter. It was going to be taller, Leedy says, "but the foundation started to give way so they made it shorter. Or they ran out of money and didn't want to be embarrassed. You never know." Inside, a larger-than-life marble statue of Garfield and his chair is the central focus of Memorial Hall. Above the statue on the rotunda wall a band of mourners, many of them ordinary people carrying wreaths, is depicted in stone mosaic, while the stained-glass windows contain allegorical figures representing states, all bearing tribute. Bas relief panels outside show scenes from the late president's life. A spiral stairway near the door rises to the rotunda balcony and then continues onto a porch from which downtown Cleveland is visible in the distance. In 1984 a Cleveland architectural firm, Gaede Serne Zofcin, completed a restoration of the Garfield Monument. One of the principals, Robert C. Gaede, helped introduce historic preservation in Ohio.

INVENTING PRESERVATION: BOB GAEDE—

The first time I met architect Robert C. Gaede, at his Cleveland office in 1988, I was working on an article on Ohio courthouses, and I needed an architectural point of view. Gaede told me about all the best courthouses—he was one of the few people who could, because he'd actually seen most of them. He drew black-ink maps and sketches; he produced lists. He also explained that architecture should not be the only consideration in evaluating a courthouse; site and condition were also important. He was right, of course.

That day he criticized the big early twentieth-century Beaux Arts courthouses as "piles". When I talked to him again six years later, he was thinking more highly of those piles; Beaux Arts had skyrocketed in his esteem. That was a lesson too. Sensibilities changing over time are part of artistic appreciation. In fact, that's one of the most important reasons for historic preservation. What looks like a dated pile today, may seem fabulous Beaux Arts tomorrow.

It was in character for Gaede to be willing to talk to me, and to have the time, as not everyone would. One result of his accessibility is that since the 1950s almost everything published on Cleveland architecture has had some mention of, or something written by Bob Gaede. He helped all the supplicant writers; he wrote and wrote again about Cleveland architecture; and all the while, he was also a practicing architect. But his most remarkable contribution was the one Eric Johannesen recognized when he paid tribute to Gaede's long-running and active tenacity as a preservationist. The fact is, Bob Gaede helped invent historic preservation.

In the beginning, it took Gaede (whose name rhymes with "lady") a long time to get his career going. Before he finished studying architecture at the University of Michigan, he'd been called up for a long stint of service in World War II. After the war, after earning his degree and working briefly in Cleveland, he helped set up the architecture program at Kent State University; and then during the Korean War he was called up again and sent to Maine for a year. When Gaede really settled down to practice in 1953, it was 15 years after his first architecture classes at the University of Michigan.

In 1953 no one ever thought of spending money on preservation, or of hiring an architect to restore a building to its original glory. In the years after the war, the one truly positive development in preservation was Congress's founding the National Trust in 1949. The goal was to pull together scattered efforts—"the ladies of Charleston," Gaede says, "the ladies at Mount Vernon [Virginia], the ladies at Savannah and Mobile. In all cases women drove the preservation ethic."

One reason Gaede became an architect, was that he had always liked old buildings. Motivated by that, and by a fascination with why towns look the way they do, he traveled regularly to look at built environments both in Cleveland and elsewhere in Ohio. He is one of the few people who have seen all but three of Ohio's courthouses. (The ones he's missed, Adams, Meigs and Monroe, are far enough from Cleveland to give him an excuse.)

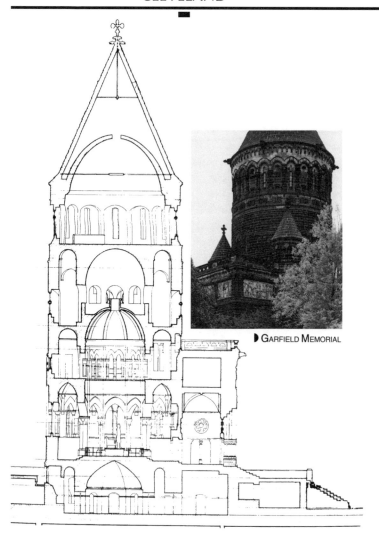

▶ GARFIELD MEMORIAL

Having explored the Western Reserve again and again, he memorized a list of early nineteenth-century Federal churches there, and then kept an eye on all of them. One upshot of all this was that he'd no sooner started practicing in 1953, than the Cleveland chapter of the American Institute of Architects named Gaede chairman of a newly formed committee on historic buildings. The committee had half a dozen members and put together a local walking tour.

But in those days, preservation was not the idea of the moment. By the late 1950s what was becoming popular in America was urban renewal. The shabby, dirty old city of yesterday, the city from the Depression era and the wars, was to be erased by demolition; and in its place architects and planners would build the marvelous city of tomorrow. "We were easily beguiled," Gaede says. "We were into the assumption that we could throw off yesterday and start afresh. That was a disastrous theme. Today it's hard to believe intelligent beings could raise barren buildings at wide intervals and call that the ideal. Urban renewal removed enormous architectural worth in a short time, and the buildings that replaced it were banalities."

When he speaks of urban renewal, he says "we" because he remembers the euphoria and what inspired it, even though he knows that he never really lost his "compassion for the old." He could accept the removal of a few marginal buildings, but that was not what happened. What came about was an architectural clear cut, the removal of buildings that to this day haven't been replaced. The small AIA preservation committee was still there, and as its spokesman Gaede began protesting.

In the early 1960s national AIA preservation efforts were chaired by a Chicagoan named Earl Reed. "Reed and his buddies documented and recorded places, like the Historic American Buildings survey in the 1930s," says Gaede. "When we met the conversation would go, 'Well, what have you lost this month in your state? Did you get a drawing? A photo?'" When in 1963 Gaede followed Reed as national preservation chair, he tried to shift from documentation to advocacy, from a passive to an active preservationism.

In 1960, after publishing their first book on local architecture, the Cleveland AIA preservation committee gave its first award to a Federal church Gaede had spotted in Windsor Mills, Ashtabula County. A dozen people came to the luncheon and witnessed the presentation of a parchment certificate. The awards now have a grander scale: six or eight presentations at, Gaede says, a "big event in the Oak Room." When the national AIA met in Cleveland in 1958, Gaede chaired a preservation breakfast for about 40 people. The breakfast has become a tradition,

though now it's usually in a ballroom. And it's not just a chat, but a forum for five-star speakers.

By 1970 urban renewal had begun to crumble. "More and more," says Gaede, "it was seen as something that didn't deliver. And the preservation movement was growing. Renewal was giving it fresh ammunition all the time." The Historic Preservation Act of 1966 authorized state preservation offices, which every state set up as it saw fit within a few years—Ohio's Historic Preservation Office, which maintains the state's National Register of Historic Places files, is part of the Ohio Historical Society. And starting in 1972 taxes, which had always favored demolitions, also encouraged preservation. "Then there was greed on the side of preservation," Gaede says. "Isn't that wonderful?"

Needless demolitions still happen, but gradually preservation became national and broad-based, and the concept of reusing buildings, not just as museums, gained credibility. Ultimately the new profession of architectural restoration evolved, and routinely architects are paid now to oversee building renovations and restorations. Gaede's firm restored the Garfield Monument (1984) and the Miami County Courthouse (1976-82); in 1997-98 they restored the Henry County Courthouse. And sometimes a whole neighborhood comes back, one building at a time. That's what's been happening since the early 1980s in Cleveland's Historic Warehouse District, where Gaede's office is. There newly bright Italianate facades signal shops, trendy restaurants, offices and apartments.

The shabby, dirty old city of yesterday is being erased—but this time, not by demolition.

▶ CLEVELAND HEIGHTS

Cleveland Heights

Besides their architectural features, the three
buildings featured here provide a slice of Cleve-
land Heights, a large urban suburb. To reach
Cleveland Heights, take Lake View Cemetery's
south exit onto Mayfield Road and drive east.
(Alternatively, if traveling east on Euclid Av-
enue, just after University Circle turn right onto
Mayfield Road.) Drive east on Mayfield to
Heights Rockefeller Building at Lee Road and
Mayfield, northeast corner. Park Synagogue is

within a quarter mile east of Lee on Mayfield, south side; a pair of buff-brick gate posts signals the entry drive.

HEIGHTS ROCKEFELLER BUILDING, 1930

Andrew Jackson Thomas, New York
3091 Mayfield Road, NRHP
Private retail, offices, apartments

The L-shaped Heights Rockefeller Building has two-story wings facing both Lee and Mayfield Roads and a three-story central pavilion, set on the diagonal and facing the corner. Stephen Gordon calls the style Norman Revival.

PARK SYNAGOGUE, 1950

Eric Mendelsohn, San Francisco
3300 Mayfield Road, east of Lee Road
Synagogue; tours may be prearranged; 216/371-2244

As the rabbi, Armond E. Cohen, said, Park Synagogue is "virtually all dome. It envelops the congregation." Close up this dome, a hemisphere 100 feet in diameter, seems immense and improbable. By being both low—it starts just 15 feet above the floor—and high—it rises another 50 feet—it symbolizes the closeness of heaven and earth. The green of oxidized copper on the outside, it appears unadorned on the inside, though it's covered with acoustical tiles. The sanctuary under the dome is just part of a complex that also includes offices, a chapel, meeting rooms, an auditorium and classrooms. The overall layout is wedge-shaped, with the sanctuary near the point, then an assembly hall and enclosed patio in the middle, and a two-story wing of classrooms at the wide end, curving like the crust end of a piece of pie. The original intention was to expand the sanctuary for holy-day crowds by opening it to the hall and patio; but because it was too hard to hear, that arrangement never worked well. Overall the design, a combination of curves and straight lines, makes Park an always interesting place, demonstrating architect Eric Mendelsohn's remark, "Good architecture is designed around the corner." Architectural historian Walter Leedy, who is writing a book about Park Synagogue, says its dome could have been built only after the development of reinforced concrete in the twentieth century. Moreover, it needed a rocky site, like this one, to preclude settling. The dome was constructed on an elaborate wooden scaffold. The first layer was two inches of insulating cork. Steel reinforcing bars were set above the cork and pressure-sprayed with concrete. Over that went a layer of roofing felt, which was topped with preformed copper strips. The dome is a mere four inches thick. Like an egg, says Leedy, a dome "is an extremely rigid structure." At the dome's base a substantial beam rests on only six supporting columns that have a row of windows between—the dome almost seems to be resting on glass. Park Synagogue is one of only eight buildings that German refugee architect Eric Mendelsohn completed in the United States, his adopted home after 1941. Four were Jewish synagogues, of which this one, the second, is the largest. Though little known to Americans, Mendelsohn (1887-1953) was one of the giants of twentieth-century architecture. He

THE RABBI AND THE ARCHITECT

THE RABBI AND THE ARCHITECT—Hired fresh out of seminary to revitalize a declining, debt-burdened Cleveland synagogue, Rabbi Armond E. Cohen succeeded; under him, it became the country's largest conservative congregation. But Rabbi Cohen also immortalized this synagogue in architectural annals. He was the one who brought in German refugee architect Eric Mendelsohn to design the congregation's new temple at the end of World War II. During construction he helped resolve the endless squabbles between architect and building committee. Ever since it was finished, the resulting Park Synagogue has been on any short list of Ohio's best modern buildings. But another result for Cohen was becoming friends with one of the century's greatest architects. That was not so easy. Mendelsohn was a perfectionist focused completely on his work; with everyone he was at times arrogant, inconsiderate, and imperious.

Cohen first met Mendelsohn in December 1945, when he went to pick him up at the Cleveland airport. Cohen knew of the architect's work, but he'd never seen him in person. The first person off the plane was a beautiful woman in a black-and-white polka-dot dress. Mendelsohn was among the last. He was an astonishing figure: tall, with red hair to his shoulders, wearing a full-length coat and a black porkpie hat and, in Cohen's eyes, moving with the bearing of a Prussian army officer. "You must be the rabbi," Mendelsohn greeted him. Then, in a confidential tone, he added, "Did you see the one in the black-and-white polka-dot dress?"

"And that," says Cohen, laughing, "was the first thing he said to me." At Park Synagogue in Cleveland Heights, he is sitting in the office Mendelsohn designed for him, at the desk he designed. At 88, Armond Cohen, originally a New Yorker, is in his 64th year with Cleveland's Anshe Emeth Beth Tefilo Congregation.[1*] In 1949 he was given life tenure, though now he is the senior rabbi—that is, not the only one. He is wearing a full mustache, large dark-framed glasses, a conservative suit and a radical purple tie. Pictures of a younger Cohen are in the classroom hall, where he appears year after year with a succession of confirmation classes.

Rabbi Cohen loves to tell his Mendelsohn stories, which have become legendary. Cohen first heard of Mendelsohn in 1941, when he happened to see a retrospective of the architect's work at the Museum of Modern Art. At the time, Mendelsohn had just moved to the United States, so all the buildings shown were in Germany or in Britain and Palestine, countries where he worked after fleeing Hitler in 1933. Those photographs made a lasting impression on Cohen. "I was overwhelmed," he says. "I didn't know what modern architecture could be like."

Though his congregation had a fine building on East 105th Street, individual members were moving to the Cleveland Heights area, and in 1942 the synagogue followed. On land once owned by John D. Rockefeller, 13 acres that belonged to the progressive, money-losing Park School were coming on the market, and the synagogue bought them. Later it acquired additional adjacent acreage. In 1945 it solicited building proposals from Cleveland architects, but of those submitted, Cohen says, "None met our hopes. We wanted a new building that would at least equal our old one." Remembering the Museum of Modern Art retrospective,

▶ THE ARCHITECT'S IMPROMPTU SKETCH

he persuaded the building committee to let him contact Mendelsohn, who was living in San Francisco. The committee agreed to hear the architect if he paid his own way. That was all right with Mendelsohn, who cabled that he would come immediately.

At once Mendelsohn started by quizzing the rabbi. How many people came to services? What kind of program did the synagogue have? How many children in the school? He took notes as Cohen answered. Then he wanted to see the site, where he charged over the snowbound acreage, studying wooded areas and ravines. While the much younger Cohen wearied, Mendelsohn seemed to gain energy. Finally the architect was satisfied, and Cohen dropped him at his hotel and promised to pick him up at 5:30. He returned to find Mendelsohn and his luggage waiting at the curb. He had checked out because he hadn't liked the hotel's architecture or the clientele. He proposed staying with the rabbi and his family.

So Cohen took him home, to the front door, and introduced Mendelsohn to his wife. The architect looked around the livingroom. "You must be a Polish peasant," he said. "No, Lithuanian," the Cohens replied, sounding meek but feeling angry. Mendelsohn said he would move the furniture to improve the room. So for an hour that's what he did, relocating even the piano. Although the room was improved, it took the Cohens a while to recover.

That night at the committee meeting in one of the old Park School buildings, Mendelsohn gave a lecture on his philosophy of architecture, and then did a sketch—an impression of the building as it stands. One member of the committee, a judge, had arrived wheeling in a cartload of books. When local architects objected to hiring someone from San Francisco, the judge said he'd been to the architectural library and borrowed 20 books with references to Mendelsohn. He offered to read from all of them. But a builder, Frank Stein, interrupted. Reading, he said, was unnecessary. "None of us understood the lecture," Stein admitted. "But this man knows more about architecture than all of us." Stein, says Cohen, "was a clever man. He recognized genius when he saw it." And according to Walter Leedy, an authority on Park Synagogue, six months later when

Mendelsohn was hired formally, no particular plan was in hand. The leadership was opting for the man, for genius.

When Mendelsohn and Cohen returned to the house that night, the rabbi was exhausted, but not the architect, who pulled out classical recordings and prepared to listen to music. "These are my inspiration," he said. Later he showed Cohen a list of the records he had at home, along with the building each had inspired.

After the design was completed, Mendelsohn came back to Cleveland with a model of the building he proposed. Everyone was thrilled, and the plans went out for bid. But when the bids came in, even the lowest was more than three times the budget. The architect apologized—postwar inflation was a reality—but the clients balked and asked for revisions. The original design set the sanctuary on a rocky promontory next to a ravine; that's where it is. But originally the architect extended the building across the ravine with a bridge for offices and, on the far bank, class-rooms. Finally obliged to revise, Mendelsohn reluctantly eliminated the bridge and set the whole complex on one side of the ravine. That was how it was built, but it took the architect a long time to be reconciled to the change. Twenty years later, a one-time associate of his designed an extension that bridged the ravine with a gallery, an auditorium on the far bank.

Once a month during construction, Mendelsohn came to Cleveland and stayed with the Cohens. That was part of how he worked—he told architecture students at Berkeley in California that closeness to the client would help assure the building's integrity. Gradually all the Cohen family came to enjoy Mendelsohn. The children did have to break him in

to American customs. At dinner the Cohens' 11-year-old daughter said something, and the architect ordered, "Quiet. Children should not speak." The child got up from her seat, went over to him, and bowed low on the floor, kowtowing. Mendelsohn roared with laughter. After that the girl and her sister regularly joined him for calisthenics on the livingroom floor. He chose sites in the yard for shade trees. He offered to remodel the house, as a gift. The Cohens accepted, even though Mendelsohn warned that they would have to throw out all their furniture. Like the building committee, they opted for the man.

Every morning on arriving at the construction site, Mendelsohn would order one of the women in the office to go out to buy his breakfast: six radishes, black bread, three cigars, imported beer. "He gave them abusive orders but the women in the office all liked him," Cohen says. "They nicknamed him 'wild radish' or 'Prussian dictator'." Construction proceeded slowly because Mendelsohn insisted on designing everything: seats, doorknobs, kitchen equipment, all light fixtures, even trivial ones, classroom desks and chalk boards, roads, plantings. He would run his hand over bricks to check that they were even. He argued with the building committee.

"He was a perfectionist," says Cohen. "He raised hell with everybody. But we'd never have had this building if he hadn't been incredibly arrogant." The committee objected to the size of Cohen's office—it's 48 feet long—and its bay window. The rabbi, Mendelsohn insisted, shouldn't be cooped up. A committeeman who was a builder protested that sliding doors could be had for a tenth of the proposed cost. "But with *these* doors," Mendelsohn said, "you can't hear what's being said on the other side." A vociferous contingent wanted stained glass windows on the sanctuary walls; Mendelsohn insisted on clear glass, for better light and closeness with nature. Once during a money argument, everyone, including the architect, was screaming. Finally Mendelsohn interrupted with the last word. "Quiet!," he roared. "You are only the clients."

In 1950 the sanctuary was ready for dedication; the school and office wings were finished in 1953. They are still in use, though not on the scale originally imagined. Members of the congregation have continued moving farther east; for years now Park Synagogue has been sharing its program with Park East in Pepper Pike. Park East was purchased from another congregation; the building, by American architect Edward Durell Stone, also has a dome, though Cohen recalls that Mendelsohn's reaction to it was scornful: "That is not a dome. That is a pimple."

Mendelsohn, the arrogant perfectionist, could be funny. He looked at the rabbi's library and pronounced it "too much sex, too little religion." (Cohen explains that he owns the works of Freud.) The architect hated Cohen's flashy ties. "I've ordered six bow ties for you at Sulka's in New York," he reported to the rabbi. "I gave them the dimensions for your face." In New York later on a visit, Cohen went to Sulka's to pick up his customized ties, which were large and conservative. They were $82 each. "I thought I'd fall over," Cohen says. But he paid. He's never worn them, but he's always kept them.

One day in July, 1953, Cohen was playing golf in Maine when an urgent phone call pulled him off the golf course. It was Mendelsohn, calling from New York, sounding hoarse. He told Cohen he'd been diagnosed with cancer of the thyroid, and the prognosis was very bad. He asked the rabbi to come see him before he went back to California. Cohen rushed to New York, made his way to the Regency Hotel, and went to the architect's room. Mendelsohn told him that this would be their last meeting. Already he could no longer swallow; he ordered two dinners and watched Cohen eat one. He asked Cohen to do one last favor for him, to correct a mistake he had made in the building. In the rabbi's office, the bay window had two aluminum dividers disrupting the view of the woods.

"Armond, please," he begged. He wanted Cohen to replace the three panes with a single one. Finally the men parted. In San Francisco when Mendelsohn drew up his will a week before he died in September, he asked that Cohen should officiate at his funeral, unless it fell between the high holy days of Yom Kippur, atonement, and Rosh Hashanah, the new year— the busiest time of year for a rabbi. In the end, that was when he died, so Cohen had to stay in Cleveland.

In that New York hotel room Mendelsohn had a last salutation for Cohen: "Take care of the building," he said. "You have a masterpiece." As Mendelsohn asked, so Cohen has done. But the window was never changed. It remains, an example of imperfection that only the architect could see.

[*] This interview was in 1997. As 2000 began, the Rabbi was still coming in to work.

launched his career and assured his enduring reputation with his second building, the Einstein Tower, 1920, an astronomical observatory at Potsdam. Brick covered with stucco, it has rounded corners; Albert Einstein himself dubbed it "organic." The style was Expressionist; it contrasted with the straight-line austerity promoted by Germany's contemporary Bauhaus school.

Access: To reach Fairmount Boulevard drive south on Lee past Cedar Road to Fairmount; turn west/right; Tremaine-Gallagher House is within half a mile, on the right at the corner of Stratford Road.

TREMAINE-GALLAGHER HOUSE, 1914

Frederic W. Striebinger, Cleveland
3001 Fairmount Boulevard, NRHP
Private house

Fairmount Road is a showplace for substantial early twentieth-century houses in various styles. Readily visible from the street, the Tremaine-Gallagher House is one that makes every book, including Virginia and Lee McAlester's guide to American house styles, which includes

▶ Tremaine-Gallagher House

it in the Beaux Arts section. They write that Tremaine-Gallagher "reflects a common Renaissance form in which a main block is flanked by symmetrical front-projecting wings." Between those wings this two-story house has a recessed front porch with three round arches; it also has one-story porches at both ends. A parapet encloses the flat roof. Architect Frederic Striebinger (1870-1941) was a Clevelander who attended Paris's *École des Beaux Arts*. In the 1960s Martin Linsey of the Cleveland Museum of Art interviewed some of Striebinger's still living colleagues and was told he was a "successful practitioner, sound in his practice, but without creativity." One might wonder how many of those colleagues produced a house so well known and so lovely as this one.

▶ DREXMORE ROAD, SHAKER HEIGHTS, CIRCA 1915

Shaker Heights

Though Shaker Heights is surely the Ohio suburb best known nationally, it's hard to scope from a car. But there is this one house that, both visually and historically, represents what Shaker Heights was all about.

Access: To reach Van Sweringen House from Fairmount Road continue south on Lee to South Park Boulevard; turn east and drive half a mile. To reach Shaker Square from South Park Boulevard continue south on Lee to Shaker Boulevard; turn right/west and drive to Shaker Square.

VAN SWERINGEN HOUSE, REBUILT 1924
Philip Small, Cleveland
17400 South Park Boulevard, Shaker Heights
Private house

An illustration promoting the original "Peaceful Shaker Village" showed a drive winding up a mountainside with a castle at the top. It was meant to hark back to fairy tales, but the castle and the houses along the ascending road were all depicted as substantial manses in period revival styles. This was no fantasy but a real place meant to make real money for its developers, the brothers Mantis J. and Oris P. Van Sweringen. After eighth grade they started as office boys; at one point, like the Wright Brothers, they had a bicycle shop. Aged 19 and 21 at the turn of the century, they went into the real estate business. Just outside Cleveland, they found some eroded land with suburban potential, a 1,400-acre tract that had belonged to the Shakers. Borrowing to buy and improve it, the Van Sweringens gradually extended their holdings to 4,000 acres and named the place Shaker Heights. By 1929 property they'd bought for $1 million was worth $80 million. Shaker Heights was to have only architect-designed houses, with doors in front and no visible concrete block. This Shaker Heights house, the Van Sweringens' own, met those criteria; besides, it has a fine site overlooking a park with a lake. What we see is the remodeling of an earlier house into a stone Tudor Revival, with large half-timbered dormers and an octagonal tower with a crenellated top. The brothers were said to live in one end of the house; their sisters, Miss Carrie and Miss Edith, in the other end. But in fact the brothers lived at their country estate, Daisy Hill in Hunting Valley. They wanted to be remote. Historian John Stilgoe says that they employed a public relations expert to keep their names *out* of the papers. The same year he did this house, architect Small designed a group of five Shaker Heights demonstration homes for the Van Sweringens. He and partner Charles B. Rowley also remodeled Hunting Valley farm buildings into Daisy Hill mansion and designed Shaker Square, described next.

▶ Van Sweringen House

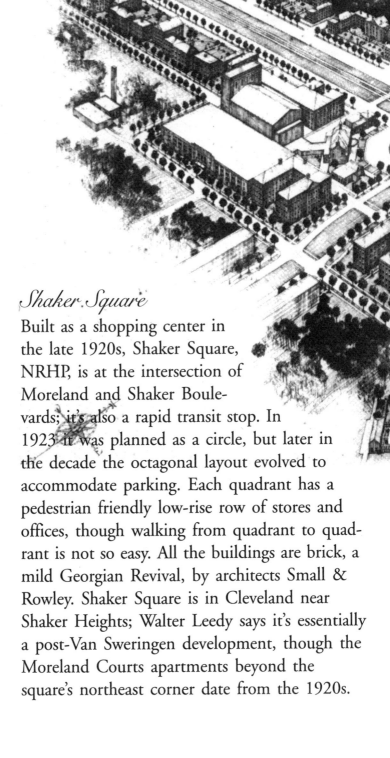

Shaker Square

Built as a shopping center in
the late 1920s, Shaker Square,
NRHP, is at the intersection of
Moreland and Shaker Boule-
vards; it's also a rapid transit stop. In
1923 it was planned as a circle, but later in
the decade the octagonal layout evolved to
accommodate parking. Each quadrant has a
pedestrian friendly low-rise row of stores and
offices, though walking from quadrant to quadrant is not so easy. All the buildings are brick, a
mild Georgian Revival, by architects Small &
Rowley. Shaker Square is in Cleveland near
Shaker Heights; Walter Leedy says it's essentially
a post-Van Sweringen development, though the
Moreland Courts apartments beyond the
square's northeast corner date from the 1920s.

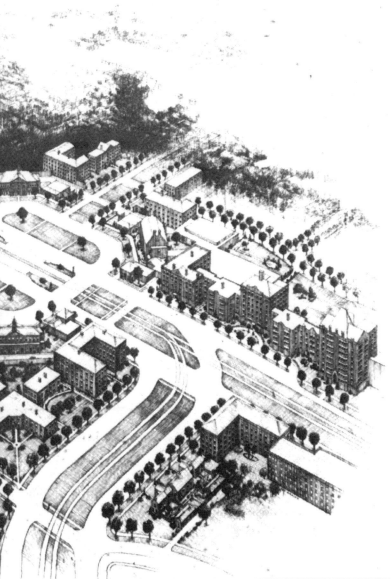

COLONY THEATRE, NOW SHAKER SQUARE CINEMAS, 1937

John Eberson, Chicago and New York
13116 Shaker Square, southwest quadrant
Movie theater; visitors may view lobby when
box office is open; 216/291-9342

▶ COLONY THEATRE

The Colony Theatre's main inner lobby, basically unaltered, has a fine display of Art Moderne at its most grandly flowing, for walls, corners, and ceiling are all curves that seem to swoosh up and away. Materials included marble and Bakelite. Converted to multi-screens in 1991, the theater has been altered; so has the outer lobby. The Colony shut down in the late 1970s, then reopened in 1981 after two years of functioning part-time and not at all. Walter Leedy thinks the theater seems to be an after-thought at Shaker Square; the lobby, an insertion.

Access: To reach Ohio City from downtown, cross the river at the west end of Superior Avenue; right after bridge take West 25th Street left/south to Lorain Avenue; the West Side Market is at this corner. Alternatively, from I-90 east-bound, exit at West 25th Street and drive north to Lorain Avenue. From the market drive west a few blocks on Lorain to St. Ignatius at West 30th, which has been cut off for a campus mall; Carnegie West Branch Library is just above Lorain at West 38th and Fulton Road. Driving distance from West 25th to West 38th is about half a mile.

Ohio City

Ohio City, which is on the west side of the Cuyahoga River, is one of Cleveland's older neighborhoods; early in the nineteenth century, it was a separate municipality. In recent decades Ohio City has had some residential rehabs and, just across from the West Side Market, has a brew pub and other attractions.

WEST SIDE MARKET, 1909-12

Hubbell & Benes, Cleveland
1979 West 25th Street at Lorain Avenue, northeast corner, NRHP
Food market with 180 stands open Monday and Wednesday, Friday and Saturday;
216/664-3386

The West Side Market is a long rectangular building, buff brick and stone, 241 by 124 feet, with a 137-foot tower at one corner. Architecturally, it has a basilica plan, with a high, 44-foot ceiling in the central hall, low-ceilinged side aisles, and high clerestory windows. Originally the slightly tapered clock tower held a water tank, but during World War II the tank became scrap metal. The market's inside walls are white tile; ceiling vaults, between elliptical supporting arches, are tan Guastavino tile in a herringbone pattern. All the tile surfaces generate "tremendous acoustical excitement," writes Joanne M. Lewis in *To Market/To Market*, her book about the market. She also points out that all the decorations depict food. An estimated two million people visit the West Side Market in a year. They come to patronize 180 food stands run by 108 vendors, selling fresh and cured meats, fish and poultry, baked goods, nuts, spices, dairy products and, in a separate adjacent arcade outside, fruits and vegetables. Famous for the ethnic variety of its personnel and foodstuffs, the market has customers ranging from the

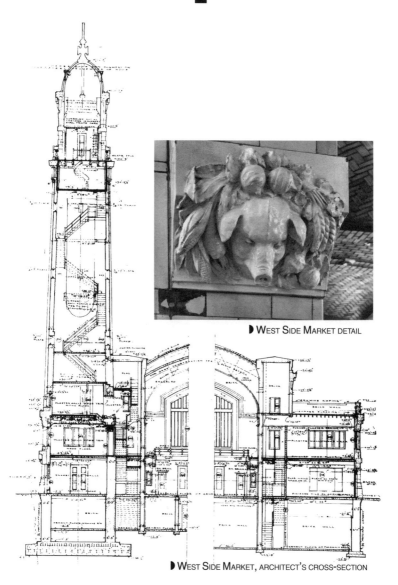

▶ WEST SIDE MARKET DETAIL

▶ WEST SIDE MARKET, ARCHITECT'S CROSS-SECTION

homeless to the very rich. So says George Bradac, the supervisor, who started cutting meat in Cleveland markets in the late 1950s and has been managing this one since 1986. He works for the city, which owns the market and rents the stands. Bradac appraises the building in a way that should make architects Dominick Benes and Benjamin Hubbell rejoice in their graves. "It amazes me," he says, "that when they were putting the building together, they certainly knew what was needed." For example, from the beginning the basement has had walk-in refrigerated storage rooms, though of course they've been updated mechanically. And the building's materials have held up. In spite of two million visitors a year, three quarters of the original quarry tile floor is intact. And just recently a vendor installing shelves checked the wall with a level. It was still perfectly straight.

▶ St. Ignatius High School

ST. IGNATIUS HIGH SCHOOL, 1888 AND 1890-91

Brother Friedrich Wipfler, Holland
1911 West 30th Street between Lorain and Carroll Avenues, NRHP
Roman Catholic Jesuit high school for boys

Once upon a time a High Victorian Gothic school like this one was a common sight in the United States; today St. Ignatius High School is a relatively rare survivor. Built to serve the local German and Irish Catholic community, it began as both college and secondary school. The college, John Carroll University, moved east to University Heights in 1935, but the high school, which draws about 1,300 students from the whole region, remains a vibrant institution. The interior has been remodeled extensively; for the architectural tourist the outside is the main attraction. From the back it's possible to see the slight variations that reveal the two stages in the original construction. The first wing

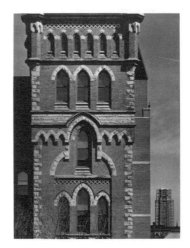

was built in 1888 facing Carroll Avenue. Two years later, the second wing, with the tower at the end, was added, forming an L-shaped footprint. (The ultimate intention, never realized, was a U-shaped building with the tower at the front center.) Four-and-a-half stories over a raised basement, the structure seems high and massive, with seemingly endless parades of windows, single, paired and in trios, some topped with pointed or slightly curved arches, running around the building in rows separated by horizontal bands of stone. The roof has windows in dormers, and even the tower roof has turret-like dormers under copper spires. High Victorian Gothic exteriors always had at least two contrasting colors, seen here in the stone and red brick. German Jesuits founded St. Ignatius in 1886. So as to have a building in the "pure" style being used in Europe at the time, they brought over a Dutch Jesuit, Brother Friedrich Wipfler, to do the design. He arrived in April, and by June 11 he had plans ready enough that foundations were being laid. Brother Wipfler could be so speedy because he didn't start from scratch; he simply recycled interior and exterior detailing he'd recently done for St. Knud's College in Copenhagen.

CARNEGIE WEST BRANCH, CLEVELAND PUBLIC LIBRARY, 1910

Edward L. Tilton,
New York
1900 Fulton Road,
NRHP/Ohio City
PD
Public library; open
daily except Sunday;
216/623-6927

This library is a wonderful building, with a flamboyant exhibition of red brick with white terra cotta. The structure's shape matches the site—triangular, rounded at the corners. The back two sides have rounded bays; the front, a formal porch with four pairs of Beaux Arts

▶ CARNEGIE WEST

columns. But these fluted columns are banded, and the banding recurs all around the building, on pilasters and attached columns. This branch library once served its neighborhood with a collection of Hungarian literature. After World War II the neighborhood changed and the library shut. That it was kept and renovated—the interior is interesting too—was, Bob Gaede says, one of the best saves ever by Cleveland's preservationists. The neighborhood is still not the best. When I was there some adults were sleeping in the adjacent park, but lots of kids were using the library. Akron's National City Bank on East Market Street has banded columns similar to these; that city's architectural historian, James A. Pahlau, calls them Mannerist.

Tremont

Tremont represents quintessential Cleveland: immigrants, ethnic churches, and nearby factories. So says Robert D. Keiser, secretary of the city's Cleveland Landmarks Commission. Starting in the 1860s, Tremont became a neighborhood of immigrants—Irish and German first, followed by Polish, Ukrainian, Greek, Slovak, Syrian, and others; by the late twentieth century, 30 different nationalities lived, or had lived in Tremont. They came to work in factories and steel mills nearby in the Flats. And they built a remarkable group of European churches, including the spectacular St. Theodosius Russian Orthodox Cathedral below. ¶ In the 1970s Tremont declined and even became dangerous; but in recent years it's been rebounding, with restaurants (for instance, on Professor Street), galleries, and new and redeveloped housing. Street names like Literary, Professor, and College, are relics of the short-lived Cleveland University, founded here in 1850.

Access: To reach St. Theodosius from Ohio City drive south on West 25th to Barber Avenue (just north of I-90) and turn left/east. At first intersection, Scranton Road, turn left/north; in a few blocks turn right/east on Starkweather Avenue and continue past West 14th to the cathedral. Alternatively, from I-71 northbound exit at West 14th Street, continue a few blocks north on 14th to Starkweather; turn east/right and drive to the cathedral.

▶ St. Theodosius

ST. THEODOSIUS RUSSIAN ORTHODOX CATHEDRAL, NOW ST. THEODOSIUS ORTHODOX CATHEDRAL, 1912

Frederick C. Baird, Cleveland
733 Starkweather Avenue, NRHP
Orthodox church; to see interior call the pastor, Rev. Jason Kappanadze, at 216/661-1575

St. Theodosius Orthodox Cathedral is one of the best examples of traditional Russian architecture in the United States. It has 13 splendid onion domes, all copper oxidized to green, atop 13 cupolas. The central dome, representing Christ, is the highest and largest; the next four, a step lower and medium in size, signify the evangelists; and the eight smallest ones, around the edges, represent the remaining apostles. All the domes are topped with crosses. St. Theodosius is said to be modeled on Moscow's Church of Our Savior. Cruciform in plan, the building is buff brick with Romanesque details, like the round-arched windows and front door. In *A Guide to Cleveland's Sacred Landmarks* author Foster Armstrong suggests that a fine view of the building is to be had from the foot of the hill just to the east, at the corner of Starkweather and West 7th Street. The church's interior, which can be seen by appointment, is unusual in having the walls entirely painted in religious murals that were done in the 1950s by a Russian artist. St. Theodosius was featured in several scenes of the 1978 movie, *The Deer Hunter.* Since 1988 the pastor has been Rev. Jason Kappanadze, whose eponymous grandfather preceded him in the job. As pastor between 1902 and 1908, the first Rev. Jason Kappanadze led in the acquisition of the land for the church, but then he decided to return to Georgia in Russia, so he was away while it was built. After the Russian revolution he returned and served as pastor again from 1922 to 1957. Thus the present Father Jason started out here himself. "I was born here, raised here and spoke Russian," he says. "Then I went into the advertising business." He later rediscovered the Orthodox church, though, and enrolled in a seminary. He was ordained in 1984, at the age of 40. Though Tremont today is reviving, Kappanadze says that as it declined in the 1970s, only two parishioners never moved away. The church continues to be viable because 400 people travel to it from other neighborhoods.

Access: To reach Lakewood from downtown, drive north on West 3rd Street or East 9th Street to intersection with the Memorial Shoreway, U.S. 6/20 and State Route 2, and drive west on the highway. Exit at Lake Avenue; West 117th Street is the Lakewood boundary. From I-90, exit at West 117th and drive north. The Mack Houses are on Lake and the parallel Edgewater Drive one block north.

Lakewood

Just west of Cleveland on the lake, Lakewood is a large suburb (about 60,000 people) that's urban in character, though it has very nice residential areas.

CLARENCE MACK HOUSES, 1925

13834 and 13840 Lake Avenue, west of Homewood Drive
13823 and 13825 Edgewater Drive, west of Homewood Drive
Private houses

The pair of houses on Lake are Georgian Revival, three stories, red brick with white trim. They are almost back-to-back with the two on Edgewater Drive. The second pair is French in inspiration, in painted brick with very steep hip roofs that in number 13825 are slightly flared. In an arrangement common in London and New York town houses, all four of these houses have the main living floor upstairs, on what we usually call the second floor. The son and grandson of builders, Clarence Mack (1888-1982) never went to college, but he traveled with his eyes open in England and France, and the houses he designed were always popular. Often before selling a newly finished house, Mack would live in it himself and furnish it. In the 1920s Mack built 23 houses in Lakewood (many in this immediate area), as well as others in Rocky River and Shaker Heights. The largest of his Ohio

▶ THE MACK HOUSES ON LAKE AVENUE

houses was Charles King's in Mansfield, now Kingwood Hall (see also; Vol. II) and, along with its gardens, open to the public. After the 1929 stock market crash Mack left Ohio and ultimately resettled in Palm Beach, Florida, where he continued building houses until he retired in 1962.

Access: To reach Detroit Avenue drive south from Lake on Nicholson Avenue. Flower shop is just to the west; Grace Avenue, two blocks east.

WINTERICH FLOWERS, 1923

13519 Detroit Avenue, just west of Nicholson Avenue
Greenhouse for flower business; now pottery shop, irregular hours;
216/521-0170

The entry to this greenhouse is so enchanting that we might expect to run into Peter Rabbit himself. The gable front is all glazed, with vertical dividers in the gable, horizontal ones in the wall. The front porch has a curved roof and two small columns. As of 1997 the greenhouse business had moved to another location, and a pottery

▶ WINTERICH FLOWERS

shop was using the building. The owner's house, behind the greenhouse at 13521 Detroit Avenue, is an 1883 Stick style.

HACKENBERG HOUSE, 1893

L.H. Moffett
1568 Grace Avenue, between Franklin Boulevard and Madison Avenue, NRHP
Private house

This is a good Queen Anne, painted in many colors, with a corner tower that has a bell-shaped roof.

THE FAN—In 1987 Craig Bobby was suddenly, seriously struck by Victorian houses, and neither Bobby nor Ohio Victoriana has been the same since. He became a hobbyist of such intensity and on such a scale, that now he probably knows more than anybody else about Ohio's Victorian houses. But as Bobby points out, a hobbyist isn't the same as a scholar; his knowledge isn't necessarily so methodical and complete. He's really in it for fun.

But this is fun that drives Bobby's entire life. It's invaded his Lakewood apartment, which overflows with his Victorian house books, his current researches, his 12,000 pictures of more than 6,000 houses in 22 states. His job as a letter carrier finances his hobby, the photographs and his travels; it's not so coincidental that his job also started in 1987. Victorian houses claim all his free time—including an hour before work even though he starts at 7:30 in the morning. When he had a two-week summer vacation, he hoped to use it for household chores, but his hobby took over. In the end he spent 40 percent of the two weeks at the library, 50 percent at county archives and only 10 percent on the chores. Not surprisingly, he feels he has to hire people to clean his apartment.

And he travels, though only in search of Victorian houses. In Ohio or Michigan or Kentucky he drives; but to see famous, far-flung neighbor-hoods, like Cape May, New Jersey, or Galveston, Texas, he pays for airline tickets. On such a trip he'll rise early and go straight to the first house he wants to photograph. Then he'll keep going until he runs out of daylight. Sometimes he shoots 15 rolls of film in two days; some days he has forgotten to eat. He can't explain why he does this, except to say that he's enthralled by Victorian houses.

Why enthralled? He likes 12-foot ceilings, window hoods, ornament in the gables, second-floor porches, slate roofs in a diamond or fish-scale pattern, asymmetry, shoulder-high carved wooden wainscoting. He likes the Gates Handyside House, an 1894 Queen Anne at 762 Broadway, Bedford, which has an octagonal second- and third-floor tower on the left front, and a 45-degree angle second-floor porch with a conical roof on the right. His favorite styles, in order, are Second Empire (with mansard roofs), Italianate (with towers), and Queen Anne. "The more ornate," he says, "the more features a house has, the more I like it."

Little about Craig Bobby is ordinary, except perhaps his job—he spends his days delivering mail in a Cleveland neighborhood where the houses are, alas, mostly post-Victorian. He has curly reddish brown hair down to his shoulders, a square jaw and set mouth, a compact, muscular build. As an admirer of Victorian houses, he is hardly alone; many people like them a lot. But being a really serious, independent student of them can be a lonely business. It involves being obsessed with facts so obscure that hardly anyone else cares. Bobby worries that he talks too much about Victorian houses, "because not everybody has the passion I do."

He does know of a dozen other architectural hobbyists in Cleveland and Ohio, but he is the only one seriously into Victorians. His Victoriana colleagues are scattered, like a man in Durham, North Carolina who is also very partial to Second Empire houses, though not the more ornate ones that Bobby prefers. He met the North Carolinian through a woman in New York who does paintings of Victorian houses. Another colleague, in Spokane, has a passion for Richardsonian Romanesque structures, which are apt to be courthouses or train stations. In Ohio Bobby knows a fellow hobbyist who loves Greek Revival and Federal. Bobby shudders. "I think they're the most boring styles I've ever laid eyes on. Thank God I don't have a formal education in architecture. I might not like the Victorians."

Essentially, for Craig Bobby being a Victorian house hobbyist means seeing as many as possible and then tracing their origins—their dates and especially, for a house that he thinks was architect-designed, the source of their design. He can do this because he has a very good memory for houses——"If ever I've seen a building I remember it," he says. By now also he's learned enough to make certain assumptions. For instance, he knows that in large cities, a Victorian house probably was done by an architect, but in small towns it was more likely built from a mail-order plan that an architect sold to many customers. In either case, design sources may be almost impossible to find, but of course sometimes he does. Even then, he may be the only one rejoicing. Tenants are rarely interested in who the architect was, and owners aren't necessarily. What he has done, is add to our store of architectural knowledge: a real, if abstract, achievement.

One way he goes about his primary research is, to spend his days off in the Cleveland Public Library going through all the issues of a turn-of-the-century magazine called *The Inland Architect*. He has done this several times, looking for Cleveland references in the "Building Synopsis" columns, which listed new construction by architect; the second and third times, he collected information

he'd earlier thought unimportant. That way he discovered, for instance, the previously unknown designer of one of Ohio's well known Victorians, the Hine House at 4624 West Prospect Street, Mantua. The architect was Cleveland's Fennimore C. Bate, whose best known work today is Grays Armory, 1234 Bolivar Road in downtown Cleveland. Another of Bobby's projects was ferreting out the date of a Lakewood Stick style house at 13521 Detroit Avenue (behind the greenhouse). To do that, he went to the Cuyahoga County Archives ("I practically live there," he admits) and checked old real estate tax records for the particular lot. Its valuation quadrupled between 1882 and 1883, which meant that the house dates from 1883.

Sometimes Bobby's researches have a real impact. In 1992 two San Francisco authors, Elizabeth Pomada and Michael Larsen, published *America's Painted Ladies*, a book on Victorian houses. They included 13 from Ohio, and of those six originally were suggested by Craig Bobby. Wrote the authors, "The state should give him a medal, better still, a grant to spend his life documenting the state's Victorians. Now what we need are forty-nine more Craig Bobbys!" As for documenting Victorians, that's what he's doing, grant or no.

A Clevelander, Bobby spent six years in college at Case Western Reserve and Cuyahoga Community College, but his academic career was unfocused. He remembers taking "101 in everything" but never got a degree. Then about the time he realized he was spinning his wheels, the post office job came along and permitted his hobby. At first he traveled mostly around Cleveland, and then he ventured to nearby towns, like Medina and Chagrin Falls. Gradually he added other places, like Mount Vernon and Lakeside and Kelleys Island. Findlay, he says, "has some of the best Victorian architecture I've ever seen." Early in 1998 he found the architect for a Findlay house; he recognized a picture of it in a 1903 magazine. In 1996 he visited Hamilton for the first time (Hamilton *is* a long way from Lakewood) and was impressed. To see the houses of Middle Bass Island he had to hire a boat. He found some Second Empire cottages there, and many mosquitoes.

Craig Bobby is Ohio's resident expert on George Franklin Barber, who was a Tennessee-based mail-order architect of elaborate Victorian houses. He first found Barber about 1994, in a book of Barber house plans reprinted early in the 1980s. For Bobby, this man is the "quintessential Queen Anne architect. I know I'm going to like what he's done." Born in Illinois, raised in Kansas, and ultimately based in Knoxville, Barber (1854-1915) published his plan books from 1888 to 1908; the books were really catalogues of houses for which he would sell detailed and customized construction drawings. He was not the first to do this; Barber was following the example, and sometimes ideas, of two East Coast brothers, George and Charles Palliser, who started issuing this type of plan book in 1876. Barber's plans were a huge success. He probably sold an average of at least 1,000 a year, so as many as 20,000 Barber houses, large and small, many in small towns, may have been built. An architect whom most of his clients never met, George Franklin Barber had an impressive output.

From looking often at Barber plan books, Bobby recognizes the architect's work. He knows of at least 25 examples in Ohio, and he regularly finds more: lately he came across two, one much altered, in Cleveland's Collinwood neighborhood. Not surprisingly, he abhors alterations that take the Barber out of the facade by, for example, replacing the porch with an office box. Bobby's favorite Barber house in Ohio was built from the same plan as the architect's own house in Knoxville; it's the Spitler House, now a museum in Brookville, Montgomery County.

One thing about being a Victorian house hobbyist, is that the challenges are ongoing; there are always more houses to see, more house pedigrees to track. And as he knows more, the more house plans he has in his head, the more he sees when he travels or reviews his own photographs. So in just one fairly typical month, Craig Bobby made three discoveries. First, he identified an unaltered Barber house at 37850 Euclid in Willoughby. Then he came across an old advertisement for the Saving and Sensible Architectural Bureau, an 1890s Cleveland-based vendor of house-plan books. Though the plans were, really, too plain to be personal favorites of his, once he knew the designs he began seeing still-standing examples—one near where he lives in Lakewood. And finally, he realized that a house he photographed a long time ago in Painesville, was actually from a 1883 Palliser, Palliser & Company plan book published in New York, by the very firm that inspired George Barber. This was Bobby's first Palliser find in Ohio. It whetted his interest. He is out there, looking for more.

CRAIG BOBBY'S FAVORITE OHIO VICTORIANS

*1. Second Empire: Hower House, 60 Fir Hill, Akron, museum

2. Second Empire: John Wright House at Historic Lyme Village, State Route 113 near Route 4, Bellevue, museum

**3. Italian Villa: Cortrite House, 131 East Main Street, Norwalk, private house

**4. Italianate and Gothic: Craig House, now Chamber of Commerce, Third and Mulberry, Mansfield

5. Queen Anne: Holmes County Historical Society, State Route 83, Millersburg, museum

**6 Bobby's favorite George Franklin Barber house: Samuel Spitler House, 14 Market Street, Brookville, museum

7. Three additional George Barber Queen Annes: **601 East High, Mount Vernon; **402 North Chestnut, Barnesville; 439 East Second, Dover, all private houses

---

*means see also in this volume;

** means see also in Vol. II

▌HOWER HOUSE

Columbus

Columbus never had the money other Ohio cites had, but it had the big daddy, the State of Ohio. So not only does Columbus have the Ohio Statehouse, the architectural focus of downtown, but it also has plums like Ohio State University. On the other hand, with the state as prime

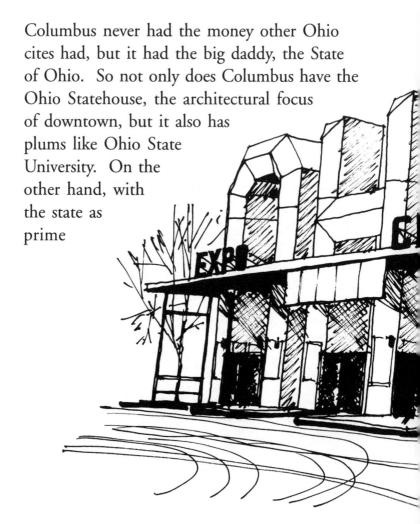

fount, the city never had much showcase architecture by non-Ohio names. ❡ What's distinctive here are the numerous instances of uncommonly interesting or thoughtful architecture—I
think of them, separated as they are, as islands
of savvy. For instance, in the Ohio Theatre and
German Village, Columbus has two rescues of
national significance. It has the picturesque
Sessions Village, which took trips to France to
design, and the imaginative Kahiki, which took
a trip to Polynesia to design. It also has a gate
that spells OHIO with four slender 32-foot-
high buildings shaped like letters. That was a
governor's inspiration. ❡ At least, when I first
wrote that paragraph,
Columbus still

▶ THE OHIO GATE AT THE FAIRGROUNDS

had the Kahiki and the OHIO gate, but now in early 2001 the first has been razed and the second is scheduled to be. Columbus is a place where preservationists live with a series of broken hearts. This tour starts with Capitol Square and Downtown, followed by the North Side, the South Side, the East Side and Westerville, in that order.

Access: Just northwest of the junction of I-70 and I-71, downtown Columbus has its hub at Broad and High Streets, the site of Capitol Square and the Statehouse, where this tour begins. To reach this corner, take Broad/U.S. 40 west from I-71 or Fourth Street/U.S. 23 north from I-70 to Broad; turn left/west; High comes after Third Street. For Atlas Building, Long is two blocks north of Broad; for Ohio Theatre, State Street is on south side of Capitol Square; for Southern Theatre, Main Street is a few blocks still farther south. This foot tour of downtown forms a loop, with buildings in suggested order. Walking is recommended; at a moderate pace the whole tour, including return to start, takes about 40 minutes, plus time at or in buildings. To shorten, drive to the Southern Theatre.

Capitol Square

Capitol Square's ten acres provide a site that enhances the Statehouse. Columbus's two best interiors, both with a state seal overhead, are here too: the Statehouse rotunda, and the Senate Building hall. As for the recently added garage entrances—conspicuous, oversized concrete maws on the lawn's east side—those I can't explain.

OHIO STATEHOUSE, 1839-61, 1996

Thomas Cole, principal designer, Catskill, New York; also Statehouse architects Henry Walter, Cincinnati; William Russell West, Cincinnati; Nathan B. Kelly, Columbus; and Isaiah Rogers, Cincinnati; consultant architects Alexander Jackson Davis, New York; Thomas U. Walter, Philadelphia; and Richard Upjohn, New York; 1996 renovation by Schooley Caldwell Associates, Columbus
Capitol Square, southeast corner of Broad and High Streets, NHL, NRHP
Ohio capitol building; guided and self-guided tours daily except holidays, starting in Senate Building on Third Street; groups of ten or more should prearrange; 614/728-2695

That the Ohio Statehouse succeeds as a monumental building is clear right away, for it has more presence than any of the new skyscrapers clustering around, paying homage. It's a massive building, a rectangular box, 184 feet wide and 304 feet long. On all four sides it has central recessed porches with Doric columns, while on top it has an unusual cupola with an almost-flat roof. The design is austere, with a quiet Doric frieze for ornamentation: a pattern of three vertical fingers (triglyphs) alternating with blank spaces (metopes) and running all the way around just below the cornice. Inside, the 64-foot-wide central rotunda has a dome soaring 120 feet over the floor, into the cupola; the state seal is visible at the eye of the dome. The Senate's chamber and offices are upstairs on the north side; the House's, upstairs on the south side. Both chambers have corner rooms with 28-foot ceilings. The House podium has an 8-foot chair built for Lincoln, who spoke in this room on his way to his 1861 inaugural in Washington. Four years later, he

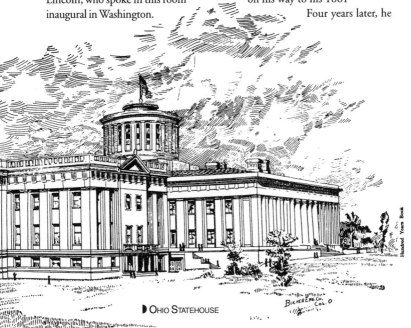

▶ OHIO STATEHOUSE

lay in state in the rotunda, and 50,000 people filed by his coffin. The Statehouse faces west, toward High Street. On the east side, a new Atrium (1993, Schooley Caldwell Associates, Columbus) connects the Statehouse with Capitol Square's second building, a 1901 annex originally called the Judiciary Building (see below). Before the Atrium was built, the National Park Service threatened that an addition might jeopardize the Statehouse's National Historic Landmark designation. The relatively discreet Atrium was built anyway, but it is freestanding and "reversible"—it could be removed with little impact on the historic buildings. The Statehouse remains a National Historic Landmark.

JUDICIARY BUILDING, NOW SENATE BUILDING, 1899-1901, 1993

Samuel Hannaford & Sons, Cincinnati; 1993 renovation, Schooley Caldwell Associates, Columbus
Capitol Square facing Third Street
Ohio Senate office building; included with Statehouse in guided and self-guided tours daily except holidays, starting in lobby on Third Street; groups of ten or more should prearrange; 614/728-2695

This structure has always had a site problem. From the beginning it blocked the east side of the Statehouse, clearly robbing the capitol not only of lawn but of some of its majesty. After the Supreme Court, originally the prime tenant, moved out in the 1970s, it had other problems as well. It was closed, neglected, scheduled for razing, and not included or even mentioned when the Statehouse was put on the National Register. Ultimately its convenient space caught the eye of legislators, who started setting up makeshift offices and moving in, in spite of water damage and dismal halls. Demolition plans were finally cancelled only when the Senate decided to use this building for their offices, rather than follow the House to the Riffe Center. Restoration that ended in 1993 brought an astounding transformation, turning the derelict hall and stairway into a splendid place. Marble that the architect in charge, Robert Loversidge of Schooley Caldwell Associates, thought must be gray because it was so dark, cleaned to white. Paint covered wall frescos, and plywood hid a beautiful leaded glass skylight: the state seal at its best. "This is one of the most spectacular entrance spaces in Columbus," says Loversidge. "And no one knew about it." Like the Statehouse, the Senate Building has classical columns. But because it was built at the turn of the century, it is not Greek Revival but Neoclassical Revival. Loversidge contrasts the two styles. He points out that the Senate Building has fancy detailing—a balustrade at the roofline, carving in the pediment, and fluting

OPTIMISM IN COLUMBUS LIMESTONE

—In 1970 Robert Loversidge, Jr., an Ohio State freshman from Red Bank, New Jersey, stood on the Statehouse lawn and snapped a picture of the monumental limestone building. Eighteen years later, he became the latest architect to take it on, though his assignment was a first. Loversidge was expected to find and retrieve the original building.

For eight years, from 1988-1996, Loversidge helped plan and then oversaw restorations in the Statehouse and its annex for Schooley Caldwell Associates. Most of the original Statehouse was intact but out-of-sight: 53 rooms chopped into 317. Loversidge, steeped in the building's past and future, also became its most authoritative host. For years sightseers in hard hats followed him through scaffolding, past piles of pipe, doors resting on the floor, and walls stripped of plaster. He told his tours just how primitive Columbus was when this building was first planned in 1838. In a state of 1.5 million people, it was a village of 6,000.

In this village, Ohio set out to build a Statehouse that is one of the nation's best examples of Greek Revival, though it took so long to build, 22 years, that when it was new, it was old-fashioned. Its eight designers included some of the nation's top architects, but it was built by amateurs, convicts from the nearby state penitentiary. In spite of all the architects, the Statehouse was not spoiled; its design has a consistent simplicity. For that, politicians may take some credit. While tending the public purse, the General Assembly incidentally helped give Ohio a great building.

The Statehouse took so long to build because it was so ambitious; it was optimism in Columbus limestone.

It was so expensive that the state could barely afford it; in fact, one year after groundbreaking, in 1840, construction was halted, mostly for financial reasons, and didn't resume for eight years. The end result was a building almost as big as the original Capitol in Washington. Its legislative chambers were even larger and the structure, higher.

Three statehouse commissioners, political appointees whose ranks changed periodically, managed construction. In 1838 the first commissioners started with a nationally advertised design contest. They promised three prizes, $500, $300, and $200. Fifty entries came in, and three winners were announced in October. First prize went to Henry Walter of Cincinnati, who the next year was appointed statehouse architect. For years Walter, who later designed St. Peter in Chains Cathedral in his home city, got credit for the Statehouse, as in *Walter et al.*

But just after World War II, a graduate student named Abbott Lowell Cummings discovered that the Statehouse wasn't Walter's design, but that of the third-prize winner, Thomas Cole. Thomas Cole is well known today not as an architect, but as a landscape painter, the founder of the Hudson River School. Recalls Cummings, "I got very excited."

As a youth he came to Ohio from New England to attend Oberlin and then OSU, where he got his PhD in 1950. To pay for graduate school, Cummings was put to work on a history of Statehouse construction. By endless hours of going through old newspapers, he unraveled the politics. In a dank basement room in the Statehouse, he discovered—and rescued—the original drawings. And in New York, in the papers of the renowned architect, Alexander

Jackson Davis, Cummings discovered that in appearance and floorplan, the Statehouse is like Cole's contest entry.

Before that day, no one knew what the winning entries looked like, because no one knew that pictures even existed, much less that they might be buried in Davis's papers. But two statehouse commissioners went to New York to consult Davis in spring, 1839, and he drew copies of the three winning designs—the copies Cummings found. All three designs were similar, with round domes. The porches were different—Cole's were recessed; the others projected.

In 1838 Cole was an established painter living in Catskill, New York. In that era, it wasn't uncommon for non-architects to design buildings. The first national capitol was by a physician; the Montgomery County Courthouse in Dayton (see also), by a horticulturist. Thomas Jefferson, hardly remembered first for architecture, was so influential in the field that an American style was named for him.

Architect Davis prepared a composite of contest entries for the commissioners, but in Columbus his version was deemed too expensive. So the commissioners did their own composite, which was closest to Thomas Cole's contest entry. It happened that one of the commissioners, a Zanesville lawyer named

William A. Adams, was an old friend of Cole's. They'd met in the 1820s, when Adams was a would-be artist in Zanesville and Cole, an itinerant painter working in eastern Ohio. Adams thought himself the only commissioner with artistic taste, as perhaps he was; all through the contest and afterward, he strongly favored Cole's plan. The results show that he ultimately prevailed.

Including Cole, eight different people helped design the Statehouse. Alexander Jackson Davis gave it additional height. Henry Walter raised the rotunda floor 7 feet. The next supervising architect, William Russell West of Cincinnati, added the low pediments over the east and west porticos. Then Nathan B. Kelly of Columbus showed he had grown tired of Greek Revival and preferred then modern frills—the ornate brackets under the House balconies are his. When the strength of his cantilevered stairway was challenged, Kelly loaded them with five tons of iron and had 40 men march three abreast, up and down the stairs, which never wobbled. He was dismissed for extravagance.

All through construction, every new architect added or removed the cupola's round dome. Architect West explained, as he took it off, that it wasn't authentically Greek. It came off permanently at the behest of two nationally prominent architects invited to Columbus in 1856. Thomas U. Walter, who the year before had designed the dome for the national Capitol, and Richard Upjohn, architect of New York's Trinity Church, urged that the Statehouse stick to its classical origins. Thus the architect hired to finish the job was Isaiah Rogers of Cincinnati, known all over the country for fine hotels and chosen here for his enduring

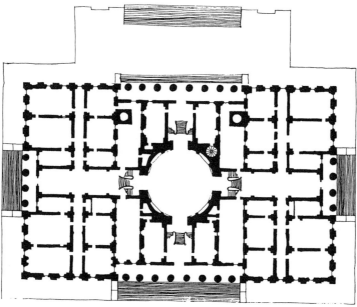

▶ First Floor of Statehouse, 1861

allegiance to classicism. He completed the Statehouse's rotunda, stairs and cupola. He intended to add fluting to the columns—Doric columns usually have these vertical grooves—but a commissioner saved $20,000 by lopping fluting.

Bob Loversidge likes to explain how the whole Statehouse, conceived in the candlestick era, was designed to use natural light. It was essentially four buildings around a rotunda. Each enclosed a 24-by-60-foot light court—an open courtyard with windows that brought light and air to inside rooms and permitted the building's massive scale. Windows were in halls as well as rooms; the building had skylights, light grates, and some translucent glass blocks. By the time it was finished in 1861, it also had hundreds of gas lamps. They'd been invented after construction began.

At a place where some plaster has been knocked off, Loversidge points out the rough stones, held together in the walls by mortar and "habit." Walls range from 2 to 6 feet in thickness; the higher they are, the thinner, because the load is less. He notes the fine ribbing made on the limestone when the blocks were cut; the hand chisels had tiny finger-like projections.

Most of Abbott Lowell Cummings's construction history is about stone cutting. For instance, when other work stopped for the winter of 1850-51, 80 convicts kept on cutting stone. The Statehouse's Columbus limestone came from a nearby quarry and is a very hard stone, taking twice as long to saw with modern diamond blades as the famous Indiana limestone. Columbus limestone is also less consistent, which means it has fossils that may be interesting but are even harder to cut than the rest.

Some critics cavil over the quirky, domeless cupola. When it was built, domes were going out of style. Then Thomas U. Walter's enormous dome, built on the national Capitol after the Statehouse was finished, during the

Civil War, inspired emulation in the states well into the twentieth century; dome and capitol are firmly linked in our minds. But for Frank Lloyd Wright, this domeless Statehouse was "the most honest of state capitols, sincere and forthright." Architectural historians Henry-Russell Hitchcock and William Seale described it as "more monumental than the national Capitol had yet become and more intrinsically coherent than it would ever be."

The original Statehouse had 53 rooms and housed the entire state government. By the mid-1980s, it wasn't even able to house all the General Assembly. By then the 132 legislators each expected his own office, and partly in a vain attempt to provide them the Statehouse had been carved up into 317 rooms.

The light courts, no longer essential for light, were roofed and filled with five floors of offices, though the rest of the building had three floors. Some large rooms were chopped horizontally and vertically. Finally much of the building was a warren of partitions, dropped ceilings and miniscule desk crannies that did not impress constituents.

Two things made a Statehouse restoration possible. One was a new tower across the street, the 1987 Riffe Center, which had offices for all the House members. The other was the Senate's decision to move its offices to the adjacent annex, the one-time Judiciary Building. From 1993-96, after authorizing $112.7 million for improvements in Capitol Square, the General Assembly met under other roofs for the first time since 1857.

The improvements included Statehouse and annex restorations, plus the Atrium, a roofed connector between the two buildings. Today's Statehouse is down to about 100 rooms.

When construction was almost finished in 1996, Bob Loversidge gave me a tour, so I could see what he and his cohorts had wrought. The basement amazed me. With room partitions and plaster from the 1930s cleared away, its wonderful brick and stone arches stood fully revealed. In the room under the rotunda the vaults rose an impressive 18 feet. The arches are all working, helping to support the building.

After admiring the rotunda and chambers, all repainted in their original colors, we set off from the second floor, climbing up a narrow spiral stairway where each step is a triangular stone. It takes us up into the cupola, which has two levels, each with a ring-shaped floor, windows on the outside and the rotunda dome's outer shell inside. In the nineteenth century the cupola was a popular place for people to visit; Loversidge wonders how crowds managed that tiny stairway. He pauses to look out a window, down at the new Statehouse roof and the west lawn 14 stories below, shaded by skyscrapers across the street.

At the cupola's upper level the walkway widens because the dome is narrower, and, below signatures of long-ago tourists, a bench lines the wall. The very last flight is a short wooden stairway that rises to look over the top of the rotunda dome, held in place by the original iron framework. From those dark braces and bolts I look up, past the supplementary artificial lights that help illuminate the rotunda, and out the glass of the roof skylight. The view beyond is a skyscraper face, the flat layers of glass and stone of the Rhodes Tower. In one glance, it is the gamut of our buildings.

in the columns—none of which the more austere Statehouse has. Both buildings incorporate the technology of their time. The Statehouse has heavy load-bearing masonry walls, as well as load-bearing arches in the basement and on the first floor. The Senate Building has a steel frame with a relatively thin skin of limestone. Loversidge observes that though the architect of the second building, Samuel Hannaford & Sons, produced a structure characteristic of their day, they matched the older building with classical styling, the same stone, and cornice lines and water tables at the same level.

Downtown

If Capitol Square is the architectural focus of downtown, the surrounding city ornaments it with good examples of late nineteenth- and early twentieth century architecture. ¶But there's no denying that this is still another beleaguered downtown. Streets around the City Center mall, especially High Street, have declined because the mall has so little connection with them. The theaters are downtown, but the restaurants and bars that should augment them are not. I remember one that tried. After a play in a downtown theater, our party of six would walk the short distance to the Vault, a bar with high windows overlooking Broad and High. Time after time, we were the only people there. Perhaps almost everyone has forgotten what cities should be about.

To see more: Broad Street Churches—About half a mile east of Third Street, Broad Street has two churches of interest. One is the tall and slender First Congregational Church at 444 East Broad Street, open weekdays; 614/ 228-1741. It's a 1931 building by John Russell Pope, New York, and Howard Dwight Smith, Columbus. Across the street at number 501 is Broad Street United Methodist Church, 1885, designed by J.W. Yost, Columbus. The stone church on Capitol Square is Trinity Episcopal, 1869, 125 East Broad; architect, Gordon W. Lloyd, Detroit.

STATE OFFICE TOWER, NOW JAMES A. RHODES STATE OFFICE TOWER, 1974

Dalton-Dalton-Little, Cleveland and Brubaker/Brandt, Columbus
30 East Broad Street
State government offices and Supreme Court; building accessible weekdays; 40th floor open as observatory

Directly across Broad Street from the Statehouse, the Rhodes Tower is central Ohio's tallest building—41 stories rising 629 feet above the sidewalk. This tower also offers an amenity unique in Columbus: it's possible for the public to take an elevator to the 40th floor, where windows provide overlooks in four directions. What was no longer available in late 1998 was easy access to the Supreme Court. It was possible to see that courtroom, but only after clearance by the State Highway Patrol. The Supreme Court planned to move to another downtown building in 2002. Clad in red granite, the Rhodes Tower is the only example of the Brutalist style in this guide to Ohio buildings. Characterized in part by heavy, rectilinear masonry surfaces, Brutalism has a name that, at least to a layman, sounds like a joke or an insult. Ohio does have other Brutalist buildings; one, also in Columbus, is the Ohio Historical Society, 1970, by architect W. Byron Ireland; it's visible just west of I-71 above Seventeenth Avenue. For a skyscraper, the Rhodes Tower has an uncommon floorplan. Service towers for ducts and elevators project from the north and east walls—the back and one side. Because these services usually preempt the middle of the building, this one is exceptional in having an unblocked, open, five-story hall inside the entry. Ohio State's Douglas Graf compares this space to an Italian palazzo's courtyard. In the middle, there's what Graf calls a well, where escalators connect to the lower level, which has a restaurant and an underground pedestrian passage to the Statehouse garage. He especially likes the public space outside in front: the "porch" there provides pedestrians shelter in rain and has granite piers, perpendicular to the wall, guiding people indoors. Then if they turn around and look back, they see the Statehouse through the glass wall, which frames it.

CHAMBER OF COMMERCE CAFE & RATHSKELLER, NOW RINGSIDE CAFE, 1910

Carl E. Howell, Howell & Thomas, Columbus
19 North Pearl Street
Restaurant and bar; lunch offered weekdays and early evenings; 614/228-7464

Pearl Street, an alley, runs along the Rhodes Tower's west wall, and there you'll find the Ringside Cafe, which would seem small even if central Ohio's tallest building weren't next door. One-story high, the Ringside has one room plus a basement. It's brick and stone, with an arched stone entry at the corner. Cafe & Rathskeller is carved in the stone, along with grape vines; originally

▶ Ringside Cafe

the name was Chamber of Commerce Cafe, but the Chamber objected to a saloon's adopting its name. The Chamber, in an 1889 Richardsonian Romanesque building that was razed in 1969, was located where the Rhodes Tower is now. The Ringside is just as charming inside as out. It has stained glass in the windows, oak paneling, tables and wooden booths, a bar along the far wall, and a diminutive open kitchen in the corner. All this is in a room that's about 25 by 30 feet. Stairs at the west end lead downstairs. On the west side of the barroom, the tiny door to the ladies room blends so well with the paneling that it's hard to find. The alleys here, Pearl Street and the one paralleling Broad behind Rhodes Tower, provide Columbus's best urban spaces. That's so, though they're not optimally used—for one, I've seen lots of litter.

COLUMBUS SAVINGS & TRUST BUILDING, NOW ATLAS BUILDING, 1905

Frank L. Packard, Columbus
8 East Long Street at North High, NRHP
Office building

Early skyscrapers often were modeled on the parts of a column, with base, shaft and capital, as architect Frank L. Packard has done in the Second Renaissance Revival style Atlas Building. The first three stories, in a heavily rusticated, or grooved red stone, represent the base. The shaft, seven stories mostly in brick, is plainer. The top, representing the capital in white terra cotta and white stone, is the most ornate section, with a heavy bracketed cornice. Be sure to see the lobby, in white marble with a coffered ceiling. This description comes partly from a Columbus *Dispatch* series by Robert E. Samuelson, an associate professor of architecture at Ohio State. The articles were related to Samuelson's work as project director for *Architecture: Columbus*, published in 1976. It is a valuable resource, listing all types of

Columbus buildings, including many significant ones no longer standing, with black-and-white photographs for all.

AMERICAN INSURANCE UNION CITADEL, NOW LEVEQUE TOWER, 1927

C. Howard Crane, Detroit
50 West Broad Street at Front, NRHP
Office building and Palace Theatre (see next)

In a burst of energy in the late 1920s, Cleveland, Cincinnati and Columbus built major skyscraper complexes that Doug Graf calls Ohio's last "big display of embellishment of the city" for half a century. Of these three superb towers—Terminal, Carew, and LeVeque— Columbus's was the first to be finished. It rose 46

▶ ATLAS BUILDING

stories and 555.5 feet—enough to make it the world's fifth tallest building. For almost 40 years it was Columbus's only real skyscraper; even now, only the Rhodes Tower is taller. The Rhodes has an observation window that looks down on the LeVeque's octagonal, crown-like summit, with turrets nearby and 18-foot eagles not far below. Except for the octagonal top, the tower is square, with two 18-story wings, one extending north along Front Street; the other, running east along Broad Street, contains the Palace Theatre. It's a steel-frame building, clad in bark-textured terra cotta tiles that were sprayed with white and brown glazes. The structure rests on 44 10-foot-square caissons that reach down 112 feet to bedrock. They were built by sandhogs from New York, men with Hudson River-tunneling experience. The western part of the building lobby still has its marble; elevator doors are bronze bas-reliefs; at the west end a vaulted hall section has colorful ceiling paintings. As for the building's style, it's been given variously as Art Deco, Commercialized Gothic, and Modern Monumental. In 1926, promoters never hesitated. They simply called it "the most beautiful building in the world." The American Insurance Union was a fraternal life insurance company founded by John J. Lentz, a lawyer and politician, in 1894. Successful as it was, A.I.U. could not have afforded its

Citadel if the 400-room Deshler Hotel, on the corner at High Street, had not agreed to take 600 rooms in the tower wings. For decades the Deshler, razed in 1969, set the standard for glamour in Columbus. It had an arched bridge over the alley to connect it to the tower and its public rooms there, the Spanish Tea Room and the Hall of Mirrors. The A.I.U. went out of business during the Depression. New owners in 1946 renamed the building the LeVeque-Lincoln Tower, a name shortened after another sale in 1977.

KEITH-ALBEE PALACE THEATRE, NOW PALACE THEATRE, 1927

Thomas W. Lamb, New York
34 West Broad Street, NRHP
Theater; regular venue for Opera, Broadway series, and touring entertainment. Outer lobby ticket office open weekdays, offering peek at inner lobby; for information about tours, some free, call CAPA, 469-1045

In the early 1940s, Phil Sheridan would cut classes at North High School and take the trolley downtown, where he would buy peanuts and go to the Palace Theatre for movies and live shows—the likes of big bands or Sally Rand. "She had two dances," Sheridan recalls. "One with the featherlike fan in front of her and then one with a big ball she held up over her head. Concealing nothing." Sheridan became so entranced with show business that since the 1970s he has self-published a series of Columbus theater histories. When Katherine LeVeque was widowed suddenly in 1975, the Palace Theatre, which her husband had quietly purchased two years earlier, became hers, though to spare her from stress, she wasn't told that. So in 1978 she was very surprised to read that she owned the Palace and it was about to be torn down. Later that year, she toured the theater, then closed two years, with Phil Sheridan as her guide. Sheridan recalled walking through water and plaster from burst pipes, but afterward, LeVeque told him she had never realized how beautiful the theater was. After basic renovation it was reopened in 1980; in 1982 Phil Sheridan became manager; and in 1984, after more extensive rehabbing, Opera/Columbus moved in as a resident company. Since 1989 CAPA, the Columbus Association for the Performing Arts, has owned and operated the theater. The Palace is less ornate than its sister theater, the Ohio, but its lobby, illuminated and visible from the sidewalk on a winter evening, is an alluring sight, with the white marble and red carpet of its curving central stairway ascending to an unseen lobby and wonders only imagined. Sally Rand, perhaps.

WYANDOTTE BUILDING, 1898

D.H. Burnham & Co., Chicago
21 East Broad Street at Wall Street, NRHP
Office building

The Wyandotte Building has "bays of windows which practically ripple across its facade." So wrote G.E. Kidder Smith in his survey of American buildings. This nearly square, eleven-story Chicago Style building has a tall rectangular entrance arch with decorative terra cotta trim. State offices occupied the Wyandotte from 1917 until 1974, when the Rhodes Tower opened. In 1978 a private partnership purchased the building and rehabbed it, but 20 years later the structure was languishing, only partly used. George Nickerson, who is managing it, said that although the Wyandotte might seem ideal for a conversion to housing, the residential safety code and a lack of parking make that impractical. As for prospective office tenants, they hesitate because mechanicals—elevators, plumbing and so on—use up 40 percent of each floor. But Nickerson is sure that the Wyandotte offers something unique in Columbus: bay windows. In late 1998 the building had some good news. The local AIA chapter redid a second floor office and moved in. After the 1893 World's Columbian Exposition displayed his Beaux Arts work, Chicago architect Daniel H. Burnham was in demand across the country. That year he was hired to do Columbus Union Depot; the Wyandotte followed. The station, completed in 1897 just north of downtown, had grand Beaux Arts arches facing High Street. Razed in 1976, Union Depot was a great loss.

▶ WYANDOTTE BUILDING

OHIO STATE OFFICE BUILDING, NOW OHIO DEPARTMENTS BUILDING, 1933

Harry Hake, Cincinnati; consulting architects Frank W. Ball, Cleveland and Alfred R. Hahn, Toledo
65 South Front Street, NRHP
State office building; being renovated for Supreme Court, which was scheduled to move in 2003

In recent years the Ohio Departments Building had had some maintenance and updating—for instance, a central air system replaced 500 window air conditioners—so no one expected the outside walls to start falling off, as they did in 1995. Once it was clear that supports for the 4-inch marble blocks were rusting away, people were barred from standing near the walls while the state mulled its way to an $11 million option. In a job finished in mid-1999, the state is replacing all the marble siding with 3 inches of foam insulation and 2-inch-thick marble blocks from the same Georgia quarry as the originals. While up there, they're also replacing the windows. "The building," said project architect Bruce Ratekin, "will be a hundred times more energy-efficient." Due to reap the benefits was the Supreme Court of Ohio, which had a budgetary green light to take over the building in 2003. They'll be moving into Columbus's best Art Deco structure. This is evident outside, but it's perhaps even better seen inside, where halls and hearing rooms have Ohio history in Art Deco bronze, mosaics and marble, as well as in wall murals and paneling in, for example, Hearing Room 2 and the State Library. At 73 by 317 feet, this 13-story structure is distinctively long and narrow. Both long sides have facades, one on Front Street, the other looking across Civic Center Drive to the Scioto River. At the top two floors the windows are recessed between piers and columns; while on the very top of the building, under the green roof, a setback was designed for three stories of book stacks for the state library, which was a tenant here until the end of 2000.

▶ OHIO DEPARTMENTS BUILDING

HUNTINGTON CENTER, 1984

Bruce Graham of Skidmore, Owings & Merrill, Chicago
41 South High Street
Bank headquarters with office, hotel, retail space

At the top, the Huntington Center has a symmetrical pair of stepped extensions that rise a few stories and look somewhat like horns, giving the building a distinctive profile in the skyline.

LOEW'S OHIO, NOW OHIO THEATRE, 1928

Thomas W. Lamb, New York
39 East State Street, NHL, NRHP
Theater; regular venue for orchestra, ballet, Broadway series, classic films; for
information about tours, some free, call CAPA, 469-1045

"The theater," said Scots-born architect Thomas W. Lamb, who designed 300 of them, "is the palace of the average man." Early on he designed restrained, classical auditoriums like that of Columbus's Palace. By the time he did the Ohio, he'd changed his approach. On the outside this theater has a mild-mannered Beaux Arts facade, but the interior is unbridled lushness. The style is Spanish-Baroque, which means twisted gold columns undulating like belly dancers; large, voluptuous shells holding boxes; two golden ladies with wings at the top of the proscenium. The ceiling is red with gold and silver stars; the main chandelier weighs two-and-a-half tons, supported by a steel bar anchored above in the structure's steel beams. The Ohio became the city's premier movie-and-stage show house. But by late 1968, Loew's had two suburban theaters and was happy to sell the Ohio to a local developer; a new state office tower was planned for the site. Before the last movie ended its run February 24, 1969, a temporary save-the-theater committee had formed. At the end of March, to test the auditorium in live performance, the Columbus Symphony held an open rehearsal there; 2,000 people came and critics cheered. In May the nonprofit Columbus Association for the Performing Arts was organized, and by July 30, the theater rescue had survived a dozen crises and had the $1.75 million needed to buy the property. Then volunteers swarmed in to help ready the house for its first season of performances. One was a man from Athens, who came every week to clean a drapery, until he'd done them all. The Junior League washed chandeliers. But the Ohio wasn't really saved until the next spring, when developer John Galbreath and the Battelle Memorial Institute, a research organization, retired $1 million of the mortgage, leaving the remainder at a more manageable $250,000. That fall, the Symphony made the Ohio its permanent home. The rescue involved lots of people, including many big contributors. The local architects took out a full-page newspaper ad in support of the theater. And the previous owners made concessions at a couple of critical stages—as when they gave CAPA a break in buying the theater's equipment and furnishings. The Ohio Theatre's save and then its ongoing renovation became a national model and inspiration for groups

across the country. Though hundreds of cities have saved theaters since 1969, at that time a group of citizens rallying to preserve one was unexpected; when they succeeded, it seemed—and it was—

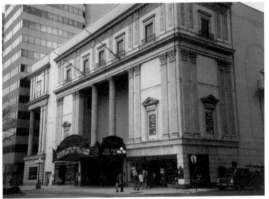

▶ OHIO THEATRE

miraculous. For many years now, this palace of the common man has been Ohio's busiest theater. The Galbreath Pavilion on the east side was added in 1984; architects were Hardy Holzman Pfeiffer Associates, New York.

U.S. POST OFFICE AND COURTHOUSE, NOW BRICKER & ECKLER, 1887, 1912, 1986

James G. Hill, 1887; James Knox Taylor, Supervising Architect, Treasury Department, Washington, 1912; Friedrich Bohm of Bohm-NBBJ, Columbus, 1986 renovation
100 South Third Street at East State, NRHP
Law firm offices; interior not accessible to the public

The Federal government built itself a stone castle that by 1977 it had evacuated, leaving behind a leaking roof and other problems. Fortunately the law firm of Bricker & Eckler saw the building's possibilities and undertook a major renovation that included fixing the roof, adding a four-story addition for utilities, and restoring the six remaining marble fireplaces. Price tag: $13.5 million.

▶ OHIOTHEATRE

SOUTHERN THEATRE, 1896, 1998

*Dauben, Krumm & Riebel, Columbus; theater interior, Menno S. Detweiler,
Columbus; 1998 restoration, Feinknopf Macioce Schappa, Columbus
21 East Main Street, NRHP
Theater; regular venue for chamber music, jazz and operettas; for information
about tours, some free, call CAPA, 469-1045*

The Great Southern Hotel opened in 1897, the pride of downtown south.
Now the Westin Great Southern, the six-story red-brick hotel has good
public spaces. Interesting as the hotel is, the best thing under this roof is the
Southern Theatre, which opened the year before the hotel, in 1896. It's at
the east end of the hotel building, behind a round sandstone arch swathed in
Sullivanesque carvings. A private developer refurbished the hotel in the mid-
1980s, while the theater, shut down in the late 1970s, stayed on hold; in
1986, it was donated to CAPA. In the mid-1990s, when state, city, and
private funds finally were all in hand, CAPA began a $10 million restoration.
The theater reopened in fall, 1998, with 933 seats. This theater is a favorite
of mine. It's unusually intimate, because no seats are really far away. The
orchestra's back row is 68 feet from the stage; at its widest, the auditorium
measures 66 feet; the ceiling over the second balcony is 60 feet above the
stage. The auditorium also has a distinctive series of concentric arches
radiating out from the proscenium to the balcony. Its second balcony is
unique in active Ohio theaters today.

NO ACCIDENT—"Psst. Want to see something special?"

For nearly 20 years, that was the usual invitation for a tour of the Southern Theatre. A flashlight-toting guide would move the piano blocking a door in the Southern Hotel lobby and lead the way into the darkened house. Cold, dirty and dim, it was a relic of its former self, but it resonated with possibilities. Even when the orchestra seats were torn out, the sound was so good that a word spoken on stage was audible everywhere. Even by flashlight, it was possible to catch sight of the round arches radiating out from the stage and the elliptical curves of the balconies. That was how the theater was when Jay Panzer, at the time a theatrical consultant from New York, saw it for the first time in 1984.

In 1998 Panzer finished a five-year stint realizing the possibilities that he'd first seen 14 years before. He oversaw the theater's restoration—"It was a *collaborative* project," he emphasizes, trying to list administrators, electricians, artists—which critics acclaimed a success. "From the beginning the charge was to create a twenty-first century performing facility within a nineteenth-century environment," Panzer says. "It wasn't about building a museum. It was about building a theater. And I think we've done pretty well."

He first had that feeling at a rehearsal. A resident chamber orchestra, ProMusica, was practicing Mendelsohn's *Third Violin Concerto* on a Saturday morning, and Panzer was listening. He was amazed and elated. "I leaned back and said, 'Well, if this is the best I ever do, that's OK.'"

One reason the Southern Theatre is architecturally interesting is because it has Chicago antecedents. While a Columbus architectural firm,

Dauben, Krumm & Riebel, planned the hotel and theater, Menno S. Detweiler designed the theater's interior. Little is known of Detweiler, but according to a contemporary newspaper story on the hotel's construction, he had worked on the 1893 World's Columbian Exposition in Chicago. Though he had a Columbus office later in the 1890s, Detweiler must have known Chicago theaters; perhaps he had even worked with Dankmar Adler and Louis Sullivan, architects of renowned Chicago houses like the Schiller Theater, since razed, and the Auditorium. At least, when Detweiler was in Chicago he was paying attention, for in the Southern he designed a theater very much like the Schiller. Given the fact that the Southern works as well as it does, Jay Panzer is willing to give Detweiler the highest praise. "There are certain things," he says, "that are not lucky accidents."

Panzer, who himself spent time analyzing the Southern's design on a computer, points out features that

▶ SOUTHERN THEATRE

enhance acoustics. For instance, the paintings that flank the stage at the front, contain reflectors that bounce sound under the balcony. That both balconies arch slightly—the first balcony is 1 foot higher in the center than at the sides; the second balcony is 18 inches higher—also improves sound. The greatest acoustical advantage comes from the auditorium's funnel-like shape, made by the round concentric arches framing the stage and then radiating up and out over the orchestra seats. It's not just that the funnel carries sound, Panzer says, but also that the faceting, or changes in level between arches, directs the sound toward the audience.

A native New Yorker, Jay Panzer studied opera and theater design at the University of Cincinnati's College Conservatory of Music. When his New York employer first sent him to Columbus in the early 1980s, it was to work on the Ohio Theatre. In 1993 he came to Columbus to stay, as it's turned out. He's become director of facility development for Columbus Association for the Performing Arts, which owns the Southern, Ohio and Palace Theatres and manages theaters that others own, including one in Chicago. He says, "Going to the theater is not relaxing for me. I'm unable to suspend disbelief because I'm looking at lighting, sound, costumes."

In early stages of "Psst, something special" tours, the someday rehab was expected to put mechanicals where the second balcony was. But from the time of a 1992 feasibility study, the intention was to put mechanicals in a separate, adjacent structure with its own foundation, so that the throbbing of equipment would not affect the auditorium. That has been accom-

plished, permitting theatergoers the uncommon experience of a second-balcony. It is not for the faint-hearted. It is high—38 stairs higher than the first balcony—and so steeply raked that railings have been installed between rows. For the brave, it offers the house's best sound.

Another feature of the restoration is the retention of the vomitories. These are four short, tunnel-like passages, seven-stairs high and one-person wide, leading up to first-balcony seating; their name, vomitory, is unforgettable. The Southern has four of these passages, and people used to suppose that in any rehab, fire and building inspectors would ban them as hazardous. But Panzer says inspectors asked how many people would be sitting in the first balcony, and the answer was 300 to 350. Then they asked how many ways out of that balcony there were, and the answer was seven, including two wide stairways, one emergency exit, and the four vomitories. That was deemed plenty.

Then too, there was the ladies restroom issue. "For years I've focused on it," Panzer says. "Flaws with theater restrooms are a consistent problem." The ladies restroom space, off the Southern's first balcony, is not a large one, but it's designed to shunt a line of users in, around and out the other side. Panzer is satisfied with it. "I've watched the line," he says. "Of course I tried not to watch too conspicu-ously. But I saw that ten minutes into a 15-minute intermission, there was no line. The point is, not that there are no lines, but that the lines are gone before the end of intermission."

Just as he says, certain things are not lucky accidents.

Access: To reach Volunteers of America drive west from downtown on Broad Street; cross the river. On the west bank what you'll see first is the science center, COSI, 1999, designed by Tokyo architect Arata Isozaki with NBBJ Design, Columbus, at 333 West Broad Street, 614/228-2674. The massive west facade is like a 960-foot beached whale, with curved vertical segments; the east incorporates the old Central High School and offers views of downtown. Volunteers of America, also on the left, comes soon after.

TOLEDO & OHIO CENTRAL RAILROAD STATION, NOW VOLUNTEERS OF AMERICA, 1895

Yost & Packard, Columbus
379 West Broad Street, NRHP
Volunteers of America offices, kitchen and dining facilities for recovering alcoholics program; visitors welcome; 614/224-8650

In 1987 the architect Paul Rudolph, from 1958-65 the influential head of Yale University's School of Architecture, strode into Columbus and told local architects that his favorite building in town was the one-time Toledo & Ohio Central Railroad Station. No doubt a few jaws dropped. The former station is off the beaten path in Columbus, west of the Scioto River, and has long been the home of a service organization, Volunteers of America, that helps the homeless. So for most local architects, it wouldn't have been the first thing to come to mind as anybody's favorite. But it is a distinctive structure. It has a front tower that bulges slightly as it ascends to its pagoda-style roof, which has broad, flared eaves; two shorter, octagonal towers flank the tall one. The building behind holds a two-story

▶ TOLEDO & OHIO CENTRAL STATION

barrel-vaulted waiting room. Outside walls are tan and brown brick, with rough-cut, irregular stone quoins. At least some of the roof, on the tower and the entry porch, is still red tile. Of this structure Rudolph pronounced, "It is one of the most fascinating things I've ever seen in my life." At least some others must agree, because the old train station rose up after two fires, in 1910 and 1975. Since the second fire, the waiting-room skylight has been lit artificially. Some of the fat bas-relief cherubs under the arch also date from the 1970s; they were restored by Pymer Plastering, a local family firm that had done the original work. After train service was consolidated at Union Depot, the Volunteers of America took over the building in 1930—very much to the building's advantage, for it has been both used and treasured. The waiting room has become banquet hall for holiday dinners—Easter, Thanksgiving, and Christmas. That the Toledo and Ohio Central Station is so unusual inspires speculation on the source of the design. One possibility, cited by Roger Farrell, an OSU engineer and an authority on architect Yost, was a sketch published in an 1893 architectural magazine, showing a proposed depot tower with a pagoda-style roof. Another possibility may have been next door to the west here on Broad Street. A somewhat similar building used to stand on the other side of the tracks. Of frame construction, it had two three-story towers with pagoda-style roofs. According to the "Franklinton, Ohio 1999 Historic Calendar", that structure was the Macklin Hotel, which predated 1895 and was razed in 1955.

North Side, Fairgrounds, Ohio State University

No other place on earth has, within a few miles, two major structures by architect Peter Eisenman and a football stadium that once upon a time won an AIA gold medal.

Access: From Broad and High in downtown Columbus, drive north on High Street to the Convention Center. Continue north into Short North area; at Buttles turn left to Goodale Park and Sells House.

COLUMBUS CONVENTION CENTER, 1993

Eisenman Architects, New York, and Richard Trott and Partners, Columbus
400 North High Street
County convention center; open to public daily except during some events; inquire at reception to see ballroom if it isn't in use; 614/645-5000

New York architect Peter Eisenman, long an outspoken theoretician, built his first major structure in Columbus, the Wexner Center for the Arts (see below). This convention center started five years later, in 1988, with a competition that Eisenman won, and the result now has been in use for years. Given the world's many disappointing convention centers and arenas, it must be hard to design an immense building that looks reasonably good. This one does. The High Street facade is an abstract version of an older streetscape like that across the street; it's broken up into parts and tilted, with rows of rectangles simulating windows. Eisenman's recurring specialty seems to be long halls, and this one doesn't disappoint. The concourse runs most of the building's 700-foot length, not at a straight shot but while using changing angles, colors, and carpet patterns to provide street-like variety. At the back, the building has a five-acre exhibit hall. Initially all meeting rooms were built to seem atilt, but users found this so disturbing that smaller rooms were restored to plumb. The tilt remains in the ballroom, deemed big enough not to make anyone seasick. Construction was tricky. Richard T. Lombardi, project head for the joint-venture contractors, summed up. "Having worked for years to teach trades to work level and plumb, we had to teach the opposite," he said. "It drove everyone bananas." In 1999-2000 the building was being extended at the north end; the addition's design, sympathetic to the original, was by Karlsberger Architects, Columbus, with Eisenman as a consultant. The addition emerged, alas, on the level.

SHORT NORTH, NRHP/SHORT NORTH HD

The Short North has more urban vitality—as measured by shops, bars, restaurants, galleries, and people on the sidewalks at night—than anywhere else in Columbus. Just 20 years ago, this was a depressed North High Street neighborhood whose most conspicuous inhabitants were derelicts. Besides its location, its only real asset was a relatively intact wall of shabby late nineteenth-

▶ SHORT NORTH

and early twentieth-century buildings. So what happened? A few important early steps included the rehabbed Short North Tavern's opening in 1981 and offering chamber music and poetry readings. A Neighborhood Design Assistance Center gave property owners free advice on facade renovations. Art galleries launched a Gallery Hop that still draws big crowds on the first Saturday of the month. Expansion northward, led by art galleries moving for lower rents, is ongoing. The Victorian Gate, at 663 North High Street, an apartment and retail complex, is a new, 1990s development, very much in the scale of the older surrounding neighborhood; it was built on a long-vacant lot. The Victorian Gate has been so successful that it's hard to believe it took seven years to realize—mostly because prospective lenders saw it as too risky because it wasn't in the suburbs. In 1997 author James Kunstler told a Columbus audience that Victorian Gate was probably the country's best urban in-fill development; he wrote about it in his book, *Home from Nowhere*. Great as the Short North is now, becoming great was a slow process involving hundreds of people. Turnaround neighborhoods that stay turned around are not one-man shows or overnight wonders.

PETER SELLS HOUSE, C. 1895

Yost & Packard, Columbus
755 Dennison Avenue at Buttles Avenue, northwest corner Goodale Park
Private house

This splendid house looks as though it was built for a showman. It was. This was Peter Sells's house; with his brothers Sells ran one of the country's largest circuses, based in Columbus. The house is brick, dominated by a red-tile roof with flared eaves; originally the front roof had three dormers, also steeply roofed. After decades as a nursery school, the house had a new owner in 1998 and became a private residence again.

Access: Continue north on High Street to East Eleventh Avenue; turn right/east and drive a little over half a mile to Ohio Gate, at south edge of fairgrounds just east of Martin Janis Senior Center, 600 East Eleventh. (Except during fair, to drive into fairgrounds use entrance at 717 East Seventeenth Avenue; a parking fee is charged when grounds are in use.) Return from fairgrounds to High Street by turning around and driving west on Eleventh to Grant Avenue; turn right/north one block to Chittenden Avenue; turn left/west to High Street.

OHIO GATE, OHIO STATE FAIRGROUNDS, 1966

Carl E. Bentz, state architect; Donald C. Welsch, supervising architect and Jack Mayle, project architect for State Architect's Office, Columbus
East Eleventh Avenue between 600 East Eleventh and I-71
Gate to state fairgrounds, scheduled for razing in fall 2001

This is a gate as sign—OHIO—32 feet tall and 100 feet long. Built of weatherproof plywood and wood framing, the block letters are each thick enough, about 4.5 feet, and deep enough, almost 8 feet, to hold a person running a ticket booth. The O's and the H arch over 9-foot roadways originally for drive-in fairgoers. What a wonderful idea this gate was. Edward J. Keirns, who was fair manager at the time, and Martha Zwick, who was his secretary, both remember it as Governor James Rhodes's brainstorm. In 1993 the letters were painted teal and magenta. And in 2000, the fair announced that, with its wood framing, the gate was unsound and would have to be leveled and replaced by a $700,000 metal arch. In early 2001 the structure still stood and plans for a successor were under review. A restoration, said spokesperson Christina Minier, was definitely out.

To see more at the fairgrounds—Just inside the Ohio Gate, the three oldest exhibit buildings parallel each other; all three are frame sheds, roofs with no walls. The southernmost, which has the Poultry-Rabbit sign, dates from 1905, when it opened with a sign reading Machinery. The middle building, now Antiques and Collectibles, was originally Power Hall, for machines powered by a central steam engine. It dates from 1888 when Columbus architect Elah

▶ THE FAIRGROUNDS

Terrell designed a number of centennial structures for the fairgrounds, probably including this one. The northernmost, 1905, now Commercial Building, was originally Machines. This information comes from Lavon Shook, fair buff and author, who also reports that the yellow, green and maroon colors applied in a 1989 restoration were supposed to be the originals. He says another building, a kiosk southeast of the Administration Building, now an information booth, was one of Elah Terrell's 1888 designs; it was one of 23 restaurants the Columbus Board of Trade built.

Access: The eastern edge of Ohio State University's main campus is High Street north of Eleventh Avenue. The Wexner Center is opposite Fifteenth Avenue and adjacent to the Oval; from there walk to Hayes and Orton halls, both on the Oval. To reach Pomerene and Oxley, go to Neil Avenue, which is beyond the library at far end of Oval, and turn left. From Oxley turn around and walk back to West Seventeenth; turn left and go downhill to see Ohio Stadium. St. Stephen's Church is a few blocks north of the Wexner Center at High and West Woodruff Avenue, northwest corner. For a map on weekdays enter campus at West 12th Avenue and go to Student Visitor Center in Enarson Hall, 154 West 12th, 614/292-3030; or at any time check web site: http://campusvisit.osu.edu/

ARCHITECTS OF OHIO—More than anyone else, Joseph Warren Yost (1847-1923) and Frank Lucius Packard (1866-1923) were the architects of Ohio. Their signatures appear in every region of the state—not in major cities like Toledo, Cleveland, or Cincinnati, but almost everywhere else. They brought good design to county seats from Canton to Bowling Green, and towns from Barnesville to Piqua; many of their works are included in this guide. For 41 years, from 1882 to 1923, one or both of them was working in Columbus; from 1892 to 1899, they practiced there as partners. It was Columbus architecture's finest hour.

Just before they became partners, Yost and Packard were commissioned separately to design buildings facing Ohio State University's Oval: Hayes Hall is Packard's; Orton Hall is Yost's. Both buildings date from 1893 and both have massive round stone entrances, but after that they're quite different. With its tall bell tower, Orton Hall is the more imposing. It's Richardsonian Romanesque, asymmetrical, in rough-cut stone. Hayes is symmetrical, a three-story central section flanked by two-story wings, in a dark red brick with stone trim. Originally Hayes and Orton were to have separate power plants, but then when the university decided on a central plant for the

Orton Hall, Ohio State University, Columbus, Ohio.

▶ ORTON HALL

whole campus, that became Yost & Packard's first job. Five years later, together, they designed another building on the Oval, the immense, castle-like Armory, which, until it was razed after a fire in 1958, stood where the Wexner Center for the Arts is now. The Wexner's fragmented red-brick towers are a tribute to the Armory.

Yost and Packard were both native Ohioans. They grew up and lived in the kinds of communities for which they later designed; in one town after another, the best architecture to this day is the Yost and Packard buildings. Though both architects ultimately had some formal education and apprenticeship, neither had the advantage of a four-year university course or travel in Europe. Yost was the older, by 19 years. Born on a farm near Clarington, Monroe County, he made houses of clay and collected pictures of buildings as a boy, but actually becoming an architect was a long way off. He taught school and spent two years at Mount Union College; then he studied engineering and architecture on his own while working as a house painter and decorator. In 1869 he spent a year with a Wheeling architect, and then he went into practice in Bellaire. It was nine years before he could support himself as an architect; then, in 1882, he moved to Columbus and opened an office there.

Packard, born in Delaware, was the son of a builder who moved his family to Columbus in 1883. Packard attended Ohio State and the Massachusetts Institute of Technology, studying architecture at both; in 1887 he apprenticed in a New York City architectural firm. Even before that, in 1886, when he was 20, he'd won an architectural competition for a building at the Girls' Industrial School in Delaware.

When Yost and Packard became partners, Yost was the senior, the well known architect. Together they were very successful, the state's leading firm for public buildings, though actually they designed virtually every type of structure and worked in many styles. Examples include the Toledo & Ohio Central Railroad Station in Columbus, the Wood County Courthouse in Bowling Green (see also, Vol. II), and the Armory, which was a massive collection of turrets, towers, and crenellated parapets built around an enormous, round-arched entry. Their work was featured regularly in the architectural press. In about 1896, Yost & Packard published a promotional book, *Portfolio of Architectural Realities*, which listed works the two men had done, separately and together. It lists over 330 projects in Ohio—from courthouses to barns—and 22 in other states.

Yost was the one who moved on. He went to New York, where in 1901 he joined with Albert D'Oench and became the active partner in D'Oench and Yost. The firm was busy—it added a story to the top of the Tribune Building; it designed the library in Sandusky—but it clearly wasn't the prominent, prestigious practice that Yost left in Columbus. So why did he leave? Roger Farrell, who did a paper on Yost while working on a master's in city planning at OSU, says that the clue may lie in a speech Yost gave at an American Institute of Architects meeting in 1896. The subject was the use of steel and glass in architecture, concepts that even today seem modern but in 1896 hinted at revolution, especially for an architect whose commissions were all revival styles. Suggests Farrell, "Yost wanted

to build skyscrapers."

Packard remained in Columbus and ran a very successful practice. Barbara Powers, a staffer with the Ohio Historic Preservation Office, is the leading authority on Frank Packard. It was she who discovered the first use of the Yost & Packard name, for the power plant at Ohio State. She's given a downtown tour on the Columbus Civic Center, whose leading sponsor was Packard. A plan to redevelop a blighted Scioto River area with landscaping and handsome public buildings, the Civic Center has been largely forgotten, though Columbus City Hall and the Ohio Departments Building, above, were part of its never fully completed realization.

Powers has also weighed the extraordinary newspaper claims when Packard died, that he had designed more than 3,400 buildings. "It's unbelievable," she says. Of course, as a 1912 bio noted, Packard's firm had "a large office force and corps of able architects." Powers thinks that his principal role was the business side of architecture: contacting clients and securing jobs. Not surprisingly, she has also tracked designs, and parts of designs, that he used more than once.

Packard died suddenly in 1923, after a late night at the office. In tributes to a local architect that seem amazing today, Packard's death made the front pages of the city's three daily newspapers; a few days later, he was interred at Green Lawn Cemetery in a mausoleum of his own design.

And within a month afterwards, at the home of his daughter in Avalon, Pennsylvania, Yost also died. An era came full close.

▶ OSU AND ITS OVAL

Ohio State University

For over 60 years, ending in 1956, two men built Ohio State University. As professors of architecture and university architects, Joseph N. Bradford and Howard D. Smith designed well themselves and oversaw the work of others. As both were men of exceptional talents, the campus they created had grace and cohesion.

Lately the university has been in the throes of a building boom whose magnitude Bradford and Smith could never have dreamed of, and whose results have been uneven. (Faculty architects, who are not permitted extra work for the university, no longer design for their own turf.)

One of the great legacies of the past that's still intact is the Oval, the focal point of the campus. It's a large oval lawn surrounded by buildings, including three here, and criss-crossed by walks whose courses were set by paths worn in the grass.

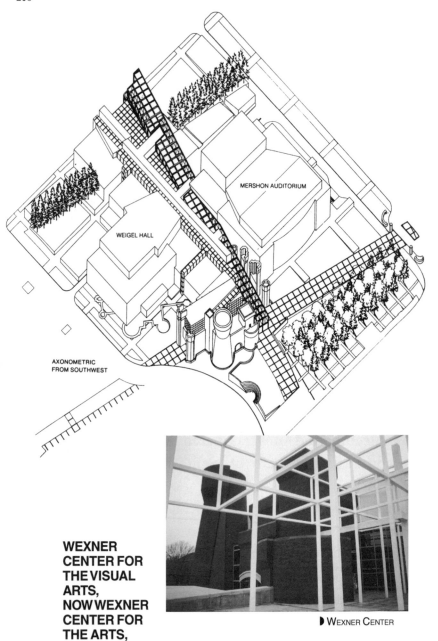

AXONOMETRIC
FROM SOUTHWEST

MERSHON AUDITORIUM

WEIGEL HALL

▶ Wexner Center

WEXNER CENTER FOR THE VISUAL ARTS, NOW WEXNER CENTER FOR THE ARTS, 1989

Eisenman Architects, New York and Richard Trott and Partners, Columbus
1871 North High Street
Gallery, theater, library, and office building; open daily; gallery closed Mondays
and between shows; 614/292-3535

Surely no other building at Ohio State University, and few if any buildings in Ohio, has received as much attention in the architectural press as the Wexner Center for the Visual Arts. That was mostly because of the architect, Peter Eisenman, who for years had been a leading architectural theorist, but who had actually built only four avant garde houses. The Wexner Center was his first major building. Pointing out that it was not at Yale or Princeton, Eisenman said, "It's a great thing about America that people in Columbus, Ohio, are building this crazy building." This project had a benefactor, OSU alum Leslie Wexner, who had amassed a fortune as a clothing merchant. Of the center's total $43 million cost, Wexner gave $25 million. The design, chosen in a competition in 1983, was at once the most daring and the most resourceful of the entries. The Eisenman-Trott team chose as its site a narrow space between the small Weigel Hall and the large Mershon Auditorium; they were able to spread out at the back, where a parking lot was, and underground. Fractured, abstracted brick towers herald the Wexner Center and recall the Armory on this site until 1958. But the structure's most striking feature is the white steel scaffolding, an oversized, multi-story jungle-gym-style scaffolding that forms a long exterior corridor between the Wexner and Mershon. The path slopes, so the perception of the built lines and their shadows holds surprises every time. This scaffolded corridor and its adjacent building are aligned with the campus grid and true north, though that means they are a little askew from nearby High Street, which diverges from true north by 12.25 degrees. Inside the building and downstairs, the truncated beams and posts that were astonishing in 1989 appear; a post interrupts the stairway itself. Downstairs, the gallery spaces line up along their own wonderful hall, which ascends, paralleling the corridor outside. Gallery spaces and, say, the arts library, have irregular shapes, which now seems the norm for conspicuous modern buildings. When the Wexner Center was under construction, critics and theoreticians dubbed it the first example of Deconstructivism, a style supposed to reveal more by, in a way, taking things apart. And what was benefactor Wexner's reaction to all this? "Left to my own devices," he said, "I might have designed a different kind of building." He was proud of the center, which he dubbed a "world-class" building, but later, when he was left to his own devices, he instigated a posh housing development in suburban New Albany, where all architecture is a revival of Georgian Revival.

HAYES HALL, 1893
Frank L. Packard, Columbus
108 North Oval Mall, NRHP
Classroom and office building

Frank L. Packard designed Hayes Hall, which is Ohio State's oldest building, at least by a few months. Red brick and brown sandstone, Hayes was built originally for manual, domestic, and mechanical training, including home economics and drawing, which Bill Arter studied here. It was named for ex-President Hayes, a university trustee, who died in January, 1893, just when the structure was needing a name. Interior has been altered.

ORTON HALL, 1893
J. W. Yost, Columbus
155 South Oval Mall, NRHP
Library, museum, classroom building

When Ohio State University opened in 1873, the president was Edward Orton, a geologist and one of seven faculty. In front of the campus's single unfinished building, Orton set up a table and enrolled 21 men and women students. He wrote down their names, their courses and later, their grades.

In his honor, 20 years later Orton Hall was built entirely of Ohio stone, in the order found in nature, the oldest at the bottom. Thus the lowest basement course is Dayton limestone from the Silurian age; the front steps are Columbus limestone from the Devonian; and the red sandstone trim is from the Mississippian. Inside the barrel-vaulted hall displays 24 decorative columns, each from a different stone; labels are on a placard near the door. Even the floor tiles were made from Ohio clay. What a splendid pride in Ohio all this showed. Orton is Richardsonian Romanesque in style, has a two-story, round-arched door and a round bell tower. It is one of the few old campus buildings in the state that retains much of its original interior. See, for example, the oak-paneled two-story library left of the entrance.

POMERENE HALL, 1922

Joseph N. Bradford,
Columbus
1760 Neil Avenue
Office and classroom building

❱ ORTON HALL, LOOKING UP AT THE ARCH

Another of this campus's good old interiors is that of the Tudor Revival Pomerene Hall. It was designed by Professor of Architecture Joseph N. Bradford, who was also university architect; clearly, he was good at his work. Hall ceilings are ornamented plaster and carved wooden doors have Tudor arches. The old women's gym, a fine unaltered room, is on the third floor. But some modern changes at Pomerene have been thoughtless. A side balcony that overlooks Mirror Lake (on this campus, perhaps *the* prime view) has evidently been accommodating bigger and bigger ventilation units for a long time now. The lowest floor has a cafeteria-rathskeller with ceramic tiles, high wainscoting in a dark, paneled wood, and ceiling arches. In spring 1999, in this romantic Medieval room, black vinyl table tops were being attached to the paneled wall.

OXLEY HALL, 1908

Florence Kenyon Hayden, Columbus; advisory architect, Wilbur Mills, Columbus
1712 Neil Avenue
Office building

Built as a women's dormitory, Oxley Hall was designed by a woman, Florence
Kenyon Hayden, later the wife of James Rector. In 1970, she told Bill Arter
that she'd been a star student of Joseph Bradford, who chose her to design
Oxley Hall. The university trustees were so incredulous that they assigned
her a male associate. After one day of trying to deal with the associate, she
locked him out of the office and carried on by herself. She finished the plans
in 17 days and then supervised construction, which came in early and under
budget. The red-brick Oxley Hall has an octagonal tower and array of
gables, large and small, under deep eaves. The interior has been altered. See
also Florence Kenyon Hayden Rector's own house, below in Olde Towne
East.

OHIO STADIUM, 1922

Howard Dwight Smith, Columbus
411 Woody Hayes Drive, NRHP
Football stadium; reconstruction due for completion 2001

Can any building in this book—or in all of Ohio—be loved more ardently
than Ohio Stadium? Probably not. This temple of football covers ten acres
of hallowed ground, where Ohio State University plays and usually wins its
home football games. Built on the Olentangy River floodplain, it was and is
largely alone, looming over surrounding flats of grass and asphalt (parking
lots on game days.) Horseshoe-shaped, built of reinforced concrete, it is
immense: almost 100 feet high and a third of a mile around. When built it
had 62,000 seats on two levels—more than a four-fold increase over the old
Ohio Field. It has classical elements: a recessed coffered half dome entrance
in the round end, and a pair of rectangular 109-foot towers at the ends of the
horseshoe's open arms. The classical references were by design, Priscilla
Smith D'Angelo says. She's the daughter of architect Howard D. Smith
(1886-1958), who as university architect and professor of architecture from
1929 to 1956, was to design over 50 campus buildings. A 1907 OSU
graduate, Smith earned a master's from Columbia and then won a Perkins
Scholarship for a year's travel abroad. Rome and Greece were his chosen

destinations, D'Angelo says, and, judging from the column pictures all over the house when she was growing up, he never lost interest. Thus Ohio Stadium was inspired by Rome. The curves are from the Coliseum; the half dome, from the Pantheon. Howard Smith's monumental design won him a national honor, a gold medal award from the American Institute of Architects. Five-story arches lined the outside wall of his stadium; above each, relatively small, boxy windows appear in the concrete wall. The stadium was handsome and also versatile. In the west wall, under the seats, it later had three levels of co-op dormitories. Ripley's "Believe It Or Not" cited the dorms for being built from the top down—the top floor was attached to the wall first; the other two were added below it. Though some stadium rooms didn't have windows, all were highly prized. In the 1960s, labs and offices were built in the east wall. Though by 1998 seating capacity had increased gradually to about 90,000, Ohio Stadium entered a construction phase that year. Though overall refurbishment was long overdue, this became a $187 million project to add 7,000 seats. Suddenly at this state university, high-priced "private hospitality suites" and "club seats" were being introduced. The scholarship dorm had to go somewhere else, as did the track. Except for the towers and half-dome, the whole building was to disappear within a 40-foot-deep enclosure, 40 feet higher than the original. It will mimic the original arches but otherwise alter the appearance. The goal is simple: more money, if only to cover the $187 million construction. This time no one is aiming for an AIA gold medal.

ST. STEPHEN'S EPISCOPAL CHURCH, 1953

Brooks &
Coddington,
Columbus
30 West Woodruff
Avenue at North High Street
Church, chapel, meeting and classrooms; building open Monday through
Thursday, sanctuary accessible; 614/294-3749

▶ ST. STEPHEN'S

It's hard to realize now just how daring St. Stephen's Episcopal Church was in 1953. At that time, *Architectural Forum* lamented, congregations usually preferred "to hide behind sentimental images from the past." The magazine featured 11 exceptions—modern churches that realized an "expression of a real faith for our times." Principal among them was St. Stephen's. St. Stephen's faces Woodruff Avenue with an A-frame gable and all-glass front wall, while a solid brick wall shuts off traffic noise on the High Street side. The church and its wings enclose a courtyard, a modern cloister, and on the far side a chapel, paralleling the sidewalk, echoes the main church with its smaller gable. This chapel is well worth seeing; with off-center windows and off-center hanging lamps, it becomes two rooms in one. Inside the main

church evenly spaced welded steel beams make a series of inverted Vs that bend to reach the floor. The sanctuary's most striking feature is the altar, its back wall illuminated by daylight from an unseen, heavenly source; the effect is perfect. The light source in fact is a tower with glass bricks on one wall, clearly visible outside. I saw St. Stephen's with friends, architects Ruth Gless, who's on St. Stephen's vestry, and Frank Elmer. She talked about design—the blue mosaic walls that flank and cover the entry; the traditional layout, with distinct and well-defined vestibule, nave, and altar. He pointed out how the architects were trying out ideas—were inventing how to design a modern church. Not only *Architectural Forum* noticed the result. So in due course did *Saturday Evening Post* and *Life*. After one of Rev. R. Cameron Miller's first services at St. Stephen's in 1989 (he recently moved on), an older gentleman introduced himself as Gilbert Coddington, the architect. He wanted to be sure that the new rector wasn't going to mess with his building. Of the architects, Brooks & Coddington, Gilbert Coddington (1907-1995) is by far the best known today, because from 1961 to 1977 he taught architecture at OSU. His partner was T(heodore) Woodbridge Brooks (1907-1985). In designing, Brooks & Coddington used charettes— several days of all-staff brainstorming, with ideas posted on the wall. So recalls retired architect Andrew Macioce, who as a student worked a little on St. Stephen's and who later joined the firm for a few years. Macioce remembers Coddington as a detail man, Brooks as a designer able to lure clients. "They made a tremendous team," Macioce says. "For a number of years that office was Columbus's most talented."

South Side

Traditionally much of the South Side has been housing for workers in nearby industries. That's reflected in these architectural sites, working-class neighborhoods of the past, German Village, and present, in the South Side Settlement House area.

Access: From downtown drive south on Third Street, which passes over the interstate and into German Village.

GERMAN VILLAGE, NRHP

When Richard Moe, president of the National Trust for Historic Preservation, toured German Village in late 1997, he could hardly contain his delight. "In my business," he announced, "it doesn't get any better than this." German Village is Ohio's most successful inner city rehab, the largest privately funded historic restoration in the country, and one of the most pleasant city neighborhoods anywhere—so pleasant that now it's hard to believe it wasn't always. The best way to see German Village is on foot, moseying along brick sidewalks, checking out alleys, houses so close (on City Park) their side gutters overlap, iron fences. Landmarks include St. Mary's Catholic Church, 684 South Third Street, and Schiller Park, at the foot of Third Street. North of the interstate, Trinity Evangelical Lutheran Church, 1858, steeple, 1876, 404 South Third Street, symbolizes the northern third of German Village, which was all torn down. Almost 50 years after that demolition, the area around Trinity still seems bleak. All of German Village is worth seeing. Third Street is the main drag, with commerce and residences interspersed; a block to the east, Mohawk has brick paving with the center

▶ GERMAN VILLAGE

line in white bricks. City Park and Jackson are among the streets with special charm; beer barons built the Queen Annes on Deshler Avenue south of Schiller Park. German Village is on the National Register of Historic Places. Be sure to stop at the German Village Society, 588 South Third Street, 614/221-8888 for a flyer with a map and/or a walking tour that takes in 42 sites; open daily except Sunday; check hours. The society sponsors group bus tours. The Visitors Center also has material on the Brewery District, a rehab area just to the west of northern German Village.

DUTCH SINGLE COTTAGE, NOW FIRESIDE BOOK COMPANY, C. 1850
503 City Park Avenue at Blenkner Street
Used bookstore open daily except Monday; 614/621-1928

The Fireside Book Company is in a genuine Dutch Single Cottage, though it happens to be an exception to the prevailing red brick. This house is frame, but with its limestone foundation, brick chimney and diminutive size, it's a good example of a Dutch Single. It also has the great advantage of having regular business hours, so it's possible to walk around inside and to see the second-floor garret. Bryan Saums, co-owner of the bookstore with his wife, Jane Landwehr, says the building has been a warehouse, flower shop, doctor's office and candle shop. Now it's housing 17,500 books.

GERMAN VILLAGE: DEFINING AND POLICING THE LOOK—

Frank Fetch invented German Village. In 1960 he set out to save this declining neighborhood—people called it the Old South End—from demolition. One tactic was a better name: German Village. Then, by driving around to scope out boundaries for a general unity of style and period, Fetch defined the place. In 40 years, what he called his "windshield boundaries" have been challenged but never changed.

Fetch founded the German Village Society, which stayed the bulldozers. As a city administrator, he knew how to lead his "village" through zoning changes and, ultimately, into designation as a historic district. He engineered a preservation commission with legal powers to review architectural changes. Fetch himself demonstrated what could be done. Over the years, he bought and rehabbed half a dozen houses—and sold them at a profit.

Gradually German Village shed its one-time shabbiness to become a planner's dream: a middle-class urban area. The National Trust gave Fetch an award for its rescue, and the Village passed Ohio State University as Columbus's leading tourist attraction.

The tourists come partly for the commerce—restaurants, corner bars, and shops—but also for architecture. German Village is an architectural ensemble: many ordinary buildings that together become something wonderful. Individually, these are largely unpretentious structures, without exact dates or known architects. Built mostly between 1840 and 1920, they were houses for immigrant German workers, many of whom manned nearby breweries. The houses are typically red brick, with limestone foundations, limestone stoops, slate roofs. What they don't have is size, for a typical cottage has only 950 square feet.

German Village houses include some Queen Annes, but most are cottages—story-and-a-half "Dutch" singles and doubles with gable fronts—and simplified two-story Italianates with shallow hip roofs. Though the mid-nineteenth-century cottages are German Village's signature dwelling, an intern who surveyed them in 1994 alarmed residents by identifying only 12 "pristine," or essentially unchanged cottages. Today Carol Gabriel, the German Village Society's preservation officer, says they've reevaluated his assessments and believe that only two or three really pristine cottages remain without additions. Perhaps the pristine cottage exists only in imagination. Its small size has both saved the cottage—people could afford to renovate it—and doomed its pristine state—it's too small.

German Village's coherent look— the nineteenth-century patina, the red brick in sidewalks as well as buildings, the village feel of alleys, trees and small yards in a place where you can see downtown skyscrapers just to the north—means higher real-estate values within Fetch's boundaries than just outside. What keeps the look coherent is, in good part, the preservation commission. It polices the look.

In German Village stop-work orders have been handed to owners in the midst of house painting or tearing off a porch. A few years ago, a woman was threatened with a 60-day jail sentence for building an over-large dormer on her cottage. The sentence was suspended after she made the dormer smaller to be less obvious from the street. The commission argued that the dormer overwhelmed the cottage's modest proportions. The owner lamented, "In all seriousness, is this really 'German Architecture' we're discussing, or something else?"

Beautiful communities have to have an underlying consensus among residents. For some people, enforcing that consensus looms as an authoritarian assault on property rights. But the chairman of German Village's preservation commission is a compact, mild-mannered man named Michael Rosen. Rosen, an architect, has been one of the seven volunteer German Village preservation commissioners since 1971. He believes that the commission helped German Village evolve as a stable, cohesive residential community without freak construction and demolitions for office and apartment blocks. Most German Village residents agree. Over the years, Rosen says, the people most thwarted and most angered by the commission were typically out-of-towners with "grandiose ideas to make a suburban-type house." German Village is not the suburbs.

"The thing I try to tell people," says Rosen, "is that although they own a building, they're really only a temporary trustee."

About a hundred Ohio localities have preservation commissions, but German Village's is the oldest and the fussiest. It's the fussiest, says Columbus's preservation officer, Diane Cole, because as a rehab neighborhood, German Village is relatively finished. "These are third and fourth renovations," she says, "so they're down to picayune things like paint color."

It hasn't always

been that way, Rosen says. In 1971 any improvement—painting, adding a family room—was welcome. "Then gradually," he says, "we went from repair and rehabilitation into restoration." Restoration is today's ideal; the old house should look as it did when it was built, at least on the outside. An attentive stroller will spot some deviations from the ideal— aluminum siding, chain-link fences, a house painted chartreuse yellow with blue shutters—but Rosen says all predate the 1989 publication of German Village Guidelines, a 164-page manual that gets down to details like mortar composition and how to nail shingles.

The commission, says Rosen, is not flatly opposed to progress. For instance, it allows for cars. "German Village was built for people who couldn't afford horses," Rosen says. "In the twentieth century people may have two or three cars. How can you tell them they can't have a garage?"

The inventor of German Village, Frank Fetch, died at his German Village home in January 1985; he was 85 years old. His public legacy included the houses he had rehabbed and German Village, the creation of his savvy. Perhaps the only real hitch in this was the name. German Village could have happened only in America.

DUTCH SINGLE COTTAGE, 1871

766 Mohawk Street just north of Columbus Street
Private house

Preservation officer Carol Gabriel cites this brick house as an example of a nearly pristine cottage (it has a tiny addition at the back.)

Access: From German Village drive east (on, say, Livingston Avenue just to the north, or Whittier Street) to Parsons Avenue; turn right/ south. Since Innis is one-way eastbound, pass it and turn right/ west on Reeb, then north to Innis. An alternative route is to drive south on High Street, then east on Innis.

SOUTH SIDE SETTLEMENT HOUSE, 1980

Robert Mangurian and Craig Hodgetts, Studio Works, Venice, California;
associated architects Feinknopf, Macioce & Schappa, Columbus
310 Innis Avenue
Neighborhood recreation and support center; open weekdays; visitors welcome;
614/444-9868

Among architects, the South Side Settlement House has generated a lot of excitement, though that's not to say it's well known in Columbus; Innis Avenue is remote from hype. In a residential neighborhood there, this gray, ship-like building, with a round section in the middle, stretches along the sidewalk. Inside, the round middle holds a kitchen, dining area and fireplace; it has a barrel-vault ceiling. A two-story gym is at the west end; a courtyard and theater at the east. The real surprise is that the concrete-block interior is so cozy and homelike. For the young architects who designed South Side, who spent weeks in Columbus staying in people's homes and accepting invitations to church dinners, it was "one of those rare times when you give your all." So recalls one of them, Craig Hodgetts, a native Cincinnatian who practices now in Santa Monica. Just out of college, he and Robert Mangurian met in New York and formed Studio Works in 1968. Later, when South Side needed an architect for their new building, a VISTA volunteer from New York suggested Studio Works. The first set of plans for South Side won a 1976 Progressive Architecture Design Award, but

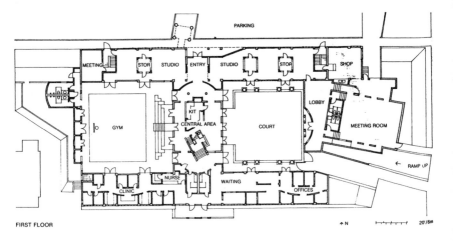

FIRST FLOOR

▶ SOUTH SIDE SETTLEMENT HOUSE

fundraising fell so short that the project was almost abandoned. Mangurian, then in Rome, and Hodgetts, in Los Angeles, started sending ideas back and forth. The settlement house reemerged less as abstract, rectilinear architecture with a capital A and more as a little Medieval town, abstracted but with two courtyards, (one the gym) flanking what Hodgetts calls "the nurturing kitchen between. It was almost like an extended household." Everyone preferred the new concept. All through construction, Hodgetts and Mangurian were on site. They did things now inconceivable and even hazardous, like getting a 40-foot multi-ton steel beam out of the nearly finished gym. The contractor balked, so the architects rallied half a dozen OSU students, collected ladders and winches, and did it themselves. They were so involved that, Hodgetts says, "We treated each concrete block as an individual entity. Every one was drawn. We searched catalogues for odd blocks." With the community collecting money in jars on store counters, the architects cut costs by lowering the structure 16 inches, which was two courses of block. Needing cheap, robust door knobs, they adapted $3 stainless masons' trowels with wood handles that they found in a hardware store. They made columns out of concrete-filled spiral metal culvert pipes first noticed in a construction yard. "We were totally mad," Hodgetts says, nostalgically. But he's well satisfied with the result. "People are using it very much as we imagined. It's a building as tool rather than monument."

East Side

East side Columbus has some of the city's more elegant old residential neighborhoods.

Access: From downtown Columbus, take Third Street (one-way southbound) one block past State Street to Town Street; turn left/ east.

TOWN STREET, NRHP/EAST TOWN STREET HD

East of Grant Street, Town Street retains much of the flavor of a late nineteenth-century residential neighborhood. The 1852 Greek Revival Kelton House, at 586 East Town Street, offers tours Sunday afternoons, fee; 614/464-2022.

615 EAST TOWN STREET, C. 1875

Private house

This Second Empire house is a personal favorite of mine. I like the convex second-floor mansard just below the tower's concave third-floor mansard, which also has four dormers. I like the three-window bay, the lintels on top of the windows—in short, just about everything there is to see.

Olde Towne East

Olde Towne East is a late nineteenth- and early twentieth-century residential neighborhood good enough not to need those extra *e*'s in its name. Lea Ann Sterling's pictorial guide, *Historic Homes of Olde Towne*, was published in 1999 by the Olde Towne East Neighborhood Association; 614/221-4411; or check the shop at the Columbus Metropolitan Library, 96 South Grant Avenue just north of Town. By stopping there you'll see the lovely Beaux Arts Carnegie library, 1906, designed by Albert Randolph Ross, New York, and Wilbur T. Mills, Columbus. The houses and Fair Avenue School below are all on National Register in Columbus Near East Side District.

▶ FLORENCE KENYON HAYDEN RECTOR HOUSE

Access: Continue east; after crossing over interstate the street name changes to Bryden Road. To see Rector House turn left/north at Eighteenth Street; drive a full block to Franklin; turn left to 878. To see AME Zion Church return to Bryden. Then continue east on Bryden, past Myers House; turn left/north on Kelton Avenue; at park turn left/west on road which becomes Fair Avenue, where school is. Just west of school take Latta Avenue north to Broad Street/State Route 16 and turn right/east.

FLORENCE KENYON HAYDEN RECTOR HOUSE, 1926

Florence Kenyon Hayden Rector, Columbus
878 Franklin Avenue two doors west of Eighteenth Street
Private house

In the annals of Ohio architecture Florence Kenyon Hayden Rector (1882-1973) is a name of distinction, for she was the state's first licensed woman architect and, through the first three decades of the twentieth century, she was the only woman practicing architecture in Columbus. As her house shows, she was good at her work. I learned about Rector from Lea Ann Sterling, an attorney who in 1997-98 wrote a book, *Historic Homes of Olde*

Towne, with 50 houses illustrated in color. Architect Rector grew up in the handsome Victorian house, c. 1888, at 870 Franklin, where her widowed mother raised two daughters, Gillette and Kenyon, apparently named for achievement on a masculine scale. ("Florence", Sterling says, was just a nickname.) Gillette went to dental school at Ohio State and ultimately became a renowned authority on periodontal disease. Kenyon also went to Ohio State, where she studied architecture and designed Oxley Hall, a women's dormitory (see also). In 1910 Kenyon Hayden married a physician, James Rector—designing physicians' offices became a specialty of hers—and they had a son and a daughter. For her own family house, built on the east part of her mother's yard, Rector designed a distinctive stucco facade with irregular windows and a recessed round-arched entry. Owner William W. Taschek showed me around the interior, which has practical features like closets and built-in drawers at every turn. They're all in a mellow golden brown gumwood, which is beautiful with golden oak floors. Another design feature was low relief—minimizing dust harbors. Taschek especially likes the house's windows, placed for natural light in all parts of the house. Every room has a fireplace, typically a small, low one, with its own decoration, such as a terra cotta braid or tiles. The third floor is mostly one large attic room. This was Rector's studio; her drafting desk is still there. Off it at the back, a parapet encloses a large open porch. The house is meticulously finished. And the element in the bathroom's electric heater is shaped like a flower, visible when it's red hot.

FIRST METHODIST EPIS-COPAL CHURCH, NOW FIRST AFRICAN METHOD-IST EPISCOPAL ZION CHURCH, 1900

George Bellows, Sr., Columbus
873 Bryden Road
Church; sanctuary normally may be seen weekdays when office is open;
614/252-2184

In the late nineteenth century, George Bellows, Sr. (1829-1913) was one of Columbus's leading architects. Even so, the name is known today largely because he

COLUMBUS, OHIO. First Methodist Episcopal Church.

▶ FIRST AFRICAN METHODIST

gave it also to his son, who became painter George Bellows. The Columbus Museum of Art owns a wonderful portrait the son did of his father as an old man. The senior Bellows, himself a member of this Methodist congregation, designed a large Romanesque Revival church, in limestone, with tracery, or stone dividers, in the enormous windows. Outside the church has a tall square tower and turrets sprouting at every opportunity. Inside the octagonal sanctuary, which seats 450 people, has a remarkable stained glass dome and fine stained-glass windows. Of the windows on the right when facing the altar, the memorial to Laura Monnet was designed by George Bellows, Jr. The sanctuary is on the Akron Plan, so that the plain wall left of the altar could open to include Sunday school classes in the service. On the far side of that wall is Fuller Hall, a U-shaped room finished in dark wood, with classrooms on two levels. AME Zion bought this building from First Methodist Church, which closed in 1968.

CHARLES FREDERICK MYERS HOUSE, 1896

1330 Bryden Road
Private house

This fine house, in brick, stone, and terra cotta, is Columbus's best example of the Chateauesque style. The authors of *Architecture: Columbus* speculate on whether Joseph Yost might have designed it. Yost's own house was nearby, at 1216 Bryden, and has some similar features.

FAIR AVENUE SCHOOL, 1890

Frank L. Packard, Columbus
1395 Fair Avenue
Public elementary school

With its central tower looming up some four-and-a-half stories, this red brick and stone school makes a romantic landmark in a residential neighborhood. Fair Avenue School is an example of Frank Packard's work before he and Joseph Yost became partners. The modern additions at the sides are not attractive.

Bexley and East Columbus

Bexley is an urban suburb, laid out on a grid in the early twentieth century, and today offering older houses with plaster walls and screened porches. It is also one of the relatively few remaining places where children can walk to school—even high school—and where people can walk to the library and the best movie theater in Columbus. In fact some people so like living near the library and walking to the movies, that they can nigh unto never leave. At least, that's been my experience.

Access: Drive east on Broad Street. Sessions Drive, a private street, has a small sign on north side of street east of Meadow Park Avenue and west of Parkview Avenue. To see Jeffrey Mansion turn north on Parkview; drive one block to Clifton, where house is on northwest corner. Kahiki used to be east on Broad, past James Road.

SESSIONS VILLAGE, 1927-1931

Robert R. Reeves of Miller & Reeves, Columbus
East Broad Street, NRHP
Private residential community; gate opens for cars during daytime; visitors interested in architecture may enter and view from the sidewalks and street

▶ SESSIONS VILLAGE

The name comes from a one-time landowner, Francis Sessions, but the concept came from an architect named Robert R. Reeves, of Miller & Reeves, who drew inspiration from old villages in France—villages he'd first seen when he won a trip as a prize for designing a monument. From the beginning, in 1927, Reeves was given a free hand in planning Sessions Village. That, as Bill Arter asserted, was "a happy decision." Sessions Village, set north of Broad on a private street called Sessions Drive, is a group of Norman Revival houses inspired by what Reeves called "the minor domestic architecture of France." Four dwellings along Broad Street—two attached houses on either side of the entrance—set the tone with steep slate roofs, stucco and half timbering. So does a second-floor extension that bridges the entry road between two of these homes. Past the bridge, houses are brick, stucco, and half-timbered. Most abut the sidewalk, though they have private walled gardens behind. Each house is different, but Reeves designed all the early ones before building any; he envisioned them as a whole. Inside the gate, the road bends away from the Broad Street and forms a Y with a plaza-like widening and even a little fountain at the fork. Eleven separate buildings, mostly close to the entry, were built in the original phase, from 1927 to 1931, when the Depression halted construction, which didn't resume until after World War II, in 1946. Then R.R. Reeves, an architect and son of Robert R., oversaw the completion of 14 more houses, which he and other architects designed. Sessions Village was just one of the places Bill Arter wrote about; it was included in *Columbus Vignettes II.* Arter was an artist, creative director for an advertising agency. In the 1960s and early 1970s he went around Columbus sketching buildings and urban settings that caught his eye. Then he'd research the site and write a chatty, fact-filled text for publication in the Columbus *Dispatch's Sunday Magazine.* Ultimately Arter collected his sketches in four books, *Columbus Vignettes,* I, II, III and IV. They seem especially valuable now because he was able to talk face-to-face with principals, such as architect Florence Kenyon Hayden Rector, who are no longer around.

ROBERT H. JEFFREY HOUSE, NOW JEFFREY MANSION, 1905, 1922, 1926

Frank L. Packard, Columbus
165 North Parkview Avenue
Bexley community center;
offices for city Recreation
Department; open and
accessible weekdays; 614/258-
5755

▶ Jeffrey Mansion

Robert H. Jeffrey started building this house in the country while he was mayor of Columbus, a job to which he'd been elected at 29. Three years after his mayoral term, in 1908, Jeffrey and some friends met on the back porch of this house and founded Bexley, (which nowadays, at least, seems disloyal for a recent mayor.) Bill Arter reports that Jeffrey, son of the founder of Jeffrey Manufacturing, was quite a remarkable rich boy. After studying in Germany and at Columbus Latin School, and after graduating from Williams College, Jeffrey worked for a year in Ohio and Illinois coal mines; then he spent another year in the company's drafting room and chain shop. He finished work early enough to walk to Ohio State to study law; at night he went to classes at Columbus Business College. After he was mayor, he had a successful career with Jeffrey Manufacturing. In 1941, 20 years before his death, he donated his house and its extensive parklike grounds to Bexley, and the next year, he moved out. Visible at the end of a straight entry drive, Jeffrey Mansion is an exuberant Jacobean Revival red brick house with stone trim. It has two-and-a-half stories, crenellated parapets, an octagonal tower. Its most prominent feature, a projecting stone entry which holds the stone stairway, was added in 1922. Except for that stairway, the interior

▶ KAHIKI SUPPER CLUB

doesn't live up to the exterior; it even seems smaller than expected. The front hall, which has an enormous stone fireplace, was the main living area. The adjacent library and diningroom have 10-foot doors with chestnut trim and high stone fireplaces. Upstairs rooms have been altered somewhat to accommodate offices. At the back an open porch was enclosed and a stone entry added in 1989. Don't miss the back of the house. Landscaping added there in 1926 includes a fine array of terraces and stairways descending to a large lawn.

KAHIKI SUPPER CLUB, 1961

Ralph Sounik and Ned Eller of Design Associates, Columbus, architects; Coburn Morgan, Columbus, interior design
3583 East Broad Street, NRHP
Former restaurant; razed in November 2000 after site was sold for a Walgreen drugstore

The curve of the Kahiki's roofline, visible from the west on Broad Street, signals a building that's not only unlike anything else in its neighborhood of strip centers, but is unlike anything else in Ohio. Or the world, for that matter. The Kahiki is a Polynesian restaurant both in menu and in total ambiance; it transports you. Polynesian restaurants were popular after World War II, for many Americans had served in the south Pacific. Today, says restaurant president Michael Tsao, the Kahiki has become historic Polynesia.

While it has stayed the same since 1961, the real Polynesia has gone on evolving. I can think of no other building whose exterior and interior so completely recreate another place. It's not surprising to read in Ohio Historic Preservation Office staffer Nathalie Wright's National Register form that all the design initiative came from the interior designer, Coburn Morgan. It was he who traveled to Polynesia with restaurant founders Bill Sapp and Lee Henry; it was he who outlined the exterior and suggested the architects. The structure is an A-frame, with curving sides sweeping low; the eight heavy wooden supporting beams, visible inside, are anchored to low concrete posts outside. The elaborate triangular facade, painted, approached on foot by a bridge over a moat, has two 20-foot Easter Island heads topped by flaming pots. Inside are five bamboo and grass tropical huts, which hold the entry, the bar, and dining areas. At the back, rows of booths along the walls look into a greenhouse rain forest (west booths) or an aquarium (east). Tables are monkeywood, chairs rattan and bamboo; ornament includes canoes, once live coconut palms, shark jaws, preserved turtles, Polynesian tapestries, and so on. Even Michael Tsao, at Kahiki since 1978, says he still finds a blowfish or turtle that he hasn't noticed before. Tsao, a native of Shanghai, started in the California restaurant business as a dishwasher. By the time a new Kahiki owner recruited him, he was managing Trader Vic's in Los Angeles. Why did he move? Because of Kahiki's architecture. He walks over to a booth next to the rain forest greenhouse in which part of a heavy support beam can be seen. "About ten years ago," says Tsao, "there was a pair of cockatiels in there and they decided to make a family. But for their nest they dug into the wood, and made a hole that big." His hands form a round shape almost as big as a soccer ball. "We caught it in time," he says. "Right away we flew engineers here. But if we hadn't found that hole, the Kahiki would fall down." He points out a metal plate now reinforcing that beam. "Now," says Tsao, "we don't put cockatiels in there. Just finches."

Westerville

Westerville is known for Otterbein College and temperance—it was the long-time headquarters of the Anti-Saloon League, whose descendant organizations disbanded in 1973. The older residential neighborhood around these sites makes an interesting walk.

Access: From Kahiki take Broad Street east to I-270; take highway north to State Street/State Route 3, Westerville. Exit; turn right/north on State Street and drive about a mile and a half to Plum Street; turn left/west to see Shinto Shrine. To see Otterbein College's Towers Hall, continue west on Plum to Grove Street; turn right/north.

▶ SHINTO SHRINE

SHINTO SHRINE, ABOUT 1962

109 South State Street at Plum
Shrine is part of Japanese Museum; much of shrine is visible from Plum Street;
museum open for group tours; fee; 614/882-2964; or Kaye Henderson, 360/577-
6731

American characters have been alive and well in the twentieth century; one of them thought Westerville should have a Shinto Shrine. It comes as a real surprise now amid Plum Street's all-American ambiance—the houses, lawns and shade trees of a classic neighborhood. But there it is: a pair of curved, red Oriental gables behind a red gate along the sidewalk. This shrine is the real thing. All 26 tons of it were fitted into 176 packages and shipped from Okinawa, where it was built to order for a Westerville Japanophile, George Henderson II. After World War II Henderson spent 28 years as an Army translator in Japan and the Far East, long enough to make him homesick whenever he was home. In 1956-58 he rebuilt his father's old medical office as a teahouse. Then he ordered this shrine, a replica of an original constructed in 638 on the island of Kyushu, Japan. Henderson put it together himself, with help from his son and Japanese language instructors from Ohio State; parts were notched to fit together like Lincoln logs. The wood is tsuga, a pine; metal detailing is brass. Henderson chose this particular shrine because it dates from a period of Chinese influence— evident both in the styling and in the paint, which seemed a sensible choice for Westerville; most Shinto shrines are unpainted. When Henderson died in 1979, his son, George III, inherited the shrine and teahouse. Though the son now lives and works in Washington state, he and his family—his wife Kaye and three children—arrive every summer to keep up the red paint and the garden. Kaye says that visitors may enter this shrine because it was never consecrated. At a real shrine in Japan, people pray outside, entering only for special ceremonies at birth and marriage.

TOWERS HALL, 1872

Robert T. Brookes, Columbus
0 Grove Street, NRHP
Otterbein College classrooms and offices; 614/890-3000

Towers Hall, Otterbein College's Old Main, really does have an address of zero on Grove Street, but it exists in fact: a big red-brick building with all-different towers. Style is High Victorian Gothic.

Dayton

Architecturally, Dayton is better than it knows. For instance, its downtown Main Street has a long and classy row of medium-high high rises. But unlike other Ohio cities, Dayton hasn't documented the origins of many of them. As for architectural talent, local historians do know that Howard Daniels and Frank Andrews, who both attained national stature, worked here early in their careers, and each designed an exceptional building downtown. But few people in Dayton know that the Olmsted Brothers had more projects here than anywhere else outside New York and their home city of Boston. And no one knows anything about the Dayton-based Whyte family, who produced exceptional architectural sculptors and designers. See the Forest Avenue Presbyterian Church below, for a glimpse of their work. ¶ In its losses to the automobile, Dayton has suffered considerably. Thus I-75 blocks the view of the Day-

ton Art Institute from downtown. The YMCA
is visible, but for the wrong reason: it stands
beyond acres of partly used parking lots. ¶ This
tour covers Downtown; the Art Institute Area
and Dayton View; and Oakwood.

Downtown Dayton

Access: Dayton is south of I-70 on I-75. For downtown exit from I-75 at U.S. 35 and drive east to Main Street/Jefferson Street exit; Jefferson is one-way north into downtown. Coming from the east on I-70 take I-675 south to 35; drive west to Main/Jefferson. Downtown Dayton has numbered streets running east-west; Monument Avenue is northernmost, then First Street. Main Street and Third, both two-way, are the principal thoroughfares; for streets, north, south, east, and west begin at that intersection. The following tour is in order for a loop tour on foot; Ludlow and Wilkinson Streets parallel Main to the west. Start at the Old Courthouse at Main and Third. Take West Third past the Arcade to Ludlow, turn left/south to Fourth Street, for the Daily News; then right/west to Wilkinson for Sacred Heart; then right/north to Second Street for other sites. Turn right there, then left on Ludlow to Monument for YMCA and finally, back down Main for Victoria and return to Courthouse. To see the Oregon District, a small, picturesque historic neighborhood with some amenities, including restaurants, drive south on Main to Fifth Street; turn left/east. Downtown maps are available at the Dayton CVB in the Dayton Convention Center at East Fifth and South Main; open weekdays; 800/221-8235; 937/226-8211.

MONTGOMERY COUNTY COURTHOUSE, 1850
Howard Daniels, Cincinnati
7 North Main Street at Third Street, NRHP
Former courthouse awaiting renovation

This courthouse is such a good example of Greek Revival—at once true to
the style and original—and was so well built, that it is not only one of the
best courthouses in Ohio, but one of the best buildings. Some people,
including Claudia Watson of the Montgomery County Historical Society, say
that the Courthouse is one of the nation's finest buildings from the first half
of the nineteenth century. In any case, from 1857 on, someone was
suggesting its demolition. The Courthouse was designed by Howard Daniels,
a Cincinnati landscape architect who also worked on his home city's
SpringGrove Cemetery and on Cleveland's Woodland Cemetery. Built of
local brown limestone used even for the roof, the two-story Courthouse has a

▶ MONTGOMERY COUNTY COURTHOUSE

formal classical porch in front, with six unfluted Ionic columns; side walls have pilasters enclosing windows. The building's most unusual features are the porches at the back corners. From the side it looks as though the back has a colonnaded portico like the one in front. Not so. At each corner it has a quarter-round porch with a single column, while the rest of the wall is relatively plain. Not having a full rear porch saved a lot of money, or permitted more space inside, or both. Daniels's solution of tiny corner porches was innovative and, Watson says, unique in Greek Revival. As was common around 1850, Daniels used Greek styling outside and Roman arches and vaults inside. Both floors have a center hall lined on both sides by three large cross-vaulted rooms, originally for the likes of the sheriff, the clerk, and juries. In the middle of the building a small round-domed rotunda contains a stairway. It was built by an immigrant Swiss stone cutter, James Louis Wuichet, who came to build the canal and stayed to install this "flying" or cantilevered staircase. A third of the full length of each stone step is imbedded in the wall, so it needs no additional support. The interior highlight is the exquisite two-story oval courtroom at the back. This room has a domed and coffered ceiling that gives it perfect acoustics. At the upper level a balcony with wooden benches accommodated spectators. The basement has brick arches that help support the building, while the attic has another 30 to hold up the stone roof, which by the 1860s leaked and was thenceforth covered with tin. In the late twentieth century the Montgomery County Historical Society used the still county-owned building for offices,

▶ BRICK ARCHES IN COURTHOUSE ATTIC

▶ MONTGOMERY COUNTY COURTHOUSE CEILING PLAN

museum, and storage. Needing more space, it moved out in 2000 and started helping the county put together $5.7 million for an exterior and first-floor restoration. "The building is our premier artifact," said Jim Dinneen, county public works director, "and we were using it as a storage locker." He hopes that after restoration, the old courthouse will become a place where people want to go for meetings and occasions.

GEM CITY SAVINGS BANK, NOW NATIONAL CITY BANK, 1981

I.M. Pei & Partners, James I. Freed, chief designer, New York
6 North Main Street at Third
bank, offices

In Dayton everyone calls this the "I. M.Pei Building", and National City Bank doesn't seem to mind. Right across from the Old Courthouse, the building has two prominent pavilions, one round and one angled, linked by a glass-faced, skylit atrium. Seven stories high, the structure is limestone with horizontal ribbons of windows.

DAYTON ARCADE, 1904

Frank M. Andrews, Dayton
28 West Third Street, NRHP
Former retail, residential and office complex; now closed

The Dayton Arcade's Third Street facade is surely one of the most colorful in any Ohio downtown. Modeled on an Amsterdam guild hall, it has a show biz, stage-set quality; it's a lure. To this day, even though the commercial arcade inside has been shut down for years, a picture of the outside makes the city's promotional literature. With entrances also on Fourth and Ludlow Streets, the Arcade's building originally housed apartments and offices as well as shops and a farmers' market. Not surprisingly, it was a big success for decades. Not surprisingly, it ultimately became run down and shabby, until it attracted a rehab that "modernized" it for a 1980 reopening. But the 1980s were a bad decade for Dayton; the Arcade held on only until 1991. Now owned by Danis Corporation, a Dayton-based contractor, it's in moth balls, opened at least once a year for a Dayton Ballet fundraiser. "The idea," says Marguerite Krein, whose realty firm represents the owner, "is to use it again." The picturesque Third Street facade is built of red-brown brick with stone trim around the windows, in quoins at the corners, as facing on the ground

▶ DAYTON ARCADE, AND DETAIL

floor. The main entrance is an arch. On top we see three curved Dutch gables and the pointed copper-green roofs of two turrets. Architect Frank M. Andrews (1867-1948), who studied architecture at Cornell and started out in New York and Chicago offices, set up his Dayton practice in 1894. His local work also included factories for National Cash Register. Designed with so many windows that they were called "glass-walled," they earned him a national reputation. Later Andrews moved to New York, where he designed many hotels and two state capitols. Just inside the Arcade's arched door there's a good corridor under a glazed ceiling. It leads to a rotunda ringed with three levels under a domed roof of iron and glass: an orderly spider web. The 1980 renovation uncovered the glass dome and added a glass elevator and an escalator. It's ironic now to see all the ink gushing over the 1980 reopening: "Reviving 'downtown' is happening throughout the country," wrote one publicist. "Dayton is coming alive downtown!" But the city was on the verge of losing a quarter of its industrial jobs.

DAYTON DAILY NEWS, 1910

Albert A. Pretzinger, Dayton
Ludlow Street at West Fourth Street, northwest corner, NRHP
Newspaper offices

Having made a success of his Dayton *Daily News*, James M. Cox wanted a new building for it. When he sought a loan from his banker, he was denied. "Newspapers," declared the banker, "have never been known to earn money." So Cox summoned his architect and issued orders: "Build me a damn bank." Albert Pretzinger succeeded. For decades afterward people were walking in, expecting a bank. They're not walking in that glorious front door today, for it's been sealed; it's in the middle of an employee lunch room wall. The way in now, past a security desk, is next door. In truth, few banks matched Cox's three-story white stone newspaper building in flamboyance: it's Beaux Arts, with Roman Corinthian columns and lush terra cotta detailing on the front. In his day, James Cox was a prominent man. By 1909 he was in Congress; four years later he became governor. In Ohio's last grand splash in national politics, he lost the presidency to a Marion newspaper man, Warren Harding, in 1920. Since Cox's death in 1957, his descendants have developed a mega communications business, the Atlanta-based Cox Enterprises; and at the request of his daughters, the old man's office at the *Daily News* has been kept just as it was when he last saw it. In winter 1998 I asked Suzanne Klopfenstein, the paper's special events coordinator, to show me Cox's office; and thus she and I found ourselves bowing in front of his desk, sniffing to catch the lingering aroma of the Governor's pipe tobacco. In the portrait over the fireplace, Cox is wearing the burgundy-colored smoking jacket that today hangs on a coat rack in the corner. His books are on the shelf—a four-volume leather-bound Bible, Truman's memoirs, *The Wright Brothers*—and his golf clubs are ready in a corner. The red-shag carpet is strictly 1950s. Though important visitors are regularly shown the Governor's office, Klopfenstein said, mine was only the second public request in five years. The first was just two weeks before: a school girl doing a paper on a historic figure.

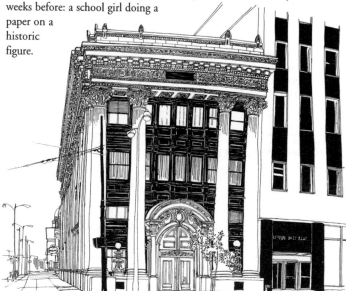

▶ DAYTON DAILY NEWS

▶ SACRED HEART CHURCH

SACRED HEART CHURCH, 1890

Charles Insco Williams, Dayton
217 West Fourth Street, northwest corner at South Wilkinson Street, NRHP
Vacant building

Sacred Heart Church's immense green domes make it a downtown landmark.
Limestone with Berea sandstone trim, Romanesque, the church has two
towers in front, both topped with octagonal copper domes. The massive
central dome and even the dome on its cupola are also octagonal and copper
green.

UNITED STATES POST OFFICE, NOW UNITED STATES
BANKRUPTCY COURT, 1915

James Knox Taylor, Supervising Architect, Treasury Department, Washington
120 West Third Street at South Wilkinson Street, NRHP
Federal Bankruptcy Court, offices

Back when post offices were architectural assets for American cities, James
Knox Taylor was in charge of their designs. He did one for Akron (now the
Art Museum; see also) in 1899; he remodeled Columbus's (see also) in 1912;
and three years after that he produced this Neoclassical Revival building.
Here the facade's central section has 16 Ionian columns, each cut from a
single block of New Hampshire granite, while the lobby has terrazzo floors,

marble trim and bronze panels from Tiffany Studios. When the post office moved out in 1975, demolition seemed the likely next step, but dextrous inter-governmental real estate swaps saved the structure. Lorenz & Williams, an architectural firm and prospective rehabber and occupant, became owner and redid the building in 1979, in 1985, and again in 1994, before renting it back to the Federal government.

MUTUAL HOME & SAVINGS ASSOCIATION BUILDING, NOW LIBERTY TOWER, 1931

Schenck & Williams, Dayton
120 West Second Street, between Wilkinson and Ludlow, NRHP
Office building

Dayton has two Art Deco buildings at Second and Wilkinson. Liberty Tower is the taller one, with tower setbacks. In 1998 it was vacant and shabby, though when I peeked in I could see the relics of a good Art Deco banking hall. How wonderful to find that by 2001, Liberty Savings Bank had taken over the building and restored interiors before moving in in 1999. The second, now the AT&T Building, is at 215 West Second Street, at the intersection's northwest corner. Massive for its height, it has a splendid entrance and a lobby with wonderful detailing. In Ohio, says Ohio State's Douglas Graf, Art Deco represents "the last burst of good stuff."

YOUNG MEN'S CHRISTIAN ASSOCIATION, NOW YMCA AND THE LANDING, 1929, 1995

Schenck & Williams, Dayton
115 West Monument Avenue between North Wilkinson and Ludlow, NRHP
Private apartments in tower; YMCA entrance on west side of building at 316 North Wilkinson

This YMCA tower is a lone sentinel in a part of downtown that was urban renewaled into parking lots in the mid-1960s. In recent years, in an arrangement much like that adopted in Akron, it's become half private apartments, half YMCA. Isolated as it is, at least this building, designed by Dayton's leading architectural firm at the time, Schenck & Williams, can be seen clearly. The footprint is U-shaped, with a 14-story tower in the middle and 12-story wings. The same pattern is echoed by a three-story U at the bottom in front of the building. The material is light brown brick; roofs are variegated red tile; trim is stone. Detailing like horizontal bands of stone, intricate iron balconies and others of masonry, and a little tower here and there, keep the eye entertained. Style is Italian Renaissance.

▶ YMCA

▶ VICTORIA THEATRE

TURNER OPERA HOUSE, NOW VICTORIA THEATRE, 1866, 1871, 1919

1919 rebuilding by Schenck & Williams, Dayton; 1990 renovation by Edward Durell Stone Associates with Lorenz & Williams, Dayton
138 North Main Street at East First, NRHP
Theater with resident ballet and dramatic companies; 937/228-7591

The Victoria is Ohio's oldest legitimate theater—it's been a venue for lectures by Mark Twain and Oscar Wilde, for performances by actress Sarah Bernhardt, basso Fyodor Chaliapin, pianist Ignace Paderewski. Though it was threatened with demolition with the 1970s, it was never shut down for long—except for rebuilding after flood, fires, or time. A fire in 1869 was so severe that it left only part of the facade; rebuilt, the theater burned again in 1918. What we see inside is the 1990 renovation, which formed a lobby by closing street-level shops; what we see outside is largely the Second Empire facade that first appeared in 1871—a couple stories shorter than the 1866 original. The auditorium seats 1,200. Across the street from the Victoria, the Schuster Performing Arts Center, designed by Cesar Pelli & Associates of New Haven, was under construction in 2001 and expected to open in December 2002, with the opera and symphony as resident tenants. Next to the auditorium, an 18-story tower was to house offices and apartments.

▶ VICTORIA THEATRE

The Art Institute Area
and Dayton View

Access: To reach Northminster Church and Dayton Art Institute from downtown, drive north/northwest on Main Street/State Route 48, continuing across the Great Miami River and half a mile past I-75 to Forest Avenue, a very sharp left turn. Drive south another half mile to Grand Avenue where church's distinctive pagoda roof appears on the right. To reach the Art Institute continue south on Forest, which becomes Riverview Avenue; at Belmonte Park North turn right into parking lot.

FOREST AVENUE PRESBYTERIAN CHURCH, NOW NORTHMINSTER PRESBYTERIAN CHURCH, 1902

George Burke Whyte, Dayton
301 Forest Avenue
Church; possible to see interior weekdays by entering through offices at back; 937/222-1171

Who were the Whytes? The whole family colluded on this church, with wonderful results. One, George Burke Whyte, was architect and sculptor. Another, John Reid Whyte, was ⬧ builder; and William Whyte was the stone mason who chose the stone. They were good at their work. The design is wonderful; the sandstone, in a multi- hued red, is the most

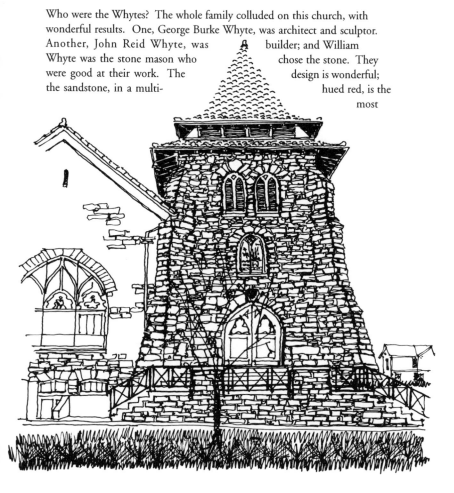

▶ DAYTON ART INSTITUTE

distinctive Ohio architectural stone. The Whytes do appear in old city directories, but otherwise, except for their work, they've disappeared. Northminster is one of five similar Arts and Crafts Presbyterian churches, all built within a three-year period, and all using the red sandstone, which came from a quarry near Mansfield. Four, including Northminster, have octagonal, Akron-plan sanctuaries. Though designed by three different architects, all four have Gothic arches, red-tile roofs, and towers with pagoda-style roofs. That's not to say Northminster is a clone. It has exceptional detailing and stained-glass and painted windows that Doug Graf admired because, with their branch-like tracery and dark-toned glass at the top, they allude to the Gothic link with the dark, mysterious forest. Two of the other churches, in Napoleon and Barnesville, are also in this guide, Vol. II. Upper Sandusky has an excellent example as well. The fifth, somewhat different, is in Shelby. The Whytes also reappear in Vol. II, for the family is credited with the fabulous stone carving at the Wood County Courthouse in Bowling Green, and with less extensive carving in Piqua.

DAYTON ART INSTITUTE, 1930, 1997
Edward B. Green, Buffalo; 1997 addition by Levin Porter Associates, Dayton
456 Belmonte Park North, NRHP
Art museum, open daily; 937/223-5277 or 800/296-4426

The Dayton Art Institute goes back to the good old days, for it had a grand benefactor, Julia Shaw Patterson Carnell, whose lifetime extended from the Civil War to World War II. For years Carnell made up the Institute's annual deficit; she donated much of the collection. She provided the $1 million that built the museum. And she went to Europe with the architects and brought back many of the doorways, iron railings, columns and other trim, mostly reproductions but including a few real antiques. So closely did she superintend construction that at the dedication she could say, "I feel that I am giving you one of my children." Edward B. Green, whose firm also did the Toledo Art Museum and its additions (see also), had a particular advantage in Dayton: he could select the site. He opted for an irregular lot on a hill overlooking the river and then made the most of it. Inspired by Italian villas, Green gave the Dayton Art Institute a spectacular entrance: a double stairway ascending the hill to ground-floor doors that happily are still kept open. Above them is the facade's focal point: a recessed porch fronted by three high round arches; its balustrade echoes those of the stairs. Second Renaissance Revival, the building is a tan Ohio sandstone under a red tile roof; two adjoining wings recede back at an angle. The only problem with this great stairway is that it's hard to view. I couldn't find a good vista for it from the downtown side of the river, and walking from the parking lot on the opposite side of the building takes a certain single mindedness but is highly recommended. Be sure to see the former front hall inside and its porch, the auditorium, and the Italian cloister. The museum is laid out as an eight-sided ring, like a diamond with flattened corners. The auditorium extends across the middle, forming two courtyards. As built originally the octagon had only five sides; in 1996-97 a $16.7 million construction project added the other three. Architect Levin Porter Associates tore down an entrance they'd done on the parking-lot side in the 1970s; it had a large abstract bracket and other whimsicalities of that era. The new and larger entrance, named General Motors Entrance Rotunda, seemed "too corporate" to former museum staffer, Marianne Lorenz. She ameliorated that by calling in an artist: Dayton sculptor Hamilton Dixon did the rotunda's hand-forged steel balustrades.

Dayton View

In the mid-1990s, Dayton preservationists prepared a wonderful set of historic district walking tours in residential areas; one covered the Dayton View neighborhood. To check availability of these tour brochures, call Brian Inderrieden in the Dayton planning department, 937/443-3672.

To see Dayton View, Access: The now depressed neighborhoods south and west of the Dayton Art Institute were once a choice place to live. From the museum turn south/right onto Riverview; turn right onto Central Avenue to see the fine Queen Anne, in white shingles with a copper green tower dome and trim, at 338 Central. Return to Riverview and continue one block to Salem Pike Avenue; turn right; after less than a mile turn left at Harvard; take first left; at next corner Traxler Mansion, 1911, a Chateauesque house with a Chateauesque garage, is at 42 Yale. Continue another half mile northwest on Salem Pike to Red Haw Road and the Dayton View Library.

DAYTON VIEW PUBLIC LIBRARY BRANCH, 1929

Pretzinger and Pretzinger, Dayton
1515 Salem Avenue, NRHP/Dayton View HD
Branch library; open daily except Sunday

This library is in a romantic Tudor Revival, with irregular stone on the lower parts of the walls, brick above, some half timbering, beamed ceilings indoors. The central section has a stone entry; the side wings both end with large window bays.

Access: From downtown take Main Street/State Route 48 south to Oakwood, where street name changes to Oakwood Avenue. Volusia Avenue, on the left, is the first street in Oakwood and part of the Schantz Park Historic District in the suburb's northeast corner. When Oakwood Avenue veers off to right, stay on 48 as it becomes Far Hills Avenue. Turn right at Park Avenue (if you're on Park Road you've gone too far; turn back) to see Municipal Building and Wright House. To see some Olmsted streets, continue on Park Avenue to Oakwood; turn left/south; then you're on one. It intersects Ridgeway Road, another, and then bends to the left as Forrer Road, still another. The parks, Elizabeth Gardens and Houk Stream, are at that intersection. Take Ridgeway south to the Kettering line; turn right/west to Oak Knoll Drive, which links to Deep Hollow Road, another Olmsted plat; take a sharp, 45-degree right turn onto Deep Hollow.

Oakwood

OSCAR F. FOCKE HOUSE, 1914

Louis J.P. Lott, Dayton
100 Oakwood at Volusia Avenue, NRHP/Schantz Park HD
Private house

Oakwood's first historic district is Schantz Park, in the northeast corner. Developed mostly between 1914 and 1924, Schantz Park is a neighborhood of houses in different styles, almost all designed by architect Louis J.P. Lott. With its corner site, this Swiss Chalet at 100 Oakwood was meant as a showpiece to attract home buyers to Volusia Avenue. At this corner see also Lott's Craftsman/Arts and Crafts style gates, identifying the subdivision. Schantz Park was the brainchild of Adam Schantz, a brewer who envisioned a suburb in 1880, when he bought 100 acres in what is now Oakwood. Schantz himself platted and planted the land. After his death in 1903 his son, Adam Schantz, Jr. took over and developed 188 lots east of Oakwood Avenue on five east-west streets, Schenck, Ridgewood, Schantz, Volusia, and Irving, the Dayton boundary line. We know more about the Schantz subdivision today because of C. William Hager, Oakwood's historical activist, who has funded research into Oakwood's architectural history. The project started in 1978 with an inventory and led to Schantz Park's National

Register listing in 1992. A Realtor whose office is in Oakwood's miniscule Park Avenue business district, Hager has found Oakwood skittish on preservation; in 1997 the Historical Society barred National Register activities. The ban was lifted the next year, and Hager began sponsoring a survey in central Oakwood.

OAKWOOD MUNICIPAL BUILDING, 1921, 1930S, 1968

Attributed to Schenck & Williams, Dayton
30 Park Avenue
Municipal building

Oakwood's picturesque Municipal Building evolved in three stages, the oldest at the east end, the newest at the west. Older interiors have been altered. Incredibly, in 1998 the city was planning to tear down this wonderful Municipal Building in 2000.

ORVILLE WRIGHT HOUSE, HAWTHORN HILL, 1914

Schenck & Williams, Dayton
901 Harman Avenue at Park Avenue, NHL, NRHP
Private house

Schenck & Williams gave Oakwood's most famous resident the fine house he deserved. It sits up on a hill, with its becolumned porch overlooking a broad, treed lawn. Wilbur and Orville Wright planned this house with their sister Katharine, but Wilbur died before it was built. Orville and Katharine kept a close eye on the construction; they would picnic on the unfinished roof. In 1914 they moved in with their father. A photograph taken not long after shows Orville, in suit and tie, and Katharine, in the long skirt of the day, in rocking chairs on one of the side porches. Locally, the house was famous for Charles Lindbergh's visit after his transatlantic flight in 1927. By then, Katharine had married and moved to Kansas City. Neoclassical Revival in style, the house has open porches at both ends, balustrades on the roofs, and four two-story Ionic columns under a pediment on the front porch.

▶ HAWTHORN HILL

THE LATE ROMANTICS: DAYTON, OAKWOOD AND THE OLMSTED BROTHERS—

Driving around Oakwood on a rainy December day, Doug Graf declares that this city just south of Dayton is "one of the nicest late romantic suburbs in the country." He's just passing Elizabeth Gardens, where even in the rain a park bench in a wooded ravine looks inviting. Along its curving roads the neighborhood has other small parks, wooded hills and ravines, with twentieth-century houses set among them. Then Graf pulls up at a quiet three-way intersection enclosed by trees and shrubs, with no building visible at all. He is delighted. Geographically in the middle of metropolitan Dayton, the intersection seems to be in the country. It is a perfect illusion.

That day Graf was unaware that this neighborhood was laid out primarily by the Olmsted Brothers. The son and nephew of Frederick Law Olmsted, co-designer of Central Park, the Olmsted Brothers succeeded him and for decades produced high quality landscape architecture. Their involvement gives this part of Oakwood very good credentials indeed.

That the Olmsted Brothers worked extensively in Dayton was researched in the mid 1980s by Noël D. Vernon, then at Ball State University in Muncie, Indiana, and now at California State Polytechnic in Pomona. One of the country's relatively few landscape historians, Vernon had help in Dayton from garden clubs, who did field work. She had access to the archives of local landscapers, Siebenthaler Company and Woolpert Consultants. She also spent a summer at the Olmsted archives, which the National Park Service maintains as part of the Frederick Law Olmsted National Historic Site in Brookline, Massachusetts.

At the archives Vernon found mention of 302 possible Ohio projects between 1894 and 1930; of those 188 were in Dayton. The 188 possibles led to 70 landscape plans, of which 50 were installed, and not all remain. Even so, in a 1993 study of Hills and Dales Park, Vernon and co-authors Malcolm Cairns, Glenn Harper, and Sherda Williams concluded that today Dayton has "one of the largest collections of historic Olmsted Brothers designed landscapes outside of New York and Boston." In possible projects, it had the highest number outside those East Coast cities.

The reason was John Patterson, the head of National Cash Register, who wasn't the Olmsted Brothers' only client in Dayton, but he was the biggest. Alarmed in 1893 by employee arson and sabotage, Patterson moved his own desk into the NCR factory, where he soon realized that harsh treatment of wage earners was hurting the company. Pay raises and cleaner, safer working conditions followed in short order; ultimately Patterson provided his employees adult education and on-site health services. But in some programs, such as weighing employees twice a year and providing a morning malted milk for underweight ones, he seems meddlesome.

But Patterson also thought his employees should have an attractive environment, and in the architectural and landscape projects he undertook to achieve that, he seems very enlightened indeed. When Patterson called in Frank Andrews to design factories with lots of windows for light, and the Olmsted Brothers to design better landscaping, he saw himself as implementing his improved personnel policies. At the time, social reformer Jane Addams praised those policies. Retrospectively, Doug Graf has high praise for the design results. He acclaims NCR for having the nation's first campus style industrial park, representing a new approach to planning. Alas, it's gone now, mostly razed.

On land he owned south of his factory, Patterson asked the Olmsted Brothers to lay out Hills and Dales Park for his employees. The park had campgrounds, plantings, bridle paths, woodlands, and meadow; it had mounted security officers who restocked the bird feeders. In 1918, four years before his death, Patterson gave Hills and Dales* to the city of Dayton. Of the nearly 300 acres, 230 were later turned into a golf course that, Vernon found, helped preserve the Olmsted landscape.

Patterson also wanted his executives to have fine housing nearby, so he asked the Olmsteds to design a subdivision that is now southwest Oakwood, adjacent to Hills and Dales Park; some of Oakwood was originally in the park, as was part of Kettering to the south. When Noël Vernon compared maps in the Olmsted archives with today's Oakwood map, she found that many of the roads were the same. Those that were included Ridgeway at Forrer, where Elizabeth Gardens is— the place where Doug Graf became so enthusiastic. Though not all the Olmsted Brothers' map was realized, the part that was, Vernon wrote, defines the character of the neighborhood.

Marion Schaeffer, an architecturally minded woman who was a 20-year resident of Oakwood, recalls that she and architectural historian Loren Gannon learned of the Olmsted

Brothers' role in Dayton and Oakwood only in 1988. While giving a bus tour for visitors attending a National Trust meeting in Cincinnati, they heard two women from Atlanta gushing over Olmsted projects in Dayton, which then were better known to Olmsted scholars nationally than to local historians. Marion Schaeffer has made up for the omission since. She can confirm that the Olmsteds laid out Oakwood's Ridgeway Road as a bridle trail called Panorama Drive. At the city's western boundary, they laid out Deep Hollow Road. Forrer Road and Oakwood Avenue north to Park were their work, as were the parks at the intersection of Ridgeway.

So not only is Oakwood one of the nicest late romantic suburbs, but it's a place whose plat has good credentials.

*Early in the 1920s a Canton developer named T.K. Harris saw Hills and Dales, and he went home to emulate it in a residential suburb. He kept the name, too (see also, Canton).

Toledo

The most amazing fact about Toledo architecture is that here large landmark buildings stood vacant for as long as 20 years; and then suddenly in the 1990s a bunch of them were rehabbed and useful again. That these buildings—the likes of the Bartley House, the Oliver House, the Lasalle department store—were not demolished is by itself surprising; that at the close of the twentieth century they had all turned around was almost incredible. ¶ It didn't hurt that Toledo had a strong Mister History, Ted Ligibel, a preservationist who was also a great publicist, the author of ten-best lists in the Toledo *Blade* and of a wonderful, compact downtown walking tour. "People told us we were crazy," Ligibel says, of the era when major buildings stood unused and unrazed. "They said nobody would ever want to move into those old buildings." Mothballing does work, he says, but it's slow. ¶ The most important turnarounds have been downtown, where a former department store and two hotels all became apartments. Tara Barney, who's in charge of downtown for Toledo's Development Department, says that the failure of Portside, a riverfront shopping center, tipped the downtown development push from retail to housing. Portside opened in 1984 with promises to "fix" downtown, and closed ignominiously in 1990, leaving downtown unfixed. After that, starting in 1993 with the former offices in the old Valentine Building, housing conversions became the order of the day. "We have the cleanest, safest downtown in the state," brags the enthusiastic Barney. "It's an easy commitment for our pioneers. Now the focus will be on the street level—something every 40 feet." ¶ As for Portside, it too has turned around. In 1997 it reopened as COSI Toledo, a science museum. ¶ This guide divides Toledo into three sections: Downtown; Museum of Art-Old West End; and, for a few scattered sites, Far-Flung, which includes the zoo, East Toledo, and the lighthouse.

To see more in Toledo—Ted Ligibel wrote an excellent "Discover Downtown Toledo Walking Tour"; in 1999 copies were still available at the Toledo-Lucas County Public Library, 419/259-5266. Call that number also for summertime downtown tours.

Toledo 1: Downtown

**Access: To reach downtown Toledo from I-75 northbound, take exit
201B, bear right onto Erie Street, get into right lane for right turn
onto Washington Street. Berdan Warehouse is at that corner. From
Washington turn right onto Summit Street; after two tenths of a
mile turn left on Oliver to Broadway and the Oliver House. Pick up
Ottawa at the foot of Broadway and turn left to see Owens Corning.
Follow Ottawa, which turns north onto Monroe, past the new
Toledo Mudhens stadium, under construction in 2001, to Melcher-
Loman Block below; then turn right on Ontario. Buildings below
are in order for touring. All (starting even with Berdan Warehouse,
for the stalwart) may be done on foot. Tour may be done by car
through Valentine Building, with remainder on foot.**

BERDAN WAREHOUSE, 1902

George S. Mills, Toledo
601 Washington Street at Erie, NRHP
Vacant warehouse

The likely inspiration for the Berdan Warehouse was Boston architect H.H.
Richardson's Marshall Field Warehouse, built in Chicago in 1887. The
prototype, which helped define Richardsonian Romanesque, was in
rusticated stone; the Berdan Warehouse, in brick, was an early example of
reinforced concrete construction. English-born architect George S. Mills
(1866-1939) came to Ohio to teach at the Toledo Manual Training School;
ultimately he became very much the man about town. He was one of the
group who in 1909 persuaded John North Willys to move his auto company
from Indiana to Toledo; no sooner had the Willys-Overland Company
arrived than it needed more space. Between 1910 and 1920, Mills's
architectural firm, Mills, Rhines, Bellman & Nordhoff, did 167 plants and
additions for Willys, as well as houses for some company officers. This story
comes from Charles H. Stark III, who in recent years was president of Mills's
successor firm, Bauer, Stark & Lashbrook. He adds that for years Mills
played pinochle every afternoon at the Toledo Club with Willys and glass
tycoon Michael Owens. What he brought back to the office was more
business. "Mills," says Stark, "spent 40 years not designing."

OLIVER HOUSE, 1859

Isaiah Rogers, Cincinnati
27 Broadway, NRHP
Brew pub open daily for lunch and dinner; 419/241-1253

Ted Ligibel spent 17 years, from 1974 to 1991, as a professional
preservationist in Toledo. The Oliver House was always on his agenda; in
the end, it was the greatest save in his era. "It's Toledo's *most* historic
building in terms of architectural importance and character," he says. Before
the late 1960s, no one realized just how important this sometime warehouse
and wheel-and-rim factory really was; but then, with the discovery of its

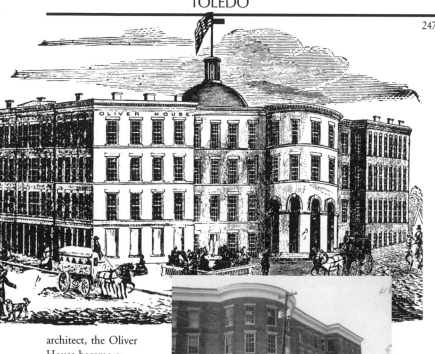

▶ OLIVER HOUSE

architect, the Oliver House became a Cinderella building. The designer was Isaiah Rogers of Cincinnati, famous for his Boston, New York, and Cincinnati hotels, as well as Nashville's Maxwell House, still known to coffee drinkers. But while once those hotels may have been more famous, the Oliver House had the staying power—it's Isaiah Rogers's only surviving hotel. Originally a grand hotel, the Oliver House was just barely hanging on in the 1980s. In 1989 the owner decided he had to get rid of it right away—tear it down or sell it. "We put on a scramble," Ligibel says, remembering the urgent meeting he called. One of the people who came was Patricia Appold, a long-time volunteer preservationist. She said she might be interested. She had to be tentative, because she wasn't a developer. But when her husband, Jim, who runs a cookie factory in McComb, asked what she wanted for her birthday and Christmas that year, she asked for the Oliver House. The Appolds bought the property for $240,000. From the beginning they planned a brew pub, but for starters the building needed, at least, a heating system. The red-brick Oliver House, three stories plus a raised basement, is an elegant building, A-shaped, with a round corner bay connecting two wings. Before it opened in 1859, the Toledo *Blade* ran a story every day for two months—this new hotel had 170 rooms, gas lights, and running water. It survived as a hotel into the 1890s; by 1919 it was a rooming house. It's over a century since the Oliver House was last as successful as it is now as a brew pub. The building also has two stores and seven townhouse apartments, all rented, and after the Appolds bought the Oliver House, Owens Corning built new headquarters across the street, bringing a thousand office workers into the immediate neighborhood. But in those days when Pat Appold was a volunteer, one thing she never dreamed of, was that when she was a grandmother in her mid fifties, she'd prove her preservation mettle by going into the brewery business.

▶ MELCHER-LOHMAN

OWENS CORNING, 1996

Cesar Pelli & Associates, New Haven, Connecticut
1 Owens Corning Parkway, across Swan Creek between Washington and Monroe Streets
Corporate headquarters

Set at the confluence of
Swan Creek and the
Maumee River, this
250,000-square-foot
headquarters building is a
glass skyscraper on its
side—it's only three
stories high, and a
thousand employees walk
up and down stairs.

▶ OWENS CORNING

"Staircases are energy
efficient," architect Cesar Pelli told Toledo *Blade* arts writer Sally Vallongo.
"They are social meeting places where people can stop and chat." The main
building, which has an arc-shaped footprint and an undulating wall along the
river, is fronted by smaller ones. Be sure to walk around to the back, where a
path offers views of the building's curves and views of the river. The
streetside focal point is a red tower that fortuitously looks like both a ship's
funnel and the Owens Corning logo; it's a striking sight at the end of
Washington Street.

MELCHER-LOHMAN BLOCK, 1875

Carl Schon, Toledo
607-11 Monroe Street, NRHP
A. Rensch & Co. at 607 is a grocery; for hours call 419/241-4931

Even though their facades are interrelated, these started as three separate buildings. The style is High Victorian Italianate; the cornices are very fancy. Still in the family, A. Rensch, a specialty grocery with Swiss cheese as a staple, was founded by preservationist Ted Ligibel's great-grandfather, who came from Switzerland; not surprisingly, it is as it was. During Ligibel's time as an active preservationist here, he became *the* authority on old Toledo; he's been called "the premier local historian" and the "guru" of local history. All that started with this store, for Ligibel's grandfather, Mr. Rensch, ran a grocery catering to the carriage trade in early twentieth-century Toledo. Everyone of importance was a customer, and their names—now the streets of Toledo—slipped into the annals of the Ligibel family. When Ligibel launched his own career, all people needed to know was that he was Mr. Rensch's grandson. That character voucher got him his first job.

Access: Burt's Theatre and Pythian Castle are at Ontario and Jefferson; continue on Ontario to Madison, where Pilkington Building is at corner; turn left to library; then right on 11th Street; right on Adams to courthouse; left on Erie to Beech; right to Superior and Toledo Blade at corner. Continue on Superior to Adams; turn left to Valentine Building and Theatre. Turn back on Adams to Huron, and, if driving, park and walk for rest of tour.

BURT'S THEATRE, NOW CAESAR'S SHOW BAR, 1898

George S. Mills, Toledo
725 Jefferson Avenue at Ontario Street, NRHP
Bar

For Burt's Theatre, architect George S. Mills took his design theme from the Miami/Erie Canal, which once ran along Ontario Street and made him think of Venice. He modeled this theater on Ca d'Oro, a fifteenth-century Gothic palace there. Now

▶ BURT'S THEATRE

all that remains is two stories of extraordinary ornamentation on the facade. The inside has been completely altered; a bar occupies the ground floor. Kenny Rogers' song *Lucille* was written here. It begins, "In a bar in Toledo across from the depot..." Burt's Theatre was the last building Mills designed. One day, thumbing through an old architectural book at the office, Charles Stark found a marker at the page with a picture of the Ca d'Oro.

PYTHIAN CASTLE, 1890

Norval B. Bacon, Toledo
801 Jefferson Avenue, NRHP
Vacant building

"I just got stuck on it," said the late Robert Shiffler, an independent rehabber who bought the Pythian Castle in 1996, even though it had been empty for 20 years. He decided, "It's just not going to be a wreck anymore." By year end he had a new roof on it; he had installed dozens of new floor joists; he had begun to save the Pythian. "Be careful what you wish for, Jane," he said to me. What I was wishing was that Robert Shiffler might succeed, but he ran out of

▶ Pʏᴛʜɪᴀɴ Cᴀsᴛʟᴇ

money and died in 1997. But it's easy to see how this building could inspire such effort. A tall castle looming over its end of downtown, the Pythian is good both from a distance and from close up. It's Richardsonian Romanesque, with rough-cut sandstone and arched windows in the lower part, and red brick, turrets and pointed dormers at the top. Above it all looms a high tower with a conical roof that peaks 125 feet above the sidewalk. Before Schiffler came along, water damage inside was enormous, but the shells of two auditoriums, one on the third floor, one on the fifth, both with stages and balconies, remained. Altogether the building has six stories and, at the level where the dormers are, an attic. The architect was Norval B. Bacon (1837-1909), an upstate New Yorker who studied in Boston and other cities, and practiced in Toledo from 1873. For 60 years the Knights of Pythias, a fraternal order, used the top three floors of the castle they'd built; until 1971 piano dealers, music classes, and recitals used the lower floors. Then came a cultural center for youths and after that, a free university (leatherwork and Indian philosophy) that foundered after a series of drug arrests. In 1976 a developer anticipated Shiffler by buying the building and then being unable to develop it. Though a 1998 poll found that the Pythian is Toledoans' favorite empty building, it's still empty. At least, the building stands secure under its new roof, behind its new windows and repainted trim. Shiffler's legacy, averred Kathleen Kovacs of Neighborhoods in Partnership, was an important one. He saved the Pythian.

LIBBEY-OWENS-FORD, NOW PILKINGTON BUILDING, 1960

Skidmore, Owings & Merrill, New York
811 Madison Avenue
Office building

It's fitting that one of Toledo's great glass companies should build a headquarters with the stuff that made it famous—even the spandrels, the segments below windows, are Vitrolux glass, a Libbey-Owens-Ford product. The building is in the International Style: a glass box mounted on pillars above an open plaza. Starting in 1953 with New York's Lever House, Skidmore, Owings & Merrill became *the* firm to hire for a prestigious International Style office building. Little altered, this 15-story tower is probably Ohio's best example, though its impact has been muted by the multitude of glass boxes built over a period of about 20 years. Libbey-Owens-Ford was acquired by Pilkington, an English company, in 1986.

▶ PILKINGTON BUILDING

TOLEDO-LUCAS COUNTY PUBLIC LIBRARY, 1940

Alfred A. Hayes of Hahn & Hayes, Toledo
325 Michigan Avenue
Public library; 419/259-5200

Set in its own city block, the Art Deco Toledo Public Library is built of limestone with trim in aluminum, an innovative material in 1940. Mercifully the interior was never subject to a major alteration. The main floor atrium is ringed with colored glass mosaic murals that are said to be unique; more are in the children's room. I was impressed by detailing, like the Art Deco hardware on the ladies room door. At the turn of the twenty-first century the library was building an addition to the west, on the far side of 10th Street; a glass connector will link the two structures. On completion of the new building in 2000, the old one is to be restored and to reopen in 2001.

▶ TOLEDO PUBLIC LIBRARY

▶ LUCAS COUNTY COURTHOUSE

LUCAS COUNTY COURTHOUSE, 1897

David L. Stine, Toledo
Courthouse Square, Adams Street at Ontario, NRHP
Public courthouse

In 1893 architect David L. Stine (1857-1941) went to the Columbian Exposition in Chicago, soaked up all the classical palaces, and came home to design this Beaux Arts courthouse. So says Ted Ligibel. That the domed courthouse can be seen from a block or two away on Ontario Street is also a Beaux Arts feature; that approach makes the building all the more impressive. Toledoans are  especially fond of a frog mosaic in the main entrance floor: a reminder that the site was once a frog pond. In fact, Toledoans are generally fond of their courthouse. In the mid 1980s, when the city and preservationists assigned 505 downtown buildings scores for architectural merit, with bonuses for

▶ TOLEDO BLADE

interior and historical importance, the courthouse came out way ahead, with 119 points out of a possible 120. Second place went to the library, just above, with 113.

TOLEDO BLADE, 1927

Langdon, Hohly & Gram, Toledo
541 North Superior Street
Newspaper office

In a part of downtown with enough parking lots for a Super Bowl, the Toledo Blade asserts some class. The main entrance, facing the corner of Superior and Beech Streets, connects two facades with rows of high arched windows. The material is limestone, the style is Renaissance Revival with Spanish touches—like the curved gables and urns at the top. Whenever Ohio State's Douglas Graf sees a picture of the Blade building, he has something very nice to say, like "beautiful."

VALENTINE BUILDING AND THEATRE, 1895

E.O. Fallis, Toledo; theater rehab by Charles Stark, Bauer, Stark & Lashbrook, Toledo
419 St. Clair Street, NRHP
Renaissance Apartments (1993); Toledo Cultural Arts Center's Valentine Theatre, reconstruction completed 1999

This block-long building was E.O. Fallis's stab at the Chicago Style, and the man designed with distinction. It's a four-story structure in a light brown brick, with a cornice at the top and ground-floor shop windows between brick pillars. Above the shop level, the windows are slightly recessed; except for sills, they are without ornamentation. The effect is striking. "It was so simple," says Ted Ligibel, "that at the time it was revolutionary." Originally the Valentine was an office block, completed in 1892 and surrounding a theater, finished three years later; for a while the famous Toledo Mayor Samuel "Golden Rule" Jones had his office here. (Right, Jones was renowned for integrity.) Later the

▶ VALENTINE BUILDING

building was a hotel, then city offices, then a candidate for demolition rescued by the Save the Valentine committee, which sought support by giving tours in the empty, unheated building. In 1993 National Church Residences built Renaissance Apartments, 54 affordable apartments for the elderly. Though the exterior was plain, the theater was fancy. It had a then innovative cantilevered balcony, which eliminated the need for view-blocking support posts. According to Reynold Boezi, a consultant who spent 15 years turning around both the Valentine building and theater, architect E.O. Fallis himself sat under the balcony opening night, though he made his family stay home. Whether or not he really doubted its stability, the balcony's still in place. Almost all other original features were lost in a 1940s movie theater makeover in a Chinese mode, so in the late 1990s a major rehab largely funded by the state ($18.5 million) virtually had to start over. Boezi showed me around while the theater was still being prepared for renovation in late 1996. With a bulldozer where the stage and orchestra pit were to go, reconstruction began as a dusty business. But even under scaffolding and plaster debris, the grand stairway was grand; and we really did glimpse a bit of coffered ceiling. Ted Ligibel is such an admirer of architect E(dward) O. Fallis (1851-1927) that he did a 1981 master's thesis on him at Bowling Green. Fallis, Ligibel says, "tried to give Toledo one good example of every style"—several are in this guide. Indiana-born, trained in a Toledo apprenticeship and on a European study tour, Fallis always practiced in Toledo and lived to be Ohio's oldest architect. Ligibel found 107 documented Fallis structures (not all surviving) in Indiana, Illinois, Kansas, Michigan, and New York, as well as Ohio, where he did courthouses in Paulding, 1887, and Williams, 1890, counties.

LASALLE AND KOCH DRY GOODS CO., 1917, NOW LASALLE APARTMENTS, RENOVATED 1996

Starrett & Van Vleck, New York
513 Adams Street at Huron Street, NRHP
Apartments; street-level retail

With this building, Lasalle and Koch department store brought New York to the streets of Toledo. It has stone colonnades near the top and an arcade along the sidewalk, brick in between, and a crowning copper cornice. Renaissance Revival in style, the nine-story structure has the grand New York mercantile look. New York architects Goldwyn Starrett and Joseph Van Vleck were renowned for department stores. Lasalle's was one of the last

▶ LaSalle

done before Starrett's death in 1918, but the firm kept on doing stores, like Polsky's in Akron (see also). Michael Young, former Toledo city planner, reports that Atlanta has a twin to the Lasalle, except that Atlanta's is still Macy's. Of the two, the Toledo version has the more elegant touches—for instance, polished granite rather than limestone on the first-floor columns. An old-time Toledo store, Lasalle's was acquired by Macy's in 1924. So it remained for 60 years. After Macy's closed, the vacant building went to the city; but it was another ten years before much happened. Then the city spent almost $1 million to replace the roof and remove asbestos—investments that made the building all the more attractive to Wisconsin developer Randy Alexander when he came to town to look at warehouses. "Hey," called Alexander, as his car passed the Lasalle on the way to warehouses, "what's that?" To him, it looked like housing right away. The Alexander Company renovated the Lasalle, capitalized the *S* in the name, and came up with 130 apartments that people started moving into in early 1997. Counting the initial $1 million, the LaSalle turned around with a substantial city investment. But it also sparked other major downtown housing rehabs— Hillcrest Hotel, also by the Alexander Company, and the Commodore Perry Hotel—that needed less city outlay.

Madison Avenue

Slightly narrower than other downtown streets, Madison Avenue has a largely intact wall of high rises. If you've trekked around New York City's Wall Street, you won't find Madison a great canyon, but it has a distinctive group of turn-of-the-century buildings. Madison is one-way west-bound; if you're driving you'll have to see these in reverse order. The next four buildings are all in the Madison Avenue Historic District; a couple are individually listed on the National Register.

▶ SPITZER BUILDING

SPITZER BUILDING, 1896, 1904

Thomas Huber, Toledo
520 Madison Avenue at
Huron Street, NRHP
Office building; ground floor
arcade open to public

The Spitzer is a ten-story Chicago Style building. On the Madison Avenue side, note the arched arcade entry ornamented in terra cotta.

GARDNER BUILDING, 1893

Charles Gardner, Toledo
506 Madison Avenue at Superior Street
Office building

Almost torn down in the 1980s, the Renaissance Revival Gardner Building is famous for its innards, among the first to consist of reinforced concrete. The six-story Gardner Building is the earlier of two Ohio buildings that represent pioneering use of reinforced concrete; the other, Cincinnati's Ingalls Building, 1903, (see also) is ten stories taller. Both are civil engineering landmarks.

▶ OHIO SAVINGS

NORTHERN NATIONAL BANK, NOW KEY BANK, 1916

Mills, Rhines, Bellman & Nordhoff, Toledo
245 Superior Street at Madison
Bank with regular business hours

The Neoclassical Revival facade faces the cross street, Superior. See the elegant 1930s lobby, with its high coffered ceiling and wood paneling.

OHIO SAVINGS & TRUST COMPANY, NOW NATIONAL CITY BANK BUILDING, 1930

Mills, Rhines, Bellman & Nordhoff, Toledo
405 Madison Avenue at St. Clair Street
Office building

The architects took their cues from Eliel Saarinen's unsuccessful but influential entry in the Chicago Tribune Tower design contest of 1922. Thus this is a limestone Art Deco tower that setbacks make narrower as it rises: a "man-made mountain," as historian Leland Roth called it. But no mountain has decorative arches ornamenting the lower levels; here the main entry is an especially large recessed arch. The projections above are gargoyles. The Depression forced the Ohio Savings Bank to close a year after the new building was finished. But amid the euphoria of its opening, the bank issued a celebratory pamphlet on Toledo's history and their success. They had 18 branches, billions in capitalization, and now Toledo's tallest building, 368 feet high, a "cathedral of finance". Just above street level, the main banking room was by Graham, Anderson, Probst & White, Chicago. Running the length of the building, it offered an elegant concoction of marble and travertine, arcades of 25-foot arches, an elaborate beamed ceiling. It's all gone now, though a few of the mosaics have been recovered and installed in the building's cafeteria.

TOLEDO EDISON STEAM PLANT, 1897

D.H. Burnham & Co., Chicago
Water Street below Madison Avenue
Redevelopment in process
in early 2000

▶ EDISON STEAM PLANT

Designed by Daniel H. Burnham, one of the great names in American architecture—or at least, by his office—this riverside building is a good example of the dignity utilitarian structures once had. It's not ornate or elaborate, but it has arches and other detailing to enhance the brick expanses. The Alexander Company is taking it on as their third downtown Toledo project, as a restaurant or entertainment venue.

The Old West End and Museum of Art

This tour includes the true high points of Toledo architecture; with the superb museum, fabulous cathedral, and fine historic residential area, it is one of Ohio's best relatively compact architectural tours. All of the Old West End is listed on the National Register, including all these buildings except Frank Gehry's Center for Visual Arts. Right, *the* Frank Gehry.

▶ MUSEUM OF ART

Access: From downtown, take Monroe Street/State Route 51 west to Collingwood Boulevard and, on the left, the Toledo Museum of Art and Center for Visual Arts. Alternatively, I-75 has signs for the Museum of Art; if you're coming from the south, the Bancroft Street exit takes you onto Bancroft just west of Glenwood in the Old West End. To see Scott High School and Rosary Cathedral, turn north on Collingwood.

THE TOLEDO MUSEUM OF ART, 1912, 1926, 1933
Green & Wicks, Buffalo, with Harry W. Wachter, Toledo
2445 Monroe Street
Museum open daily except Monday; free; 419/255-8000; Peristyle not normally accessible but open frequently for evening concerts

From either direction on Monroe, the approach is urban drear; the Toledo Museum of Art contrasts its street as day does night. Set back on its expansive, well-treed lawn, the building is a Neoclassical bulwark against disorder and the ordinary: copper frieze and copper roof, recessed porches fronted with tall Ionic columns—16 in the center, six on each wing—and an unadorned facade in white marble. It could only be an art museum. And as such, it is no slouch. The American Association of Museums ranks art museums on collections, quality and size, and the Toledo Museum of Art is one of the top eight, according to Barbara Van Vleet, the former publicist. So is the Cleveland Museum, making Ohio and New York the only states with two institutions among the Big Eight.

▶ THE PERISTYLE

BUILDING ON GLASS—The Toledo Museum of Art rests on a glass foundation, and while Edward Drummond and Florence Scott Libbey were not its only patrons, it is hard to imagine this institution in the big leagues without them. From the museum's founding in 1901 to his death in 1925, Libbey was president of the board. At the beginning, the museum had two works: a painting of a sheep, and a mummified cat. For almost a decade, it rented quarters. When the time came for a building, Libbey announced his own large contribution and called for the people of Toledo to donate half as much; the response was so enthusiastic that he added works of art to his gift and his wife donated the land her father's house had been on. Community donors included 10,000 children who gave $500 in pennies, nickels and dimes, which museum Director George Stevens displayed in a heap in a bank window downtown.

Specifying a style, "Greek Ionic of the Periclean period," Libbey commissioned the architect, Edward B. Green of Green and Wicks, who had done Buffalo's Albright Art Gallery in 1905. Completed by January 1912, the building they did for Toledo is now the front half of the center section. The first expansion, the back of the center section, included the 14 columns above the Grove Place entrance from the parking lot. One of Libbey's last actions in late 1925 was to inspect this addition, still under construction, when he returned from abroad with a cold. Not long after, Libbey died of pneumonia.

A Bostonian, Libbey went into glass manufacturing with his father and then inherited the business. Toledo was trying to lure industry, and it had what a glassmaker needed: cheap gas and good sand. So in 1888 the Libbey Glass Manufacturing Company packed up and moved from Massachusetts to Toledo. A brass band met the train the workers came in on, and everyone paraded four miles to the new factory. By the turn of the century, every self-respecting middle-class home in America had Libbey cut glass. Libbey himself became a co-owner in other glass businesses; his Owens Bottle Company patented the first machine that produced uniform glass bottles.

Two years after coming to Toledo, Libbey married well. His bride was Florence Scott, also in her thirties. Her grandfather was Jesup Scott, founder of the University of Toledo; her uncle platted the West End; her father was a real-estate magnate; but this marriage that brought together two fortunes produced no children who survived. The true legacy of Edward and Florence Libbey is the Toledo Museum of Art. They were its principal builders; they launched the collections, including the superb one in glass art; most of their wealth was left to run the museum and fund acquisitions. Mr. Libbey's friends often urged that the museum be named for him, but he insisted that, to assure community support, it remain Toledo's. He was right, of course.

Florence Libbey survived her husband, living until 1938, and it is her contributions that elevate this building architecturally from the good to the very, very good. That was not necessarily Mrs. Libbey's first objective in 1930, when early-Depression Toledo had 10,000 unemployed. Mr. Libbey had left $2 million to construct east and west wings, and in 1930 Mrs. Libbey released that money—the income was supposed to be hers during her lifetime—for immediate construction to "do the greatest economic good," as she put it. Then for two years, 2,500 people were at work building the museum's wings, completed by January, 1933.

It was probably unprecedented for a museum to triple its floorspace for collections yet to be acquired, but Mrs. Libbey knew acquisitions would be provided for. For the time being the west wing that architect Edward Green and his son designed was teaching space, minimally finished on the interior, while the east wing had a Classic Court and an auditorium called the Peristyle. The west wing was completed in 1991 with enhanced architectural features and fine materials, as in the oak, ebony, and walnut parquet floors.

By undertaking construction to provide employment in the depths of the Depression, Florence Libbey proved forevermore the quality of her character. But she also assured a building with an uncommon unity—a steel-framed structure whose entire 658-foot facade was all the work of one architect, all in Vermont marble.

That was not all Mrs. Libbey accomplished, for the Peristyle was her pet project. This 1,700-seat auditorium counts as one of Ohio's most extraordinary spaces. Mrs. Libbey specifically wanted a setting for music and, according to museum staffer Sandra Knudsen, a specialist in ancient art, the benefactress knew what she wanted it to look like. She rejected the first proposals and told the architects to draw as if they were Iktinos and Kallikrates—the creators of the Parthenon in the 5th century B.C., no less. So the Peristyle is basically a classical room. A raised, U-shaped balcony embraces the main floor seating; above the last row of balcony seats a colonnade follows the U. The frieze matches the one outside. Chairs are in a Greek style with a splayed metal leg. Perhaps because Mrs. Libbey, unaccustomed to children, wanted the seats covered when young audiences came, the original seat fabric is still in place.

Even if Iktinos and Kallikrates might feel at home in the Peristyle, they could not have done the ceiling. Plain, coved, it's really a suspended acoustical ceiling, a pioneer in its day. It works. The acoustics are so perfect that entering concertgoers are offered throat lozenges with soft, non-crackly wrappers.

▶ CENTER FOR THE VISUAL ARTS

UNIVERSITY OF TOLEDO CENTER FOR THE VISUAL ARTS, UNIVERSITY OF TOLEDO, 1992

Frank O. Gehry & Associates, Santa Monica, with The Collaborative, Toledo
620 Grove Place
Accessible daily; 419/530-8300. Gehry also designed the sculpture studio across
Grove Place just to the east: a plain rectangular box with a rear porch whose
columns look like telephone poles.

The art school, Center for the Visual Arts or CVA, used to be inside the
museum; since 1992 it's had its own building off the east wing. It was the
first Ohio project by Toronto-born, California-based Frank O. Gehry, who is
the most original architect working in the United States today. Gehry gave
the museum its largest sculpture: a helter-skelter pile of blocks with few
windows and beautiful siding—copper galvanized with zinc—that was shiny
and coppery at first, then gray, and gradually, as the copper erodes through
the lead, should turn greenish. The colors, and that of the green glass wall on
the CVA's south side, are striking next to the old building. In its complexity
and shunning of right angles, CVA is a truly modern work. It has only one
square room, a first-floor gallery. A second-floor office is U-shaped, working
its way around posts—"gehrymandering" is the word Art Department chair
Tom Lingeman uses. That office also has a window overlooking the lobby;
the occupant keeps a bird cage in it. The architect picked the colors, like the
red, orange and white around the supply store. He also designed the library
shelves and carrels and specified the quarter-sawn wood, with its fine parallel
lines. The library basks in light reflected by a concrete wall opposite its large
window; librarians wear sun glasses in summer. Though few windows are
evident outside, Toledo *Blade* arts writer Sally Vallongo found that inside,
each room had a window with a carefully framed, postcard-like view. She
especially liked the city vista from a tiny third-floor balcony, a student
smoking porch. For construction superintendent Pat Bolger, CVA was "not
just another strip mall." Bolger told Vallongo that this project was in his

head "day and night, 24 hours a day, all year. Nothing's the same. Nothing's standard." Some walls are meant to be out of plumb; some are curved; hall walls aren't parallel; no two offices are alike; and on the outside, the building has 44 corners. Bolger had to deal with a thousand pieces of steel, almost all different and each requiring its own drawing. Bolger knew he would miss the challenge afterwards. He said, "Everything from here will be downhill." The CVA received some awards, including a 1996 American Institute of Architects' Honor Award—*Architecture* magazine described it as "complex, damn-the-right-angle Modernism." The building also topped *Time's* citations for best design of 1992. Besides, says Lingeman, in the mid 1990s it was the number-one favorite of 35 Dutch artists touring all Gehry's U.S. buildings.

JESUP W. SCOTT HIGH SCHOOL, 1913
David L. Stine, Toledo
2400 Collingwood Boulevard at Machen Street

During the time when Edward Libbey headed the Toledo School Board, the architect who had done his house, David L. Stine, designed two landmark city high schools, both Collegiate

▶ Scott High School

Gothic in brick and terra cotta: Waite in East Toledo, and this one, which has been altered less. The highlight of the tour Principal Stanley Woody gave me was the cafeteria, a room whose wainscoting, arched doors and high dark-beamed ceiling would be the pride of any college— except for the between-beam ceiling panels. This inner-city school had a good ambiance, with everyone in the hall greeting the principal with "Hello Mr. Woody" and a smile. The 1,375 students, he said, are not so many that he can't know them all.

ROSARY CATHEDRAL, OR OUR LADY QUEEN OF THE MOST HOLY ROSARY CATHEDRAL, 1940
William Richard Perry of Comes, Perry and McMullen, Pittsburgh
2535 Collingwood Boulevard at Islington Street
To see the sanctuary on weekdays, ask at the parish office in adjacent school (this handsome 1914 school was designed by the same architectural firm); tours may be arranged for groups of at least ten; 419/244-9575.

This, says Larry Adams, is the world's only Spanish Plateresque cathedral— Toledo's Spanish name inspired the architects. Adams, an ordained deacon who in 1989 moved from Archbold to Toledo mostly to be closer to Rosary Cathedral, knows a lot about this building. He gives more than a hundred tours a year; he is probably the only person on earth who could do a six-and-a-half-hour tour, as he did once but won't again. Construction began in 1925

▶ Rosary Cathedral

and walls had risen only to the cornerstone, three feet above the sanctuary floor, when the 1929 stock-market crash threatened to dry up pledges. "Desperate times," says Adams, "called for desperate measures." So the bishop and the rector canvassed rich Old West End parishioners and in one day collected enough money for tickets to Europe. Then the two clerics departed for Lisieux, France, to offer a 30-day perpetual novena to St. Theresa, the Little Flower—"perpetual" meant that at least one of them was praying every moment of the day and night. Why France? One reason was that St. Theresa's 1925 canonization coincided with the cathedral's ground breaking. Another, says Adams, was that new saints are reputedly more responsive. In their prayers, the bishop and the rector promised that if St. Theresa would help assure the money to finish their cathedral, she alone of all the saints would have a shrine in the sanctuary. So it is. The cathedral was completed in 1940, though German woodcarver August Schmidt kept working until 1948; he did the pulpit and its canopy, the large crucifix overhead, figures on the sanctuary wall and a mural in the sacristy. Smaller carvings—rosettes or the 1,500 spindles over the glass in doors—were done by local craftsmen. As a style Plateresque is, in the words of architectural historian Eric Johannesen, "a wild mixture." Thus this church combines the classical, three-part Palladian windows with Gothic tracery (curving stone dividers), a combination you won't see often. The name *Plateresque*, from the

Spanish word for silver, means ornamentation resembling a silversmith's work; Rosary Cathedral adapts that concept by using gold edging. The structure is all stone, with no supporting steel. The front facade has delicate, almost lacelike stone carving, especially above the gable and in the rose window. It is an opulent building. Johannesen loved this church. He called it one of Toledo's "most splendid" buildings, with an interior that "looks more like a painting than like sculpture or engineering."

Houses of the Old West End

The Old West End is a mostly intact array of large, luxurious late nineteenth- and early twentieth-century houses. It is unique because it was designed almost entirely by an exceptional group of Toledo architects, including the trio that Ted Ligibel calls "the three heavies"—E.O. Fallis, George Mills, and David Stine, plus Harry Wachter and the unsung Lawrence Bellman, who both came a little later. For the work of all five, Toledo is far and away the best showcase.

Access: The residential Old West End is north of Monroe, west of Collingwood. Touring tips: The Old West End residential district extends fairly far north, but the really big older houses are mostly south, closer to Monroe. See Glenwood, Robinwood, Scottwood, and Parkwood, especially south of Virginia. Collingwood Boulevard used to be the principal showcase, but now it has the most gaps. Foot touring is practical because distances are short; the area between Monroe and Virginia totals less than half a square mile. Driving is easy too, except that streets may be blocked or change direction—devices introduced years ago to thwart through traffic. All houses here are private and not open to the public, except as noted for Mansion View. The Women of the Old West End publish a walking tour available from the Chamber of Commerce, 419/243-8191. They also sponsor a Christmas tour the first Sunday in December. Call Toni Moore at 419/242-8088. The Old West End Association sponsors a festival and house tour the first full weekend in June. Call Dennis Lange at Pumpernickel's Deli, 419/244-2255. Houses here are listed by street, starting with Collingwood on the east and starting with lowest numbers for each street. All but one of these sites are below Virginia Street; cross streets of Bancroft and Virginia both have two-way traffic.

▶ MANSION VIEW

THE BARTLEY HOUSE, 1905, 1997

E.O. Fallis, Toledo
1855 Collingwood Boulevard at Jefferson Avenue

With its steep roof ascending 40 feet above the house, E.O. Fallis's
Chateauesque Bartley House stands at the gateway to the Old West End.
Built for Rudolph Bartley, a German immigrant who sold a lot of groceries, it
later passed through periods as a funeral home and, more recently, a vacant,
city-owned property. The city was an inattentive caretaker. It sent a roofing
crew that repaired the wrong place, left open a roof hatch not visible from
the ground, and failed to check the gutters. Water damage was so severe that
almost all the interior had to be scrapped when the Bartley was redeveloped
as ten apartments in the 1990s.

REYNOLDS-SECOR HOUSE, 1887, NOW MANSION VIEW

E.O. Fallis, Toledo
2035 Collingwood Boulevard
Mansion View available for rentals and tours; 419/242-0495

This is E.O. Fallis's demonstration of how to do Queen Anne in brick; even
the carriage house is a gem. After the Jay Secor family bought the house in

MANY PAVILIONS—Toledo, says William Frisk, a life-long resident of the Old West End, was "the Silicon Valley of the 1890s. Success was guaranteed." The most successful moved to what is now the Old West End, the neighborhood platted in 1882 by Frank J. Scott. The neighborhood became a showcase. "This," says Frisk, "was the first blush of money."

From the 1880s to 1925, the Old West End was Toledo's classy residential neighborhood; today, preserved and restored, it is largely intact. The houses are substantial, distinctive, and designed by architects: a visual banquet. Michael Young, who lived on Parkwood Avenue when he was head of planning for the city, did at least 500 walks during his four years in the neighborhood. "Every time," he says, "I saw something new architecturally." Until he moved to San Diego in early 1997, Young's house was at 2255 Parkwood. Designed in 1887 by architect David L. Stine, it has six fireplaces, eight bedrooms, and a total of 22 rooms. Young could sit on his front porch and look down through all the porches on his block. From a covered second-floor porch, he could watch storms coming in.

In the early 1990s, the scuttlebutt was that the Old West End was not succeeding as a rehab neighborhood. But when I was visiting and revisiting in 1996-98, I found it a clear success. Virtually no property below Virginia looked derelict. In 1995 Mike Young visited five houses on the Christmas tour. Three years earlier, when he himself was house-hunting, three of those houses had been vacant and vandalized. Now they were so well restored they were on the tour.

On the other hand, many of the neighborhoods around the Old West End, which extends north to Central Avenue at least on Collingwood Boulevard, are rough. But Young said that when his family moved in and came to know their neighbors, they felt secure.

The first few West End houses were built in the 1870s; in the 1880s, people still thought they were moving to the country. In the twentieth century a newer area farther west became the West End, and this, the Old West End. What really saved the Old West End was Rosary Cathedral—Catholic families wanted to stay near the church. So says Toledo architect Charles Stark, who adds that though some houses became tenements, many never did.

The area was among the first historic communities with a neighborhood organization; the Old West End Association dates from the early 1940s. Judge Andy Devine says it was founded with what now seems the immoral goal of keeping the neighborhood white. When Devine moved in in the early 1950s, he challenged the association to change its course and promote peaceful integration—if it didn't, he and his faction threatened to found a competing group. So the old board resigned, and a new Old West End Association emerged. Residents today are proud of the neighborhood's diverse population. With their family gone, Devine and his wife left their ten-bedroom house in 1991 and went to the suburbs, where he is pining for the Old West End and its spirit of community—the spirit, he says, that saved the neighborhood.

Today the Old West End offers a still largely intact array of large luxurious houses. Ohio State's Doug Graf describes the Old West End as a whole with many pavilions. Architecturally speaking, he says, it's probably Ohio's best residential district.

▶ MANSION VIEW

1904, all the old-fashioned Victorian interior was updated, except for the hall and stairs. After six years as a bed and breakfast, the house was donated to the Old West End Association in late 2000.

EDWARD FORD HOUSE, 1901
George S. Mills, Toledo
2205 Collingwood Boulevard at Bancroft

Plate-glass tycoon Edward Ford's formal, Renaissance style house has dark terra cotta trim contrasting with its light brick.

LEEPER GEDDES HOUSE, 1903
Thomas F. Huber, Toledo
2116 Parkwood Avenue between Floyd and Bancroft Streets

A Neoclassical house fit for a prince. You'll see Corinthian capitals and balustrades, appearing and reappearing at different levels.

▶ LEEPER GEDDES HOUSE

CRATZ HOUSE, 1897

Harry W. Wachter, Toledo
2150 Parkwood Avenue south of Bancroft

Neighborhood resident William Frisk estimates that half the houses in the Old West End are by architect Harry W. Wachter (1868-1941), a Toledo native. The Cratz House has several distinctive features that may help you spot some of Wachter's other work. For instance, note the flared eaves; the decorated bargeboards (boards running along and emphasizing gables); the three-sided mini-Gothic windows on the second floor—you'll see these again and again in the neighborhood. Frisk's estimate on Wachter's substantial contribution is unlikely to be documented. He says that when Wachter's son Horace, also an architect, was closing the office in the 1980s he threw out drawings for perhaps 800 houses, including many around here.

EDWARD LIBBEY HOUSE, 1895

David L. Stine, Toledo
2008 Scottwood Avenue south of Bancroft, NHL, NRHP

This stone and shingle house is just barely visible from the front door of Edward and Florence Libbey's principal legacy, the Toledo Museum of Art. An Ohio native, architect David L. Stine studied in Chicago and later, with Libbey, was a co-founder of the Museum.

DUNN-BLAIR HOUSE, 1915

Mills, Rhines, Bellman & Nordhoff, Toledo
2049 Scottwood Avenue south of Bancroft

This house is a copy of an early twentieth-century addition by architect Edwin Landseer Lutyens to an eighteenth-century English manor house. Jim and Pat Appold, owners of the Oliver House, lived in Dunn-Blair for 16 years. They visited the English prototype, now a girls' school, and were surprised to see detailing they had at home, such as the same stair rails. The biggest exterior difference is that this version has a lower roof.

ARTHUR SIEBEN HOUSE, 1902

George S. Mills, Toledo
2109 Scottwood Avenue south of Bancroft

Here's a shingle house with a heavy stone porch and several elongated conical turrets, some along the side wall of the house.

JOHN BARBER HOUSE, 1897

David L. Stine, Toledo
2271 Scottwood Avenue at Virginia Street

Eric Johannesen very much liked this house for its unlikely combination of Colonial Revival motifs that are classical in origin, with Gothic designs in the ornamental wood carvings.

▶ TILLINGHAST-WILLYS HOUSE

TILLINGHAST-WILLYS HOUSE, 1900

Brown, Burton & Davis, Cincinnati, with George W. Netcher, Tiffin
2210 Robinwood Avenue at Bancroft

The Tillinghast House's roof has three chimneys with chimney pots that owner Michael Murray says are as tall as a person. One day in the early 1980s Murray noticed a man dressed in top hat and tails, walking up and down across the street, studying his house. Then the stranger approached and told Murray his house had the most beautiful chimneys in Toledo—so beautiful that the man, a chimney sweep, wanted to have his wedding on top of them. He explained that a platform big enough to hold the wedding party of eight men, eight women and the minister, could rest securely on the pots of the middle chimney. Murray assented, but when the day came he climbed out a third floor window and had everyone sign liability releases on their way up. He noticed that the bride wore tennis shoes with her white dress; the men, all chimney sweeps, wore top hats and tails with red scarves. Along with 2,000 other people, Murray watched the ceremony from the ground. From above, a CNN crew in a helicopter taped it. Later the tape appeared as part of a Russian television documentary on the American way of life. A real estate agent and founder of the local Harley club, Murray bought this house, the Old West End's most conspicuous mansion, in 1977. He paid the highest price ever in the neighborhood, $77,000. Even then, he believes, had the house been in another neighborhood, the price would have been three to four times as much. Since then West End values have appreciated faster than those elsewhere in Toledo, but they had further to go. Murray gave the neighborhood's 1996 price range as $40,000 to $300,000. Murray's house— Ted Ligibel says it's a mix of Tudor, Chateauesque and Gothic—was built by licorice, the source of Alvin B. Tillinghast's fortune. Outfitted with cane, spats and high hat, the Licorice King would walk up and down outside, watching his house being built. Alas. His company failed and he never lived here. Among later owners, one was auto manufacturer John North Willys. Murray bought the house from the Society of Oblate Fathers, who used it as a retirement home for priests; when Murray first saw the livingroom, it held 11 recliners, 11 foot stools, and 11 pedestal ash trays. The Oblate Fathers made a few changes in the house. The little confessional window in the library wall is still there. So are the liturgical signs on the third-floor ballroom beams, though the room is no longer a chapel. The first floor has two glazed porches; the diningroom is chestnut; the livingroom, mahogany; the library and hall, quarter-sawn golden oak; and all the woodwork upstairs is solid cherry. The second floor has five bedrooms and four baths; the third floor, which Murray rents, has four bedrooms and one bath, plus the 25- by 45-foot ballroom.

THE EMERSON, 1913

2308 Robinwood Avenue north of Virginia

▶ THE EMERSON

Two levels of columns and four levels of porches span the height of this apartment building; at each corner there's a square tower. Old West End apartments were elegant in their own right; this one was among the first to have an elevator.

HOUSE, 1892

2228 Glenwood Avenue just north of Bancroft

Probably I noticed this house in late 1996 because the aluminum siding had just been pulled off, and it was looking spiffy. William Frisk reports that the siding went on with great fanfare in the 1960s, when the house was improved as an urban renewal showcase. Altogether, as he recalls, $15,000 in Federal money was spent to strip detailing and shorten the porch, which ran all across the front. Then when the house was a perfect example of modern excellence, the governor showed up to cut the ribbon. Of course in 1996, every bit of what seemed an improvement 30 years earlier, had to be undone. Who knows for sure what will happen 30 years hence.

J.J. FREEMAN HOUSE, 1896

Mills and Wachter
2274 Glenwood Avenue at Virginia

This house shows what wonderful work the six-year partnership of two young architects, George S. Mills and Harry W. Wachter, could produce. From the ground up to the fat turret and the three dormers with their elongated roofs, the house has an offering for the eye at every turn. ¶ Mills and Wachter met when both were teachers at the Toledo Manual Training School. In 1892 they became partners. Their first job was the Snell Bicycle Works; the first payment, a bicycle. The partnership brook up in 1898 partly because Wachter was ailing after an appendectomy; ultimately surgeons removed a sponge left in him in the first operation, and he recovered fully.

▶ FREEMAN HOUSE

Access: Return to Monroe Street and turn right/west to see the former First Church of Christ, which is just past the museum at Lawrence Avenue. After that Monroe's next large intersection is Bancroft Street; turn left; University of Toledo and University Hall are about two miles west; short-term street parking is available in front of University Hall.

FIRST CHURCH OF CHRIST, SCIENTIST, NOW UNITED MISSIONARY BAPTIST CHURCH, 1899

E.O. Fallis, Toledo
2705 Monroe Street at Lawrence Avenue, NRHP
Church

A freeway access makes this stone church seem alone at its site: a fat, stalwart sentinel. It has a square four-story tower flanked by two deep gables, one facing left, the other right. Ted Ligibel describes the sanctuary's leaded glass dome as "magnificent." This was Ohio's first Christian Science Church.

UNIVERSITY HALL, UNIVERSITY OF TOLEDO, 1930

Mills, Rhines, Bellman & Nordhoff, Toledo
2801 West Bancroft Street
University classes and offices open during regular hours

Sixty-thousand people, one fifth of the population of Toledo, came to University Hall's inaugural five-day open house, where one attraction was elephant rides. At a time when many educational institutions were, like the

▶ UNIVERSITY HALL

University of Toledo, ordering buildings in Collegiate Gothic, few got 217-foot towers like this one. The building celebrated the university's consolidation on a new campus, and for a few years the whole institution tucked itself into the 337 rooms on six floors. As for the elephants at the open house, Mark Yeary, a university lab coordinator, has no doubts, because he's watched old movies. In the mid 1990s Yeary helped repair the tower clock (that meant pulling off the hands, rebuilding the shafts, and installing a new motor), which gave him time to become a devotee of the tower. One cold, wet, dark December afternoon—later than we had planned—Yeary led two women from the communications office and me up into the tower by way of a spiral staircase in one corner. The good part was seeing the enormous mullions—the stone dividers in the open tower windows; from the ground they don't seem nearly so huge. The bad part was the hand railing, encrusted in pigeon droppings. Faced outside in Wisconsin lannon stone with Indiana limestone trim, University Hall has been altered inside, though college seals still line the street-level hall. The recently restored Doermann Theater is at this level too. It's not readily accessible, but I arranged to see it and was disappointed; the handicapped ramps are disfiguring. Charles Stark attributes University Hall to Lawrence Bellman (1876-1951), the principal designer for Mills, Rhines, Bellman & Nordhoff. Stark, who started with the firm as a part-time draftsman when he was in high school, in 1951, poked around in company history, and came to recognize Bellman's hand in much of the firm's best work. "As I dug in I kept finding more and more design by Bellman, and less and less credit for him," Stark says. "No one else had his sensitivity." He explains that that isn't uncommon in architectural firms, where customers like to think the older partner they know is doing the design, while actually it's probably a junior employee. The older one simply doesn't have the time.

Toledo 3: Far-Flung: Zoo, East Toledo, Lighthouse

Access: The Toledo Zoo is southwest of the city center. From downtown take State Route 25 and follow signs. Alternatively, take Broadway (at the Oliver House) to Zoo entrance and parking.

▶ Zoo Amphitheater

TOLEDO ZOO AVIARY, 1937
Paul S. Robinette, Toledo
2700 Broadway
Zoo open daily; fee; 419/385-5721

Architecturally, the seven Spanish Colonial Revival structures are the big attraction at the Toledo Zoo. Not surprisingly, the zoo is more interested in showing off its animals than its buildings, so these structures are all hard to see, and all have been altered extensively. They do offer good glimpses: arches, curvy gables, interesting stone and brick work. Originally the 1937 Aviary, or Aves, was a Works Progress Administration project, designed by an unemployed Toledo architect, Paul Robinette. It used wood recycled from a railroad shop or salvaged from an abandoned lumber yard; bricks came from a huge chimney at Milburn Wagon Works. Not all the materials were scrap. Under the eaves red bricks outline diamond-shaped windows: the first glass brick Owens-Illinois ever made. Of the other Spanish Colonial buildings, the Elephant House, 1924, and the Carnivora, or "cathouse", 1928, pre-date the Depression—in 1925 President Theodore Roosevelt's son Kermit, a big game hunter, came to turn the first spade for the Carnivora. Today it's a restaurant. The Depression-era structures all had Federal help from the WPA and other agencies; besides architect Robinette, 1,300 people found work building the zoo. The Reptile House was completed in 1934; the Amphitheatre opened in 1936, with a reflecting pool separating the stage from the seats. The Museum of Science opened in 1938; the Aquarium, in 1939.

EAST TOLEDO

East Toledo was where immigrants lived, near their jobs, for this was the industrial side of the river—iron plants, coal and rail yards—"all the dirtiest stuff," as Don Monroe says. Monroe grew up here in a house 180 feet from a refinery fence; as a boy he shopped at the Weber Block, then a dimestore, for sodas and goldfish. As an adult he started out in the window cleaning business but ended up trying to save East Toledo. Since 1979 he's been director of River East Economic Revitalization, a private nonprofit. Monroe lures new companies with the area's low rents, and he redevelops property; but his biggest challenge is keeping businesses already there.

Access: East Toledo is accessible from downtown by going east on State Route 51, which joins with State Routes 2 and 65 to cross the Maumee south of downtown; then turn left/north on Oak Street which bends and becomes Front Street. Alternatively, I-280 exits onto Front Street; drive south to Main Street.

WEBER BLOCK, 1888
101 Main Street at Front, NRHP
Ground floor retail; offices upstairs; for tour call Don Monroe, 419/698-2310

At a prime location in East Toledo, the Weber Block presents a fancy facade that easily qualifies it as one of Ohio's best Queen Anne commercial buildings. Three stories high, brick, it has recessed second- and third-floor balconies. The Weber Block was built on spec by two downtown merchants, John

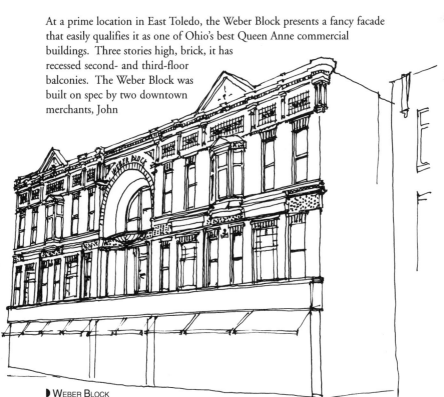

▶ WEBER BLOCK

and Gustave Weber, who rented it to a drygoods store. Other tenants included the East Side Business College, opened in 1895, and a railroad workers' hotel that ran from 1918 until it was shut down by the health department in 1932. The third floor has a couple large halls originally intended for fraternal-order meetings. One, 40 by 90 feet with 14 windows facing downtown, became a gym in the 1910s and 1920s—the sign on the wall reads "No Free Workouts". According to legend boxer Jess Willard trained here in 1919; but given that he lost his title bout with Jack Dempsey, perhaps he didn't. In the 1930s the Bulgarian Socialist Workers of America met in the smaller hall—Bulgarians were among East Toledo's many ethnic communities; the writing on the stairs says "watch your step" in Bulgarian. The Weber Block has been one of the projects of Don Monroe's River East Revitalization, which in 1997 owned and rented a quarter million square feet in seven buildings altogether. River East bought the Weber Block in the mid 1980s, after it sat empty for most of a decade and its imminent demolition hit page one of the Toledo *Blade*. Built in 1888 for $5,000, it was to be razed for $45,000. Rehabbing seemed an impossibility—just the kind of challenge Monroe likes. Today one third of the Weber Block's 51,000 square feet has been restored. Though the large third-floor halls and the Alvin Theater, added at the rear in the 1890s, remain to be redone, the building has seven business tenants on the first floor and another seven on the second. Not only is the building looking good, it's paying for itself.

FRIEDMAN BLOCK, 1892

117 Main Street, NRHP
Medical offices and apartments

Two doors from the Weber Block, the Friedman Block, red brick with two large corner towers, is another late nineteenth-century commercial building. A JC Penney store until 1967, it's owned by River East. Saving the neighborhood doesn't progress straight uphill. When I talked to Don Monroe, a departing tenant had just trashed the second-floor apartment. Later a court forced the tenant to make repairs. A new tenant was in health services.

FIRE STATION NO. 13, 1899

2154 Front Street at Paine, NRHP/Birmingham HD
Business quarters and apartment

This is one of Toledo's grand old firehouses; of those built in 1899 it wasn't the grandest, but survival counts. It's a high building with an even higher tower at the back for drying hoses. Ornamental bargeboards on the gables are mostly intact. In 1996 an electrical contractor bought the building from River East for his business and, upstairs, his living quarters.

Access: Seeing the Toledo Harbor Lighthouse from land requires binoculars and great weather. Best place is beach at Maumee Bay State Park, reached by driving east from East Toledo on State Route 2; turn left/north on Curtis Road, as marked, to park. (To reach East Toledo and State Route 2 see East Toledo access.)

▶ TOLEDO HARBOR LIGHTHOUSE

TOLEDO HARBOR LIGHTHOUSE, 1904

U.S. Army Corps of Engineers
Lake Erie, NRHP
The U.S. Coast Guard has this lighthouse on the market, but as early 2000, no buyer had appeared

This building is so wonderful that it was the one selected for the cover of a guide to 100 eastern Great Lakes lighthouses. Its picture sells T shirts at the gift shop in the Oliver House brew pub. And Randy Hinderer, an exhibit producer for COSI Toledo, who's actually been *in* it—he went to see the lens, now on display at the museum—has seen lighthouses from Istanbul to China, and this, he says, is "the most unique." The structure is two adjoining brick buildings, one three stories high and topped by the light tower, which rises to 69 feet; the other only one story and built for the fog signal. Both have roofs rounded at the eaves with a roll of metal: a detailing that's both unusual and striking. The walls of the taller building have pairs of slightly recessed arches enclosing three floors of windows. Once dredging made Toledo Harbor accessible in 1897, a lighthouse to mark the channel became a necessity. Construction began in 1901 with the sinking of a crib that was filled with stone, gravel, and sand until it became an island for the lighthouse to sit on. Work on the house was underway by 1902 but not finished that December, so the building had to be boarded up and "made snug for the winter." (So says a history in Coast Guard archives.) The light was installed in spring, 1904. A keeper was resident until the operation was automated in 1965. At that time the Coast Guard put a dummy, dressed in uniform, in the window, to discourage trespassers. Sure enough, some passing lakefarers took that dummy for a ghost.

Youngstown

In 1798 John Young, a 35-year-old New Hampshire native living in Whitestown, New York, bought a township in the Connecticut Western Reserve. Two years later, he founded Young's Town in the middle of his township. He laid out two main streets, Federal and Market, both 100-feet wide; at their intersection, he put a 250-by-400-foot square. As it turned out, after Young's wife joined him the next year, she didn't like frontier life; and in 1803 the family returned to Whitestown. So although John Young left no descendants in Youngstown, he did leave the framework for a great downtown. It became just that in the early twentieth century, as steel mills crowded into the Mahoning Valley, spewing out wealth that helped build a wonderful group of medium-high skyscrapers around John Young's square. Today the founder's plat is still there; the wonderful buildings are still there; but downtown—downtown

▶ FEDERAL SQUARE, BEFORE DOLLAR BANK REMODELING

as measured by energy, things to do, and people after 5—has left. ¶ Beyond downtown, Youngstown has an almost quirky collection of good buildings, ranging from an opulent log house to a Postmodern museum. Rebecca Rogers told me about them; later she visited most of them with me. For over 20 years Rebecca Rogers, who lives in an old house in Poland, has been focusing on her region as an architectural historian and consultant. A native of Hudson, Rogers trained as an architect at the Massachusetts Institute of Technology and was a historical architect for the National Park Service. But when she moved to Youngstown in 1975, she was no longer able to practice. Local firms had no woman architects and were unwilling to change. ¶ This guide divides Youngstown into two sections: Downtown and Wick Avenue, and Youngstown West.

Access: From either direction on I-680 follow signs for U.S. 422; for downtown Youngstown exit at Wick Avenue/U.S. 62 and drive about half a mile south to the square called Federal Plaza, which is also the name of the flanking east-west street. South of the square, Wick Avenue becomes Market Street. Central Plaza area should be toured on foot; Center of Industry and Labor and rest of Wick Avenue are an easy walk but may be done by car.

Central Square, now Federal Plaza

While northeast Ohio has many nineteenth-century squares, Youngstown's is the only one surrounded by a group of "landmark towers of approximately the same height and mass." So wrote Cleveland architectural historian Eric Johannesen, whose claim could have been more sweeping, for no other Ohio city has a square with buildings like Youngstown's. Johanessen cited seven high rises from a period of just over 20 years—1906 to 1929. One has eight stories; one has 18; and the others, 12 or 13 stories. They were designed by nationally known architects, including Albert Kahn and Walker & Weeks, and by local architects, notably Morris W. Scheibel, whose work was nationally recognized. D. H. Burnham & Co., Chicago, did two, half a block west at the corner of Phelps Street. All the Central Square/Federal Plaza buildings mentioned here, except the altered Dollar Building, are on the National Register, listed as Seven Early Office Buildings at Central Square TR.

CENTRAL SAVINGS AND LOAN COMPANY BUILDING, NOW METROPOLITAN TOWER, 1929
Morris W. Scheibel, Youngstown
1 Federal Plaza West
Office building; bank

All the cities in this guide, except Canton, have high-quality Art Deco skyscrapers. The Metropolitan Tower was Youngstown's. It was built at a time when, says Ohio State's Douglas Graf, "even a small city was so much more significant. A building like this would be big news if built now—it was normal then. How much more successful cities were, when they could mount large and successful projects just as a matter of course." At 18 stories the square's tallest high rise, Central Savings was also the grand finale. It has setbacks at the top and good detailing that can be seen at the ground level—

▶ CENTRAL TOWER

including claws at the bottoms of the first-floor window mullions, or dividers. Inside, the banking room has been redone, but the lobby is worth seeing. From outside take the side door at the back; the lobby has Art Deco elevator doors and ceiling designs in polychromed plaster. Born in New York City, architect Morris W. Scheibel (1887-1976) lived and practiced in Youngstown from 1911 on. Between this tower and the Realty Building across the street, he proved himself. Eric Johannesen wrote that, "judged purely as works of art," the square's two best designs were Scheibel's.

MAHONING NATIONAL BANK BUILDING, NOW SKY BANK, 1910; WIDTH DOUBLED, 1924

Albert Kahn, Detroit
23 Federal Plaza West
Office building; bank

Built and long occupied by a locally owned bank, for years this 13-story high rise had tall red rooftop letters reading: MAHONING BANK. After April 2000, the new owner, Sky Bank, took advantage of the same opportunity. Before Albert Kahn became internationally famous for sleek factories (see also Ohio Steel Foundry Roll Shop in Lima; Vol. II), he designed this Chicago Style skyscraper clad in white terra cotta. On the ground floor two-story-high windows look inward on a perfect view: the banking room, its splendor intact. It has paneled columns, coffered ceiling, and bankers—every time I've looked during business hours, bankers in white shirt sleeves were working at their desks. To see more at Central Square/Federal Plaza: Also on the west side, the First National Bank Building, now Bank One, 1925, by Cleveland's Walker &
Weeks, 6 Federal Plaza West, has a good ceiling in the banking room. On the other side, to the east, the Realty Building, 1924, Morris W. Scheibel, 47 Federal Plaza, is brown brick with an ornate terra cotta cornice; the Stambaugh Building, 1906, Albert Kahn, 44 Federal Plaza, built as eight stories with four more added in 1913, is brick and terra cotta.

Central Square
and Commercial National Bank Building,
Youngstown, Ohio.

▶ MAHONING NATIONAL BANK

DOLLAR BANK, NOW NATIONAL CITY BANK BUILDING, 1906, REHAB 1976

Charles H. Owsley,
Youngstown
16 Wick Avenue
Office building

The eight-story Dollar Bank, the masterpiece of Youngstown architect Charles H. Owsley (1846-1935), was Central Square's first high rise. It was swaddled in a red terra-cotta facing that, says architectural consultant Rebecca Rogers, made it "the most delicious building you ever saw." The deliciousness disappeared under gray and black granite sheathing, applied in 1973-75 in broad alternating verticals. No doubt the bank thought modern 1975 customers would be happier doing business in a modern-looking building. Author William Brenner disapproved. The bank, he charged, made a costly "investment in historical destruction that, in economic terms alone, it probably wouldn't have approved for one of its borrowers." English-born

▶ MAHONING COUNTY COURTHOUSE

Charles H. Owsley was the senior of a remarkable father-son team of architects who practiced in Youngstown during a period of over 70 years. After apprenticing under Gilbert Scott, a leader in England's Gothic Revival, the father came to North America in 1868 and the next year settled on a Trumbull County farm. As the Mahoning County seat was moved from Canfield to Youngstown in the mid-1870s, Owsley was named courthouse architect and began practicing in the city. He retired in 1911 and lived to the age of 88, rarely missing communion at the First Presbyterian Church and becoming the oldest Fellow of the American Institute of Architects.

MAHONING COUNTY COURTHOUSE, 1910, 1991

Owsley and Boucherle, Youngstown; 1991 restoration 4-M Company, Youngstown
120 Market Street, just south of Federal Plaza, NRHP
County courthouse; open weekdays; 330/740-2158

What a fine courthouse Mahoning County has. Second Renaissance Revival in style, it has rusticated, or deeply grooved stone at the ground floor level, and a slightly projecting center section with six fine Ionic columns. True to 1910, it's granite and marble over a steel frame. Don't miss the inside, which has been sparkling since a 1991

restoration. The highlight is a four-story central hall under a glazed dome. The third floor has only half its potential space; the rest is allocated to increased height for second-floor courtrooms. One fine example is Courtroom No. 1, which has mahogany wainscoting, a deeply coffered ceiling, and a mural depicting Indians who were frightened away from this area after Council Rock, site of thrice-yearly inter-tribal feasts, was cleft by lightning in 1755. This courthouse was signed by Charles H. Owsley and his long-time partner Louis Boucherle, but it was really the work of Charles H.'s son, Charles F. Owsley (1880-1953), who practiced with his father only seven years, starting in 1904. A University of Pennsylvania graduate, the younger Owsley studied at the…École des Beaux-Arts in Paris. The…École was the training ground for many of America's best architects; it emphasized good planning, quality construction, and expressive ornamentation. Back in Youngstown, Charles F. founded the local Rotary Club and married a department-store heiress, Kate McKelvey. Besides the courthouse, two of his designs are in this guide, one in Youngstown (see the Isaly Dairy below) and one in Mineral Ridge, Trumbull County (the Mahoning Valley Sanitary District's Purification and Pumping Works, Vol. II.) Charles F. did enough schools, houses and other buildings that, in the years before his death at 73, he could entertain himself with drives around the countryside, to see his designs again. Though the Owsleys designed much of the best stuff in Youngstown, it's relatively hard to find out about them. That's partly because Joseph G. Butler, Jr., author of a great local history, one of whose volumes contains 808 pages of biographies, never mentions them. Rebecca Rogers, who noticed this omission, speculates that courthouse cost overruns may have so annoyed Butler that he omitted the Owsleys out of spite. But if Butler hadn't been feuding with the Owsleys, Ohio today might not have any public buildings by the renowned McKim, Mead and White of New York. Butler was the one who called them in to design both the Butler Institute of American Art (see below) and the McKinley Birthplace Memorial in Niles (see also, Vol. II).

PEGGY ANN BUILDING, 1930

Morris W. Scheibel, Youngstown
101 Federal Plaza West, NRHP
Commercial building

Here's an Art Deco confection in white terra cotta tile. Two stories tall, it has delectable bas-relief decoration between the two floors.

WARNER, NOW POWERS AUDITORIUM, 1929-31; REOPENED 1969

Rapp & Rapp, Chicago
260 Federal Plaza West, NRHP
Theater, now used by Youngstown Symphony; to see interior call for an appointment or, suggests the woman at the box office, buy a ticket; 330/744-4269

Hollywood's Warner Brothers were really Youngstown boys; what better gift to their home town than a splendid movie theater. Today Powers Auditorium has such an awful outside alteration that you won't expect much; but the interior (except for the added sound baffles in the auditorium) is wonderful, especially the Hall of Mirrors. Rescued by Mr. and Mrs. Edward W. Powers after it closed in 1968, it became their gift in turn.

Access: **Go north on Wick, past Commerce Street and uphill to Wood Street. Turn left/west to Center of Industry and Labor. Elm Street intersects Wood just after the Cathedral.**

YOUNGSTOWN HISTORICAL CENTER OF INDUSTRY AND LABOR, 1989 (MUSEUM OPENED 1992)

Michael Graves, Princeton, New Jersey, with Raymond Jaminet & Partners,

Youngstown
151 West Wood Street
Ohio Historical Society
museum and library
focused on regional
steel industry; open
daily except Monday
and Tuesday; fee; 330/
743-5934

Michael Graves is a
celebrated American
architect, the only
widely known one
with a degree from on

▶ YOUNGSTOWN HISTORICAL CENTER

Ohio architectural school, the University of Cincinnati. After Cincinnati, graduate work at Harvard and two years at the American Academy in Rome, Graves began teaching at Princeton in the early 1960s; he is still there. Of his Ohio projects, the Youngstown Historical Center of Industry and Labor is the most interesting. The site for this Postmodern museum and library building is a steep hill descending from Wood Street, where the front entry is, down to Commerce Street, where the back is. The building faces into two different neighborhoods: downhill is Commerce Street, which is mostly the backs of buildings and loading docks; uphill is Wood Street, where St. Columba Cathedral, 1958, Diehl and Diehl, Detroit, is just opposite the museum. In fact, the museum's arched roof line echoes the cathedral's. This uphill facade is respectable and museum-like, solid and symmetrical. On the downhill side, the most conspicuous neighbor is the brick wall of Powers Auditorium's stagehouse tower a little to the west. In contrast to the front, the museum's back is an asymmetrical hodgepodge of industrial allusions: smokestacks, cylinders, sheds, factory walls. A boxy rear cupola looks like an industrial gatehouse; it also echoes a cupola on top of Powers Auditorium. In spite of its two personalities, a few features work to unify the building. One is colors, which also reflect those of the neighbors. The museum's brick and artificial stucco surfaces range in color from light yellow-tan to terra cotta orange. Another unifier is the round cupola at the front; recalling a steel mill's operations control center, it's an industrial allusion for the uphill side. Both this cupola and the square one at the back function as skylights. The front of the building houses the lobby and, upstairs, the library. See the second floor's fine domed rotunda, accessible by stairs off the lobby and located directly under the round cupola. The octagonal, glass-brick enclosed stairway at the rear is another good space; Rebecca Rogers describes it as "exquisitely designed."

Wick Avenue

Access: Continue north on Wick Avenue to the Butler Institute and
the Arms Museum.

JONES HALL, YOUNGSTOWN STATE UNIVERSITY 1931

Paul Boucherle, Youngstown
410 Wick Avenue at Lincoln Avenue, NRHP
Office building

This 1931 Jacobean Revival castle was Youngstown College's first building;
it's become a university symbol.

BUTLER INSTITUTE OF AMERICAN ART, 1920

McKim, Mead and White, New York
524 Wick Avenue,
NRHP
Art museum; open daily
except Monday; free;
330/743-1711

Youngstown
industrialist Joseph G.
Butler not only made
money; he also wrote a
local history and
collected art. And how
better to house his art
collection than to hire
New York's McKim,
Mead and White to
design a museum. So
the earliest part of the
Butler Institute of
American Art is a
Second Renaissance
Revival building in
Georgia marble. The
facade has three arches
fronting a recessed
porch, and the lobby
has a beamed

▶ BUTLER INSTITUTE

Renaissance ceiling. Originally the side rooms were galleries with high
vaulted ceilings; but in 1952 they were sliced crosswise into two floors. The
museum has had many additions. McKim, Mead and White scholar Leland
Roth says the Butler Institute was modeled on a sixteenth-century Italian
villa. In the early 1920s, Albert Kahn modeled his University of Michigan
library on the Butler Institute.

GREYSTONES, NOW MAHONING VALLEY HISTORICAL SOCIETY ARMS MUSEUM, 1905

Meade and Garfield, Cleveland
648 Wick Avenue, NRHP/Wick Avenue HD
Local historical society museum; afternoon hours daily except Monday; fee; 330/ 743-2589

▶ GREYSTONES

Descended from Youngstown pioneers and money, married to money, Olive Freeman Arms capped off her good fortune by living to 95. When she died in 1960, she left her house to the historical society, endowed it, and named it the Arms Museum. It was a house whose design she herself had shaped. In 1904 she started preparing drawings; she called in Meade and Garfield because they agreed to use her ideas—and because she needed them to assure structural soundness. "If you leave the house to the architect," she wrote, "he is inclined to build merely for *himself*—he builds *his house not yours.*" (Her emphasis.) This Arts and Crafts house's interior has only relatively brief glimpses of the original style, seen in the sitting room, diningroom and especially in the dark, low-ceilinged front hall, swaddled mostly in dark woods. Olive Arms redecorated the adjacent library/livingroom six times; it endures in her last choice, Tudor. In accord with her will, the second floor was converted into a historical museum, display cases and all. Olive Arms had a sister, Laurabelle, who married a financier named Henry Robinson. In 1906 the Robinsons settled down in Pasadena in a house by two Cincinnati-born brother architects who were practicing there, Charles and Henry Greene. Greene and Greene were designing mostly wooden houses today revered for their craftsmanship and their Arts and Crafts-related style, often called Craftsman or Western Stick. So in Youngstown people supposed—or *wished*—that Olive might have copied Laurabelle's house, giving Youngstown a Greene and Greene clone. But in fact Olive's house preceded her sister's, and the two are quite different. Where Olive found her ideas is a mystery, says Joan Reedy, the MVHS's assistant director, who suggests that Olive's house is more in the English Arts and Crafts style than the American. Olive did leave a picture of an unidentified house that's like hers, but no one knows whether it spawned Greystones, or vice versa.

Access: To reach Wick Log House drive north on Wick Avenue past U.S. 422; then, in less than a half mile, turn left on Illinois Avenue.

WICK LOG HOUSE, 1886

Owsley and Boucherle, Youngstown
57 Illinois Avenue
Private rooming house; interior may be seen with advance notice if owner Louis
Kennedy is available (try weekends); 330/747-8016

The Wick Log Cabin presents its side to the street now, but when it was built it was the only place around, and faced downhill for a lordly view. It was an Adirondack style country house for the families of Caleb B. and Henry K. Wick. The outside was rustic—poplar logs from Pennsylvania— but the interior, still largely intact, is high-style. The little window panes are beveled glass; the fireplaces, tiled. The north parlor is oak; the octagonal hall is cherry; and the south parlor, says owner Louis Kennedy, is a wood that may have been imported, for none of his visitors have recognized the grain. Somewhat to his surprise, Kennedy bought this house in

▶ Wıck Log House

1985. He'd been a tenant there, and the landlord was eager to sell, so Kennedy paid $51,000 for an irreplaceable house that the experts figured would cost half a million to replace. Now he is the landlord, renting rooms to artists and art students. "I'd have been an idiot not to buy it," he says. "It's a terrific cottage. The fireplace is imported from Italy. It has pocket doors." Besides, he's proud that sometimes, he says, "I'll be going through books and wow, there's my house."

Youngstown West

Access: To reach Isaly Dairy, drive west from downtown on Federal Plaza; turn left on Fifth Avenue, which crosses the Mahoning River and becomes Mahoning Avenue; bear right at fork after river. Follow Mahoning to Isaly at corner of Glenwood Avenue.

ISALY DAIRY, NOW U-HAUL, 1941

Charles F. Owsley,
Youngstown
1033 Mahoning Avenue
at Glenwood
Office building

▶ ISALY DAIRY

The Isaly Dairy is an astonishing yellow building with a rounded tower: a structure hard to match for sheer élan. Built as a dairy plant with an ice cream shop at the corner, the building flaunts delight both in ice cream and in having this clean, modern place for making it. The style is a sleek Art Moderne; siding is yellow terra cotta tiles with orange detailing. At the fifth-floor summit of the round tower the boss's office symbolizes a ship captain's bridge; the tops of its floor-to-ceiling glass-brick windows can be seen from the ground. U-Haul bought the building for its regional headquarters, which occupies the wing with brown metal facing. Much to its credit, in the early 1990s U-Haul also made a substantial investment to keep water out of the whole building, including the parts it's not using.

Mill Creek Park

Access: From Isaly Dairy/U-Haul, turn left/south on Glenwood Avenue and enter Mill Creek Park at second stop light, Falls Avenue. Map available at police station there; a Volney Rogers statue is nearby. Then turn left/south on park road, (East Glacier Drive; then name changes to Robinson Hill Drive) to see Slippery Rock Pavilion. Continue south; road crosses Mill Creek and comes to Pioneer Pavilion. Both pavilions are well signed. To reach park from I-680, exit at Belle Vista; drive south on Belle Vista Avenue to park entrance on left, at Calvary Run Drive. Turn right/south on park road (West Glacier Drive) to bridge and cross for Slippery Rock Pavilion; and pick up tour above. To secure maps ahead of time, as well as other park literature, like trail and garden guides, contact Mill Creek MetroParks, P.O. Box 596, Canfield, 44406; 330/702-3000.

▶ SLIPPERY ROCK PAVILION

SLIPPERY ROCK PAVILION, 1911

Charles F. Schweinfurth, Cleveland
Robinson Hill Drive, east side of park

This is an open-air Arts and Crafts picnic pavilion that shows architect
Charles F. Schweinfurth's fanciful side. Pillars of bulging sandstones support a
flared red-tile roof. The enclosure at the chimney end is kitchen facilities.

PIONEER PAVILION, 1821, 1893

William B. Ellis, Youngstown

This stone building with a barn-like gambrel roof was built as a woolen mill;
when it came into the park in the 1890s, it was derelict. What we see today
is its happy reconstruction as a party house, with ballroom upstairs, dining
area down. Two stories high, the ballroom is paneled in dark wood; the
ceiling's hammer beams, flaunting a full complement of braces and cross
beams, accentuate the gambrel roof. Flooring is oak; at room's end, a broad
red-brick chimney rises from the fireplace to the ceiling. Normally Pioneer
Pavilion is locked. I saw the inside because I happened along as it was being
prepared for a party. Visitors not so lucky may call park headquarters in
Canfield, 330/702-3000; it may be possible to set up an appointment to see
the interior.

THE JEWEL OF YOUNG-STOWN—The first time I saw Youngstown's Mill Creek Park, I drove west across the city to reach it. At first, I was passing through desolate areas, but then the neighborhood began to improve. Finally it became very nice indeed, and then I was at Mill Creek Park. It seemed to be a place so good, that its aura spilled out into its surroundings.

As it turns out not all Mill Creek Park's perimeter is so handsome, though most of it is; but the park itself is an excellent place, designed in the late nineteenth century to provide public access without disrupting the superb natural setting. The preserve follows Mill Creek as it twists its way through mostly wooded ravines, flowing north to the Mahoning River. Roads follow the creek, usually winding along both sides; occasionally they cross it—one crossing is by a picturesque little Suspension Bridge, built in 1895. The park also has three lakes formed by dams along the creek.

Mill Creek Park was wholly the creation of one man, Volney Rogers. By profession Rogers was a lawyer; by avocation he was the single-minded developer of the park. He discovered the place, assembled the land, and persuaded the Ohio General Assembly to pass a law that would permit it. Then he put his money in it, helped build it, and spent the rest of his life trying to defend it.

Born in 1846 in Columbiana County, Rogers discovered this place on his own in 1890. "One summer day," he recalled afterward, "I decided to explore Mill Creek valley on horseback, and there being no road which I could follow, I rode for the most part in the bed of Mill Creek from its mouth to Lanterman's falls, a somewhat hazardous but very enjoyable experience." Then, while

working in the area, he explored the creek on daily morning and evening walks. He came to believe that, to preserve it as it was, this place should become a public park.

When later in 1890 Rogers heard that the creek's east bank was to be logged, he immediately bought the timber on a strip of land almost two miles long, and left the trees standing. He heard then that the sandstone cliffs near the falls were to be quarried, and that logging was to start on the west bank, so he took options to purchase those areas. As quietly as possible, he secured options from 154 of the area's 196 individual owners.

Organizing a park took more than land. For instance, it required a change in Ohio law to make it possible for a municipality or township to develop a park. Rogers took care of it. He drafted a Township Park Improvement bill and successfully shepherded it through the General Assembly—this was several years before the first Ohio state park. Then, with the approval of local voters, the township began issuing bonds in 1891. Rogers bought $25,000 worth, specifying that his were to be the last repaid. By purchase, condemnation, and appropriation, Mill Creek Park began coming together.

Rogers called in two of the country's best landscape architects, whose participation Rebecca Rogers (to her regret, no relation to Volney) confirmed by going through all the park bills up to 1915. One was Charles Eliot of Boston; the other, H.W.S. Cleveland of Minneapolis. Both had worked with the co-designer of Central Park, Frederick Law Olmsted, who was the father of landscape architecture in this country. In 1893, a couple years after Eliot worked for

Volney Rogers, he went back to the Olmsted firm as a partner.

Eliot described Mill Creek park as "one of the finest park scenes in America"; in 1891 he wrote to his wife commending the energetic and enthusiastic Rogers: "He has done a fine thing." Eliot died in 1897, at a relatively young 37. Five years later his father, Charles William Eliot, the president of Harvard, published a biography of his son; it was the source of these quotes.

Construction began in the park in 1892; to be sure, Rogers oversaw that, too. When stone was set in place, he checked that it was clean, so that mortar would adhere well. When branches were to be pruned, he wanted to direct which branches. After the Panic of 1893, construction was accelerated. Because so many people were out of work, Rogers proposed moving up the sale of long-term park bonds to provide jobs right away; as a result, much of the park was constructed in 1893-94. Some additions came later; in one, Boston landscape architect Warren Manning, who also planned Stan Hywet's grounds in Akron (see also), designed the environs of Newport Lake, developed in the 1920s.

Volney Rogers died in 1919, with Mill Creek Park securely established. To this day it shows the possibilities of a horseback ride along a streambed.

PIONEER PAVILION

Photography and illustration

While every effort has been made to trace the copyright holders of photographs and illustrations reproduced in this book, the publishers will be pleased to rectify any omissions or inaccuracies in the next printing.

Germania Building, page xiii, drawing by David Day
Ringside Cafe detail, page xv, drawing by Frank Elmer

Akron—First National Tower, 5, James A. Pahlau collection; Akron Civic Theatre, 6-7, James A. Pahlau collection; Polsky Building, 8, James A. Pahlau collection; Summit County Courthouse, 8, Tom Patterson; Crowne Plaza Quaker Square, 9, Akron Hilton Inn; Hower House floor plans, 12, Hower House; Hower House, 12, James A. Pahlau collection; Goodyear Hall, 13, Jane Ware; National City Bank, Walker & Weeks drawing, 14, Cleveland Public Library; Goodyear Airdock, 16-17, Wilbur J. Watson, "Building the World's Largest Airship Factory and Dock," 1929; Glendale Cemetery Memorial Chapel, 19, Jane Ware; Glendale Cemetery, 20, James A. Pahlau collection; Stan Hywet drawing, 22-23, Stan Hywet Hall and Gardens; Stan Hywet, 23, Stan Hywet Hall and Gardens.

Canton—First National Bank Building, 26, Andrew Borowiec; Renkert Building, 27, Andrew Borowiec; Palace interior, 28, Jay Paris; Palace exterior, 28, Andrew Borowiec; Timken Senior High, 29, Andrew Borowiec; Bender's Tavern, 30, courtesy Bender's Tavern; Canton *Daily News*, 30, Andrew Borowiec; McKinley Memorial, 31, Ian Adams; Timken Stables, 32, Frank Elmer drawing; Timken Stables, 32, Jane Ware; Carriage Hill Club, 33, Andrew Borowiec; T.K. Harris's 1926 house, 34, Andrew Borowiec; T.K. Harris's 1930 house, 34, Andrew Borowiec.

Cincinnati —Union Terminal, 39, *The Architectural Forum*; Union Terminal drawing, 40, *The Architectural Forum*; Union Terminal detail, 41, Robert Flischel; Union Terminal, 42, Orange Frazer Library; Taft House, 44-45, Historic American Buildings Survey; Taft House, 45, Robert Flischel; Cincinnati, Gas & Electric, 47, Eric Weinberg; Dixie Terminal, 48, Eric Weinberg; Ingalls, 49, Orange Frazer Library; Gidding Jenny, 50, Eric Weinberg; Carew Tower, 52, Orange Frazer Library; Proctor & Gamble, 53, Robert Flischel; Gwynne Building, 54, Mary Ann Olding; Salvation Army Citadel, 55, Jane Ware; City Hall, 57, Mary Ann Olding; Isaac Wise Temple drawing, 59, Historic American Buildings Survey; Isaac Wise, 59, Paul Briol, Orange Frazer Library; Germania, 60, David Day drawing; Music Hall, 62-63, Robert Flischel; Memorial Hall drawing, 64-65, David Day drawing; Memorial Hall, 65, Mary Ann Olding; Over the Rhine, 66, Robert Flischel; Hatch House, 67, Jane Ware; Fairview School, 69, Robert Flischel; Hughes High School, 70-71, Orange Frazer Library; Aronoff Center, 71, drawing, Dugan & Meyers Construction Co.; Calvary Episcopal, 73, Jane Ware; Probasco House, 74, Jane Ware; Probasco House drawing, 74, Orange Frazer Library; Temple of Love, 76-77, Eric Weinberg; Zoo, 78, Mary Ann Olding; Zoo, 78, Orange Frazer Library; Spring Grove, 81, Jane Ware; Spring Grove, 82, Mary Ann Olding; Mount Adams, 84, Robert Flischel; Elsinore, 85, Mary Ann Olding; Art Museum drawing, 86-87, Cincinnati Art Museum; Art Museum, 86, Cincinnati Art Museum; Art Museum interior, 86, Robert Flischel; Rookwood Pottery, 89, Mary Ann Olding; Walnut Hills, 90, Mary Ann Olding; Gruen Building, 91, Mary Ann Olding; Observatory, 95, Mary Ann Olding; Ault Park, 96, Mary Ann Olding; McKinley School, 97, Jane Ware; Mariemont plat drawing and photographs, 98-101, Mariemont Preservation Foundation; The Emery

Church, 104, Jane Ware; Glendale plat, 106, R.H. Harrison, *Titus' Atlas of Hamilton County, Ohio*, 1869; Wyoming Baptist Church, 108, Wyoming Baptist Church; Hartwell plat, R.H. Harrison, *Titus' Atlas of Hamilton County, Ohio*, 1869.

Cleveland—Arcade drawing, 110, Historic American Buildings Survey; Terminal Tower etching by Louis Rosenberg, 114, The Western Reserve Historical Society, Cleveland, Ohio; Terminal Tower, 114, Orange Frazer Library; Terminal Tower, 115, Cervin Robinson, October 1987, Cleveland Museum of Art; Arcade, Superior Street entrance, 116, Cervin Robinson, March 1988, Cleveland Museum of Art; Arcade drawing, 116, Historic American Buildings Survey; Arcade interior, 117, Cervin Robinson, March 1988, Cleveland Museum of Art; State Theatre interior, 119, Cervin Robinson, July 1988, Cleveland Museum of Art; Hunting-ton Bank, 120, Cervin Robinson, February 1988, Cleveland Museum of Art; Huntington Bank, 121, Huntington National Bank, Score Photographers; Old National City Bank, 122, Cervin Robinson, March 1988, Cleveland Museum of Art; Old National City Bank interior, 123, Cervin Robinson, October 1987, Cleveland Museum of Art; Federal Reserve Bank, 123, Cervin Robinson, July 1987, Cleveland Museum of Art; Key Tower, 124, Key Bank, Mort Tucker Photography; Society for Savings Building, 125, Cervin Robinson, March 1988, Cleveland Museum of Art; South end of Mall, 126, Cervin Robinson, July 1988, Cleveland Museum of Art; U.S. District Courtroom, 127, Cervin Robinson, February 1988, Cleveland Museum of Art; Cuyahoga Courthouse, 128, Cervin Robinson, October 1987, Cleveland Museum of Art; Cuyahoga Courthouse, 129, Columbus Circulating Visuals Collection, Columbus Metropolitan Library; Rock and Roll Hall of Fame, 130-131, Pei Cobb Freed & Partners and the Rock and Roll Hall of Fame and Museum; Bradley Building, 132, Jane Ware; Trinity Cathedral, 134, Columbus Circulating Visuals Collection, Columbus Metropoli-tan Library; Mather Mansion, 135, The Western Reserve Historical Society, Cleveland, Ohio; Tavern Club, 137, Frank Elmer drawing; Prospect Row houses, 138, Jane Ware; Wade Park plat, 139, The Western Reserve Historical Society, Cleveland, Ohio; Wade Park, 138, Cervin Robinson, October 1987, Cleveland Museum of Art; Epworth Church, 141, Cleveland Library, Walker and Weeks Collection; Epworth Church, 141, Cervin Robinson, April 1989, Cleveland Museum of Art; Severance Hall, 142-143, The Cleveland Orchestra Archives; Art Museum, 144, Cervin Robinson, May 1988, Cleveland Museum of Art; Art Museum, 145, Columbus Circulating Visuals Collection, Columbus Metropoli-tan Library; Clark Hall drawing, 146, Eleanor Shankland; Mather Memorial Building drawing, 147, Eleanor Shankland; Mather Gymnasium drawing, 148, Eleanor Shankland; St. Mary Seminary, 149-150, Catholic Universe Bulletin; Wade Memorial Chapel, 151, Columbus Circulating Visuals Collection, Columbus Metropolitan Library; Garfield, 153, Cervin Robinson, October 1987, Cleveland Museum of Art; Garfield drawing, 153, Gaede Serne Architects, Inc.; Cleveland Heights, 155, Cervin Robinson, October 1987, Cleveland Museum of Art; Park Synagogue drawing, 158, Arnold Whittick, *Eric Mendelsohn*, 2nd edition, 1956, used by permission of McGraw Hill Companies; Tremaine-Gallagher House, 161, Jane Ware; Shaker Heights, 162, Cervin Robinson, October 1987, Cleveland Museum of Art; Van Swearingen House, 163, Frank Elmer; Shaker Square, 164-165, The Western Reserve Historical Society, Cleveland, Ohio; Colony Theatre, 165, The Western Reserve Historical Society, Cleveland, Ohio; West Side drawing, 167, Hubbell and Benes blueprints, Joanne M. Lewis, from her book, *To Market, To Market, An Old-Fashioned Family Story: The West Side Market*, 1981; West Side, 167, Cervin Robinson, February 1988, Cleveland Museum of Art; St. Ignatius, 168, Cervin Robinson, March 1988, Cleveland Museum of Art; St. Ignatius, 168, Saint Ignatius High School; Carnegie West Branch Library, 169, Cervin Robinson, October 1987, Cleveland Museum of Art; St. Theodosius, 171, Jane Ware; Clarence Mack Houses, 173, Jane Ware; Winterich Flowers, 173, Jane Ware; Hower House, 177, Ian Adams.

June 1995, Guide to the Arts); Mansion View, 268—by permission of the
Landmarks Preservation Council of the Lucas County-Maumee Valley Historical
Society, Maumee, Ohio; Leeper-Geddes house, 268, Jane Ware; Tillinghast-Willys
house, 270—by permission of the Landmarks Preservation Council of the Lucas
County-Maumee Valley Historical Society, Maumee, Ohio; Emerson house, 271,
Jane Ware; Freeman house, 272, by permission of the Landmarks Preservation
Council of the Lucas County-Maumee Valley Historical Society, Maumee, Ohio;
University Hall, 273, University of Toledo; Toledo Zoo, 274, Jane Ware; Weber
Block, 275, Frank Elmer drawing; Lighthouse, 277, courtesy of U.S. Coast Guard
Historian's Office.

Youngstown—Federal Plaza, 279, Columbus Circulating Visuals Collection,
Columbus Metropolitan Library; Metropolitan Tower, 281, *The Architect*, July
1929, page 384; Mahoning National Bank, 282, Columbus Circulating Visuals
Collection, Columbus Metropolitan Library; Mahoning County Courthouse, 283,
both by Tom Patterson; Youngstown Historical Center of Industry and Labor, 285,
Jane Ware; Butler Institute of American Art, 286, Ian Adams; Greystones, 287,
Mahoning Valley Historical Society, Youngstown, Ohio; Wick Log Cabin, 288,
Mahoning Valley Historical Society, Youngstown, Ohio; Isaly Dairy, 289,
Mahoning Valley Historical Society, Youngstown, Ohio; Slippery Rock Pavilion,
290, Frank Elmer drawing; Pioneer Pavilion, 291, Frank Elmer drawing.

Bibliography

For some buildings in this volume, I consulted the National Register files in the Ohio Historic Preservation Office, Ohio Historical Society, Columbus.

GENERAL

Elizabeth P. Allyn and Elisabeth H. Tuttle, comp., *A Guide to Historic Houses in Ohio Open to the Public.* National Society of the Colonial Dames of America in the State of Ohio, [Cincinnati], 1984.

John J.-G. Blumenson, *Identifying American Architecture: A Pictorial Guide to Styles and Terms, 1600-1945* rev. ed. American Association for State and Local History, Nashville, 1981.

Richard N. Campen, *Ohio, An Architectural Portrait.* West Summit Press, Chagrin Falls, Ohio, 1973.

Edna Maria Clark, *Ohio Art and Artists.* 1932 work republished by Gale Research Company, Detroit, 1975.

John Fleischman, "City Grit". *Ohio Magazine*, January 1992, pp. 8ff.

John Fleischman, "Forgotten but Not Gone". *Ohio Magazine*, August, 1995, pp. 20ff.

Stephen C. Gordon, *How to Complete the Ohio Historic Inventory.* Ohio Historical Society, Columbus, 1992.

Henry Howe, *Historical Collections of Ohio.* Henry Howe & Son, Columbus, 1891.

Eric Johannesen, *A Cleveland Legacy: The Architecture of Walker and Weeks.* Kent State University Press, Kent, Ohio, 1998.

Eric Johannesen, *Ohio College Architecture Before 1870.* Ohio Historical Society, [Columbus], 1969.

Ray Jones, *Great Lakes Lighthouses, Ontario to Superior.* Globe Pequot Press, Old Saybrook, Connecticut, 1994.

Sydney LeBlanc, *20th-century American Architecture: A Traveler's Guide to 220 Key Buildings.* Second edition. Whitney Library of Design, New York, 1996.

William L. Lebovich, *America's City Halls.* Preservation Press, Washington, 1984.

Virginia and Lee McAlester, *A Field Guide to American Houses.* Alfred A. Knopf, New York, 1984.

Diane Maddex, ed., *Master Builders: A Guide to Famous American Architects.* Preservation Press, Washington, 1985.

David Naylor, *Great American Movie Theaters.* Preservation Press, National Trust for Historic Preservation, Washington, 1987.

David Naylor, *American Picture Palaces.* Van Nostrand Reinhold Company, New York, 1981.

Laurie Penrose, *A Traveler's Guide to 100 Eastern Great Lakes Lighthouses.* Friede Publications, Davison, Michigan, 1994.

John C. Poppeliers, S. Allen Chambers, Jr., and Nancy B.Schwarts, *What Style Is It?: A Guide to American Architecture.* National Trust for Historic Preservation in the United States, John Wiley & Sons, New York, 1983.

John W. Reps, *The Making of Urban America: A History of City Planning in the United States.* Princeton University Press, Princeton, New Jersey, 1965.

Leland M. Roth, *A Concise History of American Architecture.* Harper & Row, New York, 1979.

Vincent Scully, *American Architecture and Urbanism.* Frederick A. Praeger, New York, 1969.

G.E. Kidder Smith, *The Architecture of the United States*, Vol. 2, *The South and Midwest.* Anchor Press/Doubleday, Garden City, New York, 1981.

G.E. Kidder Smith, *A Pictorial History of Architecture in America*, Vol. II. American Heritage Publishing, New York, 1976.

John R. Stilgoe, *Borderland: Origins of the American Suburb, 1820-1939.* Yale University Press, New Haven, 1988.

William H. Tishler, ed., *American Landscape Architecture: Designers and Places.* Preservation Press, Washington, 1989.

Damaine Vonada and Marcy Hawley, eds., *Particular Places: A Traveler's Guide to Inner Ohio*, Vol. II. Orange Frazer Press, Wilmington, 1993.

Marcus Whiffen, *American Architecture Since 1780: A Guide to the Styles*, revised edition. MIT Press, Cambridge, Massachusetts, 1992.

Katharine F. Willi, ed., *A Guide to Historic Houses in Ohio, Open to the Public*, prepared by the National Society of the Colonial Dames of America in the State of Ohio. Second edition. Odyssey Press Inc., Westerville, 1996.

Henry F. Withey and Elsie Rathburn Withey, *Biographical Dictionary of American Architects (Deceased).* Hennessey & Ingalls, Los Angeles, 1970.

SPECIFIC TO LOCALITIES

AKRON

Hugh Allen, *The House of Goodyear.* Superior Printing & Litho Co., Akron, Third Edition, 1937.

Priscilla M. Harding, "Building the Airdock". *Timeline*, November-December, 1994, pp. 46-54.

George W. Knepper, *Akron: City at the Summit.* Continental Heritage Press, Tulsa, 1981.

Samuel A. Lane, *Fifty Years and Over of Akron and Summit County.* Beacon Job Department, Akron, 1892.

Virginia and Lee McAlester, Chapter 17, "Stan Hywet Hall", pp. 218-31 in *Great American Houses and Their Architectural Styles.* Abbeville Press, New York, 1994.

Maurice O'Reilly, *The Goodyear Story.* The Benjamin Company, Elmsford, N.Y., 1983.

James A. Pahlau, "Architectural Walking Tour, Downtown Akron," Parts One and Two, August 1988.

James A. Pahlau, "Charles S. Schneider: Premier Cleveland Architect 1913-1932". N.D.

James A. Pahlau, articles in Progress Through Preservation Newsletters, 1986-1996.

Wilbur J. Watson, "Building the World's Largest Airship Factory and Dock". Goodyear-Zeppelin Corporation, Akron, c. 1929.

CANTON

M.J. Albacete, *Architecture in Canton 1805-1976.* Canton Art Institute, Canton, 1976.

M.J. Albacete, *Historic Architecture in Canton 1805-1940.* Canton Art Institute, Canton, 1989.

An Inventory of Historic Sites and Structures: A Window on Start County, Ohio 1986. Stark County Regional Planning Commission, Canton, 1986.

Eric Johannesen, "The Architectural Legacy of Guy Tilden of Canton". *Ohio History,* Summer-Autumn 1973, pp. 124-141.

James A. Pahlau, "Canton Architecture: Some Observations". Progress Through Preservation Newsletter, Akron, August, 1996.

CINCINNATI

Harry D. Andrews, "Chateau Laroche" in eponymous booklet published by Loveland Castle, Loveland, Ohio, N.D.

"The Castle That Harry Built". Ohio Magazine, December, 1994, p. 23.

The Cincinnati Union Terminal: Pictorial History. Dedication book, Cincinnati Chamber of Commerce, Cincinnati, 1933.

John Clubbe, *Cincinnati Observed: Architecture and History.* Ohio State University Press, Columbus, 1992.

Richard C. Cote, "The Baum-Taft House: An Architectural History". *The Taft Museum: Its History and Collections,* ed. by Edward J. Sullivan. Taft Museum Publications, Cincinnati, 1995.

Andrea Oppenheimer Dean, "Making a Nonentity into a Landmark". *Architecture,* November 1985, pp.34-39.

Robert W. Dorsey and George F. Roth, Jr., eds., *Architecture and Construction in Cincinnati: A Guide to Buildings, Designers and Builders.* Architectural Foundation of Cincinnati, Cincinnati, 1987.

David Ehrlinger, *The Cincinnati Zoo and Botanical Garden: From Past to Present.* Cincinnati Zoo and Botanical Garden, Cincinnati, 1993.

Angeline Loveland Faran, ed., *Glendale, Ohio 1855-1955.* McDonald Printing Company, Cincinnati, 1955.

John Fleischman, "Cincinnati's Big White Elephant Has Changed Its Spots". *Smithsonian,* June, 1992, pp. 102-3 ff.

John Fleischman, "Fourth Street Revisited". *Ohio Magazine,* November 1986, pp. 35-39 ff.

John Fleischman, "Mount Storm". *Ohio Magazine,* December 1988, pp. 28-29 ff.

John Fleischman, "Neighborhood With-View". *Ohio Magazine,* September 1991, pp. 34-35 ff.

Geoffrey J. Giglierano and Deborah A. Overmyer, with Frederic L. Propas, *The Bicentennial Guide to Greater Cincinnati: A Portrait of Two Hundred Years,* 2 volumes. Cincinnati Historical Society, Cincinnati, 1988.

Glendale's Heritage, Glendale, Ohio. Glendale Heritage Preservation, Glendale, Ohio, 1976.

Joseph T. Hannibal and Richard Arnold Davis, *Guide to the Building Stones of Downtown Cincinnati: A Walking Tour.* Field Trip 16 for the Annual Meeting, Geological Society of America. Ohio Department of Natural Resources Division of Geological Survey, Columbus, 1992.

Israel Knox, *Rabbi in America: The Story of Isaac M. Wise.* Little, Brown and Company, Boston, 1957.

Clay Lancaster, *Architectural Follies in America.* Charles E. Tuttle Company, Rutland, Vermont, 1960.

Walter E. Langsam, *Great Houses of the Queen City: Two Hundred Years of Historic and Contemporary Architecture and Interiors in Cincinnati and Northern Kentucky*. Cincinnati Historical Society, Cincinnati, 1997.

Dottie L. Lewis, ed., *Cincinnati Union Terminal and the Artistry of Winold Reiss*. Cincinnati Historical Society, Cincinnati, 1993.

Blanche M.G. Linden, "Spring Grove: Celebrating 150 Years". *Queen City Heritage*, Spring/Summer 1995, pp. 2-144.

"Mariemont—A New Town". *Architecture*, September 1926, pp. 246-274 and plates CLXXII-CLXXXV.

Jayne Merkel, "The Baum-Taft House: A Historiography". *Queen City Heritage*, Spring 1988, pp. 33-50.

Herbert Muschamp, "Eisenman's Spatial Extravaganza in Cincinnati". New York *Times*, July 21, 1996, p. 33.

Carol S. Nagel, "Oakwood: The Home of Henry Probasco", Cincinnati, 1988 and 1994.

Warren Wright Parks, *The Mariemont Story: "A National Exemplar in Town Planning"*. Creative Writers & Publishers, Cincinnati, 1967.

Queen City Tour Committee, Caroline C. Taylor, chair, *Queen City Tour: A Self-guided Driving Tour*. Cincinnati Historical Society, Cincinnati, 1996.

George F. Roth, "The Building of Music Hall", pp. 60-79 in *Cincinnati's Music Hall* by Zane L. Miller and George F. Roth. Jordan & Company, Publishers, Virginia Beach, Virginia, 1978.

"St. Peter in Chains", a brochure issued by Standard Oil Company, Ohio, 1965.

P.M. Sexton, *Mariemont: A Brief Chronicle of Its Origin and Development*. Village of Mariemont, Mariemont, Ohio, 1966.

[Beth Sullebarger and Liz Scheurer], "Art and Architecture in Cincinnati's Parks". Cincinnati Park Board, Cincinnati, 1995.

Sefton D. Temkin, *Isaac Mayer Wise: Shaping American Judaism*. Oxford University Press, New York, 1992

Don Heinrich Tolzmann, ed., *Spring Grove and Its Creator: H.A. Rattermann's Biography of Adolph Strauch*. Ohio Book Store, Cincinnati, 1988.

Gabriel P. Weisberg et al., *Art Deco and the Cincinnati Union Terminal*. An exhibition organized by the Art History Department, University of Cincinnati at the Contemporary Arts Center, Cincinnati, 1973.

Robert J. Wimberg, *Cincinnati: Over-the-Rhine: A Historical Guide to 19th Century Buildings and Their Residents*. Second edition. Ohio Book Store, Cincinnati, 1988.

Work Projects Administration, *Cincinnati: A Guide to the Queen City and Its Neighbors*. Wiesen-Hart Press, Cincinnati, 1942.

Daniel W. Young, "Historic Walking Tours of Downtown Cincinnati". Cincinnati Historic Conservation Office, Cincinnati, N.D.

CLEVELAND

Foster Armstrong, Richard Klein and Cara Armstrong, *A Guide to Cleveland's Sacred Landmarks*. Kent State University Press, Kent, Ohio, 1992.

George F. Barber, *The Cottage Souvenir No. 2*. Reprint of 1891 edition; American Life, Watkins Glen, New York, 1982.

Richard N. Campen, "He Built for the Millionaires." *The Plain Dealer Sunday Magazine*, August 16, 1964.

Richard N. Campen, "Rockefeller Building" in *The Architecture of Cleveland: Twelve Buildings, 1836-1912*. The Western Reserve Historical Society

and the Historic American Buildings Survey, [Cleveland], 1973,
pp. 61-70.

Jan Cigliano, *Showplace of America: Cleveland's Euclid Avenue, 1850-1910.*
Kent State University Press, Kent, Ohio, 1991.

"Cleveland Sacred Landmarks", special issue of *The Gamut.* Cleveland State
University, 1990.

Robert C. Gaede et al., *Guide to Cleveland Architecture*, Second Edition.
Cleveland Chapter of the American Institute of Architects, Carpenter
Reserve Printing, Cleveland, 1997.

Robert C. Gaede and Peter van Dijk, "Society National Bank building" in
The Architecture of Cleveland: Twelve Buildings, 1836-1912. The
Western Reserve Historical Society and the Historic American
Buildings Survey, [Cleveland], 1973.

Robert C. Gaede and Robert Kalin, eds., *Guide to Cleveland Architecture.*
Cleveland Chapter of the American Institute of Architects, Carpenter
Reserve Printing, Cleveland, 1990.

John J. Grabowski and Walter C. Leedy, Jr., *The Terminal Tower, Tower City
Center: A Historical Perspective.* Western Reserve Historical Society,
Cleveland, 1990.

Lee Hall, *Olmsted's America: An "Unpractical" Man and His Vision of
Civilization.* Little, Brown and Company, Boston, 1995.

Clay Herrick, Jr., *Cleveland Landmarks.* Landmarks Publishing Company,
Cleveland, 1986.

Eric Johannesen, *Cleveland Architecture, 1876-1976.* Western Reserve
Historical Society, Cleveland, 1979.

Walter C. Leedy, Jr., *Cleveland Builds an Art Museum: Patronage, Politics, and
Architecture 1884-1916.* The Cleveland Museum of Art, Cleveland,
1991.

Walter Leedy, "Eric Mendelsohn's Park Synagogue: Vision Informs Reality".
The Gamut, Cleveland Sacred Landmarks special issue, 1990,
pp. 45-69.

Joanne M. Lewis, *To Market/To Market, An Old-Fashioned Family Story: The
West Side Market.* Elandon Books, Cleveland Heights, 1981.

Martin L. Linsey, "Tremaine-Gallagher House" in *The Architecture of
Cleveland: Twelve Buildings, 1836-1912.* The Western Reserve
Historical Society and the Historic American Buildings Survey,
[Cleveland], 1973, pp. 88-95.

Kitty Makley, "Mather Mansion Revisited: The Man, His City, His House".
Unpublished typescript, 1977.

Roderic Hall Pierce, *Trinity Cathedral Parish: The First 150 Years.* The Vestry
of Trinity Cathedral, Cleveland, 1967.

Mary-Peale Schofield, *Landmark Architecture of Cleveland.* Ober Park
Associates, Pittsburgh, 1976.

David D. Van Tassel, ed. and John J. Grabowski, managing ed., *The
Dictionary of Cleveland Biography.* Indiana University Press,
Bloomington, 1996.

David D. Van Tassel and John J. Grabowski, eds., *The Encyclopedia of
Cleveland History.* Indiana University Press, Bloomington, 1987.

Arnold Whittick, *Eric Mendelsohn.* 2nd edition. F.W. Dodge,
New York, 1956.

COLUMBUS

"A.I.U. Citadel" [booklet], American Insurance Union, Columbus, Ohio, 1926.

"The Architecture of Howard Dwight Smith", brochure with design and travel sketches exhibit, Ohio State University Student Union, October 16, 1981.

Kurt Andersen, "A Crazy Building in Columbus". *Time*, November 20, 1989, pp. 84, 89.

Bill Arter, *Columbus Vignettes*. Nida-Eckstein Printing, Columbus, 1966.

Bill Arter, *Columbus Vignettes II*. Nida-Eckstein Printing, Columbus, 1967.

Bill Arter, *Columbus Vignettes III*. Nida-Eckstein Printing, Columbus, 1969.

Bill Arter, *Columbus Vignettes IV*. Nida-Eckstein Printing, Columbus, 1971.

Mary Bishop et al., eds., *The Ohio Theatre 1928-1978*. Columbus Association for the Performing Arts, Columbus, 1978.

Richard N. Campen, *German Village Portrait*. Watkins Printing, Columbus, 1978.

Abbott Lowell Cummings, *Ohio's Capitols at Columbus, 1810-1861*. Special Report for the Ohio Legislature, 1948. Unpublished manuscript held by the Ohio Historical Society.

Abbott Lowell Cummings, "The Ohio State Capitol Competitions", in *Journal of the Society of Architectural Historians*, Vol. XII, May 1953, pp. 15-18.

Jeffrey Darbee and Nancy Recchie, "A History of Ohio Stadium". Unpublished report prepared for Design Group, Inc., Columbus, August, 1997.

John Morris Dixon, ed., "Architectural Design" a collection of articles on Peter Eisenman, *Progressive Architecture*, October, 1989, pp. 67-99.

John Morris Dixon, "Memory Materialized". *Progressive Architecture*, February 1981, pp. 78-83.

"Eleven U.S. Churches". *Architectural Forum*, December, 1953, pp. 85-87.

Roger Farrell, "The Life and Architecture of Joseph Warren Yost: Focus on the Columbus Years 1883-1900", unpublished graduate paper, March 12, 1993.

"Father of Civic Center Plan Dies Very Suddenly". *Ohio State Journal*, October 27, 1923, pp. 1 ff.

Joseph Giovannini, "Beyond Convention". *Architecture*, May 1993.

John H. Herrick, *OSU Campus Buildings*. Office of Campus Planning and Space Utilization, Ohio State University, Columbus, 1979, rev. 1980, 1981, 1985, 1986, 1988, Vol. II and Vol. III.

Henry-Russell Hitchcock and William Seale, *Temples of Democracy: The State Capitols of the USA*. Harcourt Brace Jovanovich, New York, 1976.

Judith Kitchen, "Wyandotte Building". Ohio Historical Society *Echoes*, June, 1972.

Alfred E. Lee, "The Capitol", Chapter XXV in *History of the City of Columbus, Capital of Ohio*, Vol. II. Munsell & Co., New York, 1892.

Mark Mack, "Critique". *Progressive Architecture*, February 1981, pp. 84-85.

Alan Miller, "For a Change, State Saves an Edifice Worth Preserving". Columbus *Dispatch*, June 19, 1998, pp. 1J-2J.

"Ohio Stadium to Undergo Change". *Ohio State Alumni Magazine*, January/February 1998, pp. 12-14.

Nadine M. Post, "Cockeyed Optimism in Columbus". *ENR*, February 8, 1993, pp. 22-24.

Barbara Powers, "Frank L. Packard (1866-1923): 'Architectural Realities' of a Midwestern Architect," unpublished paper presented at Society of

Architectural Historians Annual Meeting, April, 1991.

David Prosser, "The Helenic Ideal: The Ohio Statehouse". *Timeline*, July-August 1993, pp. 46-54.

[Robert R. Reeves,] "Sessions Village: The Development of an Ideal," booklet, Converse & Fulton, [Columbus,] 1927.

Robert E. Samuelson, et al., *Architecture: Columbus*. Foundation of the Columbus Chapter of the American Institute of Architects, Columbus, 1976.

Robert Sohovich, "Architect Prefers Old Pagoda to Downtown's Tall Buildings". Columbus *Dispatch*, March 26, 1987.

Lee Stratton, "A Toast to History". Columbus *Dispatch*, July 2, 1997, pp. 1H-2H.

Jane Ware, "Broad & High". *Ohio Magazine*, May 1990, p. 19-22 ff.

Jane Ware, "How Ohio's Fanciest Restored Neighborhood Got Off the Ground and How It Stays There". *Ohio Magazine*, April 1995, pp. 44-51, 86.

Jane Ware, "The Packard Legacy". *Columbus Monthly*, May 1991, pp. 80-81 ff.

Jane Ware, "The Rebirth of the Short North". *Capitol, the Dispatch Magazine*, March 18, 1984.

Jane Ware, *An Ohio State Profile: A Year in the Life of America's Biggest Campus*. Ohio State University Press, Columbus, 1991.

Jane Ware, "Renaissance of the Southern". *Columbus Monthly*, February 1994, pp. 69 ff.

[J.W.] Yost & [Frank L.] Packard, *Portfolio of Architectural Realities*. Columbus, N.D.

Barbara Zuck, "Story refuels Wexner Center controversy". Columbus *Dispatch*, December 24, 1990.

DAYTON

Mark Bernstein, *Grand Eccentrics: Turning the Century: Dayton and the Inventing of America*. Orange Frazer Press, Wilmington, 1996.

Perry E. Borchers et al., *"The finest thing of its kind in America!": The story of The Old Court House, Dayton, Ohio*, Montgomery County Historical Society, Dayton, N.D.

Frank Conover, ed., *Centennial Portrait and Biographical Record of the City of Dayton and Montgomery County, Ohio*. A. W. Bowen, [Chicago], 1897.

James M. Cox, *Journey Through My Years*. Simon and Schuster, New York, 1946.

A.W. Drury, *History of the City of Dayton and Montgomery County, Ohio*, Vol. I. S.J. Clarke Publishing, Chicago and Dayton, 1902.

Robert Frame, *Craig MacIntosh's Dayton Sketchbook*. Landfall Press, Dayton, 1985.

Peter A. McGraw, "The Rehabilitation of the Old Post Office, Dayton, Ohio". *Technology & Conservation*, Fall, 1981.

Rosamund McPherson, *History of the Young Men's Christian Association of Dayton, Ohio 1858-1953*. Association Press, New York, 1953.

Stephen J. Ostrander, "The Old Courthouse", in *Timeline*, September-October 1996, pp. 38-43.

Bruce and Virginia Ronald, *Now Playing: An Informal History of the Victoria Theatre*. Landfall Press, Dayton, 1989.

Bruce W. and Virginia Ronald, *Dayton: The Gem City*. Continental Heritage Press, Tulsa, 1981.

Bruce W. and Virginia Ronald, *Oakwood: The Far Hills*. Reflections Press, Dayton, 1983.

Noël Dorsey Vernon, "Documenting the Olmsteds in Ohio". *Landscape Architecture*, September/October, 1987, pp. 94-95.

Noël Dorsey Vernon, "Landscape Architecture and Public Service: The Olmsted Brothers Firm in Dayton, Ohio, 1894-1930". *Proceedings* of the Council of Educators in Landscape Architecture Annual Conference, August 13-15, 1987.

Noël Vernon and Malcolm Cairns, *Hills and Dales Park: Historic Landscape Preservation Master Plan*. Prepared for the City of Dayton, Ohio, 1993.

TOLEDO

Patricia K. Appold, "Bauer, Stark and Lashbrook, 1982: Ninety Years of Architecture in Toledo". A University of Toledo Master of Arts Thesis, 1982.

Gill Wright Bentley, "The Oliver House". Northwest Ohio Quarterly, Vol. 42, No. 2, spring, 1970, pp. 6-9.

Eric Johannesen and Allen L. Dickes, *Look Again: Landmark Architecture in Downtown Toledo and Old West End*. Ober Park Associates, Inc., Pittsburgh, 1973.

Kathryn Miller Keller, "The Oliver House". Northwest Ohio Quarterly, Vol. 19, No. 3, July, 1947, pp. 115-28.

James K. Larson, "The History and Architecture of the Toledo Zoo Buildings: A Self-Guided Tour". Toledo Zoo, (1984).

Ted Ligibel, "Discover Downtown Toledo Walking Tour". Greater Toledo Office of Tourism and Conventions, Inc., et al., 1994.

Ted Ligibel, "Toledo's Top 10 Historic Places". *Toledo Magazine*, February 18-24, 1990.

Theodore J. Ligibel, "E.O. Fallis: Master Architect in Perspective". A Bowling Green State University Master of Arts Thesis, 1981.

Larry R. Michaels, *East Side Story: People & Places in the History of East Toledo*. Bihl House Publishing, Toledo, 1993.

"The Ohio Bank Building, Graham, Anderson, Probst & White, Chicago." *Architect*, Vol. 15, pp. 403-5, 407-25, April 1931.

"Toledo's Past and Present", including "The Story of Toledo Past" by Nevin O. Winter. A brochure issued by the Ohio Savings Bank & Trust Company, 1930.

Sally Vallongo, "New Design Era Dawns in Toledo". Toledo *Blade*, November 29, 1992, pp. 1H ff.

Sally Vallongo, "O-C Putting Management Philosophy in Solid Form". Toledo *Blade*, October 8, 1995.

Sally Vallongo, "Shock at First Sight". Toledo *Blade*, August 10, 1992.

YOUNGSTOWN

"Architectural Design Citation: Youngstown Historical Center". *Progressive Architecture*, January, 1988, pp. 122-23.

Philip Arcidi, "Steel Industry Enshrined". *Progressive Architecture*, March, 1990, pp. 84-87.

Frederick J. Blue et al., *Mahoning Memories: A History of Youngstown and Mahoning County*. Donning Company, Virginia Beach, Virginia, 1995.

William A. Brenner, *Downtown and the University: Youngstown, Ohio*.

Youngstown State University, Youngstown, 1976.

Joseph G. Butler, Jr., *History of Youngstown and the Mahoning Valley, Ohio*. American Historical Society, Chicago, 1921.

Charles William Eliot, *Charles Eliot: Landscape Architect*. Reprint of 1902 original by Books for Libraries Press, Freeport, New York, 1971, pp. 298-301.

Edward Galaida, *Mill Creek Park*. [Steffan Printing Company], Cleveland, 1941.

John C. Melnick, *The Green Cathedral: History of Mill Creek Park, Youngstown, Ohio*. Youngstown Lithographing, Youngstown, 1976.

Leland M. Roth, *The Architecture of McKim, Mead and White 1870-1920: A Building List*. Garland Publishing, Inc., New York, 1978.

Leland M. Roth, *McKim, Mead & White, Architects*. Harper & Row, New York, 1983.

Thomas W. Sanderson, ed., *Twentieth Century History of Youngstown and Mahoning County, Ohio*. Biographical Publishing Company, Chicago, 1907.

"Sights and Sites: A Guide to Historic Places of Interest in Youngstown and Mahoning County". Public Library of Youngstown and Mahoning County, City Printing Co., Youngstown, 1976.

Index

The circular frog on the back cover
is a detail in the floor of the Lucas
County Courthouse, photographed
by Tom Patterson